# Mothers and Strangers

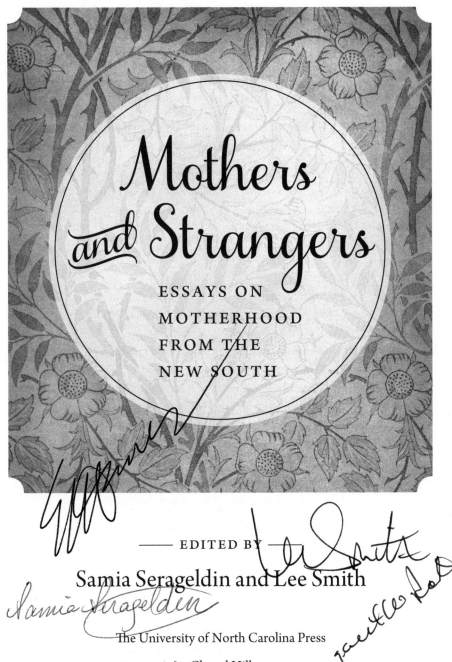

# Mothers and Strangers

ESSAYS ON
MOTHERHOOD
FROM THE
NEW SOUTH

—— EDITED BY ——

Samia Serageldin and Lee Smith

The University of North Carolina Press

Chapel Hill

This book was published with the assistance of the Greensboro Women's Fund of the University of North Carolina Press.

Designed by April Leidig
Set in Arno by Copperline Book Services, Hillsborough, N.C.
Manufactured in the United States of America

The University of North Carolina Press has been a member of the Green Press Initiative since 2003.

Cover illustration by Julienne Alexander.

Library of Congress Cataloging-in-Publication Data
Names: Serageldin, Samia, editor. | Smith, Lee, 1944– editor.
Title: Mothers and strangers : essays on motherhood from the new South / edited by Samia Serageldin and Lee Smith.
Description: Chapel Hill : University of North Carolina Press, [2019]
Identifiers: LCCN 2018051000| ISBN 9781469651675 (pbk : alk. paper) | ISBN 9781469651682 (ebook)
Subjects: LCSH: Mothers—Southern States. | Mother and child. | LCGFT: Essays. | Autobiographies.
Classification: LCC HQ759 .M873435 2019 | DDC 306.874/3—dc23
LC record available at https://lccn.loc.gov/2018051000

To the first woman in a child's life—
may her children and grandchildren
remember always.

# Contents

# Foreword

## Mama

— LEE SMITH —

MY GOOD FRIEND Samia Serageldin took me out to lunch in Chapel Hill, shortly after the death of her powerful and aristocratic Egyptian mother, along with another friend, Margaret Rich, whose own mother, a strong-willed southern matriarch, had just died at the age of one hundred in Greenville, South Carolina. "I have an idea," Samia said in her charming, lilting way. "Let's write a book about our mothers." Immediately we were in. We told other friends the idea, and they were in, too. We were all in. Because somehow we have come to that time in our lives when all the parents are gone, leaving us motherless, or fatherless, or, often now, *orphans*—suddenly out in the world alone, with nothing to stand between us and well, what? What? It is a time of reckoning. And who was she, that one who gave us birth, surely the most intimate of all physical relationships? Hers was the first face we saw, the first voice we heard . . . surely this is especially important for a writer, how we first experience language. . . . Who was she to us, or we to her? Who are we now, without her?

Samia and Margaret had powerhouse mothers—you'll read all about them here—but I had the other kind, a *mama*, the sweetest mama in the world: smart, funny, self-sacrificing, and self-effacing to a fault, yet often troubled. Though she had been gone since 1988, my early beautiful Mama—Virginia Marshall Smith, called "Gig"—came back to me almost in the flesh after that initial conversation at lunch. Early photographs of Mama show a mop of unruly dark curls, huge blue eyes, a carefree smile, and deep, mischievous dimples. Her flapper-style looks exactly fit the prevailing beauty ideal of the day. No wonder my father, Ernest Smith, fell madly in love at first sight and brought her all the way across Virginia from Chincoteague Island to his hometown of Grundy, nestled in those Appalachian peaks and hollers where she would feel a little bit homesick forever, even though she adored him, and vice versa. Mama was a very popular teacher at the high school; even boys signed up for her home economics classes. Sixty years later, at her funeral, one old man stood up and said that he had "gone to school to Miss Gig" and announced that she was a "real nice lady, for a foreigner."

I was not a foreigner. I was my daddy's girl through and through, a mountain girl, a born tomboy, though my mother kept at it, trying her best to raise me to be a lady. She sent me down to visit my lovely Aunt Gay-Gay in Birmingham, Alabama, every summer for two weeks of honest-to-God Lady Lessons. Here I'd learn to wear white gloves, sit up straight, and walk in little Cuban heels. I'd learn proper table manners, which would then be tested by fancy lunches at "The Club" on top of Shades Mountain. I'd learn the rules: "A lady does not point. A lady eats before the party. A lady never lets a silence fall. A lady does not sit *like that!*"

I didn't want to be a lady, of course. I wanted to be a boy. The only child of two older parents who had been told they could never have children, I felt too cherished, too watched over, all the time. It made me want to break things, like that white china figurine of the Japanese lady or the bowl once owned by Robert E. Lee. When I was in high school, my mother (by now suffering from anxiety, depression, and colitis) told me that she had quit teaching, which she had loved, when I was born.

"Why did you quit?" I asked, suddenly realizing that I didn't know the answer.

"Well, your daddy really didn't want me to work, once he was making enough money so I didn't have to. He thought it didn't look good in the town. He wanted me to be a real lady. And I wanted to quit, anyway, in order to raise you."

I was horrified—what a terrible responsibility for me, the "raisee," and I was not turning out so well, either. I had already flunked the Lady Lessons. I would grow up wild, drop in and out of schools, marry young, and very soon I had two children of my own, darling boys, seventeen months apart—"Irish twins," as they were called.

And then everything—everything—was different. So did I become "my mother's daughter?" Well, no, but it's a wistful "no." Now I get it. Now I'd be proud to be half the lady, and half the mother, that my own mother was. The fact is, my whole life changed forever when I had those boys. For when you have a baby, you are also born again. Children change us, they switch our focus from the inside to the outside, they bring us the world. The whole world, all over again. They hold us to life, faces to the flame. You never know what you can do until you have a child. And of course, once you have that child, you become a hostage to fortune. Now anything can happen to the child, or to you, and it *will* . . . read this book. There are many stories here, of sons and daughters and mothers and mothering, and they are as varied and surprising as life itself—well, they are life itself, aren't they?

# Mothers and Strangers

# Introduction

— SAMIA SERAGELDIN —

WHAT DO WE NOT KNOW about these most intimate of strangers, the women who raised us? What do we see when we look at them not through the familiar lens of filial relationship but as individuals in their own right and products of their time and place? How did they fit in, or stand out, or evolve in the context of their era? To what extent did they engage with their historic moment? What were the variables of the socioeconomic backdrop against which the private drama of family life unfolded? As we attempt to answer these questions, how do we account for the subjectivity of memory and the unreliability of recollection? How do we remember incidents today as opposed to how the mother herself remembers them, or how our siblings do, or even how our younger selves processed them at the time?

A distinguished roster of some of the best writers in the South and beyond set their minds to addressing these questions, with surprising results for even the most self-aware of them. As Michael Malone discovered while studying old photographs of his mother for his essay: "I finally began to see her differently. ... Although I had daily been its lucky recipient, I hadn't seen her quintessential quality."

Unique as each essay is, our contributors approached this project in a spirit that historian Jacquelyn Dowd Hall describes as, "first, the desire, always thwarted, to solve the mystery, to bring back that which is irretrievably lost; and second, the quest ... for the power to shape historical memory, to claim a place in the public record."

Beyond an exercise in fascinating personal memoir by exceptionally insightful writers, the lives of the highly diverse women depicted in this volume form a mosaic of autoethnographic accounts, a reflection of the social history of their era. They were strikingly shaped, for better or worse, by a nexus of the economic and political crosswinds of their time and place, as well as their generation and class.

# The Great Depression

For the generation that grew up or came of age during the twenties and thirties, the Great Depression was the defining event of their time. "The Depression did not need a Wall Street crash to enter the Deep South. Hard times had been a way of life for most people in the South forever, and FDR's New Deal, while a grand effort and a success, by and large, had a limited effect in some areas," James Seay notes of his mother's upbringing in Mississippi. Clyde Edgerton's mother, Truma, quit school at the age of twelve to work in a hosiery mill in North Carolina in order to help support her family—until child labor laws intervened. No family, regardless of socioeconomic background, was left untouched, but the degree varied markedly. Lynden Harris's grandfather's bank failed, as did "more than 190 banks . . . in North Carolina during the early years of the Depression. 'We've lost everything' must have been common as dirt." Though Harris puts this into perspective: "But, of course, the family hadn't lost everything. Despite their shock, they retained the land, the farm, the houses, farmworker help . . . "

How women coped ultimately depended more on character than circumstance. For Frances Mayes's mother, Flapper-era beauty Frankye, the belle of the small town of Fitzgerald, a cultivated insouciance about money left her, upon the death of her husband, in financial straits—but going to work was not, to her mind, an option. "She had the vibrancy, the looks, the determined helplessness that made you step forth to take over, even if you were eight or nine years old," Mayes recalls.

The generation that went through the Depression became one of hoarders who left their heirs the gargantuan task of sorting through their belongings. Letters are a uniquely valuable resource in that respect. As Margaret W. Rich concludes: "In . . . these letters of Mama's I see the seasons of life played out in the spates of gifts you buy and the letters you write. If you live long enough these seasons of community and connectivity start over and over. It is helpful to have that template of experience with a parent—you get to see what's reasonable to expect, or *what* to expect and something of what kind of attitude you will need to cope with the ravages of time."

# Saving Face

For a generation of women raised in the South and coming of age in the thirties and early forties, gracious manners, social convention, and "saving face" were paramount, regardless of external circumstances or inner turmoil. They were taught to be ladies, and in turn they instilled the importance of certain conventions in their daughters. James Seay's mother, Lucie, was instructed to churn butter sitting sidesaddle, so to speak, because the more practical position of straddling the churn was considered indecent.

Lee Smith relates her Virginia mother's attempts to raise her to be a lady: "She sent me down to visit my lovely Aunt Gay-Gay in Birmingham, Alabama, every summer for two weeks of honest-to-God Lady Lessons. Here I'd learn to wear white gloves, sit up straight, and walk in little Cuban heels. I'd learn proper table manners, which would then be tested by fancy lunches at 'The Club' on top of Shades Mountain. I'd learn the rules: 'A lady does not point. A lady eats before the party. A lady never lets a silence fall. A lady does not sit *like that!*'"

On a deeper level, though, saving face meant that domestic problems of alcoholism or abuse were hushed, marital infidelity and unhappiness were tolerated, depression was relegated to "bad mood" or "bad nerves," and suicide was unmentionable. "We didn't know 'dysfunctional,' but we lived it," Mayes affirms. This repression took its toll. "What wounded, what molded these adults, what had made them the way they were?" Hal Crowther asks. But they were not a generation to indulge in self-pity or to invite it from others. "Pity is the emotional charity that isolates and even humiliates its recipients," Crowther notes. So they hushed their scandals and hid their skeletons.

Divorce was still a step taken only in extremis. Sally Greene's mother, the third generation of a family of newspaper publishers, worked hard for many years to keep her unhappy marriage together for the sake of the family business and for fear of the effect a divorce would have on her son. Whatever difficulties a wife may have faced, particularly if transplanted to an unfamiliar environment, keeping up a carefully cultivated facade was a priority. As E. C. "Redge" Hanes writes of his mother, Helen, a Lutheran minister's daughter and teacher from Marion, Virginia, who married into the household-name Hanes family of Winston-Salem: "So how does a young woman, wearing a mask molded in a furnace of deep faith, modest means, and rural expanses, fit into a family of outspoken overachievers and political leaders?"

Marshall Chapman's mother felt so much pressure to produce a male heir to her husband's prominent Spartanburg, South Carolina, family that she kept having children—despite severe postpartum depression following the second daughter in a row—until, on the fourth try, she finally produced a boy. Henceforth the three daughters were left to fend for themselves emotionally. Marshall's view of her mother is that "there were two Mothers at play: the real, authentic one and the one that hid behind the mantle of being Mrs. James A. Chapman Jr." She concurs with her sister's assessment that "our mother was a terrible mother, but a great person."

Chapman's mother may have been particularly unsuited to nurturing, but her generation in general tended to be unsentimental, or at least undemonstrative, as mothers. Lynden Harris says of her mother: "She came from a generation for whom the words 'I love you' were a foreign tongue." As Hal Crowther puts it: "There were no 'helicopter' parents in the 1950s. A submarine would have made a better metaphor." Recalling her mother's constant criticism, Jill McCorkle concludes that "many women of my mother's generation thought it was a bad thing to compliment your children. I'm not sure why praise was not the first card drawn—why wouldn't it be? But perhaps it was all tied up with pride and how that *goeth before falls*."

## Social and Political Consciousness

Sometimes the social and political consciousness of that generation of southern women evolved with the times, as with Hal Crowther's mother, raised in a military family, who became staunchly antiwar in her later years; or Margaret Rich's mother, who, just before she passed away at the age of 102, thrilled at the prospect of voting for the first woman president. Michael Malone's mother was raised in an old southern family that harbored many of the typical prejudices of their day, but she earned her son's book dedication as "a Southern schoolteacher who taught that justice is everyone's right and everyone's responsibility." Lynden Harris's mother set great store by propriety all her life, and yet, at the end, lying in hospice, she corresponded with death row prisoners she came to know through her daughter's championing of social causes.

Others, like Bland Simpson's mother, fell out of sync with their children's generation on social and progressive issues. Simpson acknowledges: "Though differences between us in coming years would take on far more substantial subjects ... far more intractable and bitter, among them race, the war, and choice of career, the moments my mind turns to most often in this first decade since my mother's death at ninety tend to be ones of bemusement and odd comedy, as if one beneficent function of grief in memory is to steer the heart away from the grim and toward the light."

## Post–World War II

In the years after World War II, the ideal for women was that of homemaker. Lynden Harris's mother, once a top-secret WWII Signal Intelligence code breaker in Arlington, turned her talents to bridge clubs, garden clubs, rotary clubs, sudoku, and church activities. The stay-at-home mother was still the ideal in the sixties for women who could afford that lifestyle. Marianne Gingher recalls that her father was a doctor while her mother was a perfectly satisfied home-maker. "She delighted in her marriage and her children, had devoted friends, and filled her leisure time with their company, with arts and crafts, voice lessons, cooking, garden and bridge clubs, and volunteer work." On the other hand, Jill McCorkle's mother "worked a forty-hour week as a secretary to a pediatric group for over thirty years, and she also managed to assist with the lives of all these other people. When other mothers were staying home and doing the June Cleaver thing, my mother was at work." But Jill "never felt slighted in the least."

## The Seventies

The seventies saw a revolution in women's rights, civil rights, and antiwar and progressive causes. Working for financial security or self-fulfillment was no longer controversial. Sharon Swanson and Jacquelyn Dowd Hall are both daughters of mothers who found financial independence and escape from an untenable domestic situation—abusive marriages and economic hardship—by going to work to support their families.

But many financially secure married women were inspired in the seventies to go back to college and get a degree, start a career, take up a cause. Steven Petrow recalls that "my mother's feminism was both culinary and political, with the two often intertwined. . . . Mom's nom de cuisine was Shake 'n Bake." His mother kept a copy of *The Feminine Mystique* on her bedside table as a silent warning to husband and children. She went back to college at the age of forty to get a degree in psychotherapy, and she became an anti-Vietnam War activist.

Jacquelyn Dowd Hall's mother, Jinx, looked back at the seventies as the best time of her life, when she headed the Labor Action Coalition of New York. Dowd Hall writes about her mother's activism in the broader context of "one of that history's central tropes: the eruption, against the odds, of ordinary women into public life." Against the odds was very much the case for Jinx, who grew up in Oklahoma with parents who had little education or economic advantages to offer their daughter. Yet she was able to overcome the challenges that faced her, including "the escape from a bad marriage and a small town [and] the poverty about which she never complained."

Stephanie Elizondo Griest was simply mystified as to what her mother did at work. Griest, whose Tejano immigrant mother, Irene, held a high-powered job at IBM, only later discovered as an adult the roots of Irene's workaholic compulsion: a traumatic childhood of insecurity and picking cotton in hundred-degree heat for nine cents a pound.

# Revolutions, War, and Displacement

Beyond the borders of the United States, the broad strokes of turbulent history were also at work upending lives, as revolutions and war reshaped the stories of hyphenated Americans. The 1952 revolution in Egypt turned Samia Serageldin's mother's heretofore idyllic life into a decades-long nightmare of political persecution. In the seventies, Melody Moezzi's pathologist mother and obstetrician father were among the "brain-drain" wave that fled postrevolutionary Iran; her parents' brains, as Moezzi puts it, were their tickets to the American Dream. For Omid Safi's mother and his physician father, the Iranian Revolution of 1978 was not enough to drive them away from their comfortable life and close-knit family; the turning point came six years later when Iran, in the throes of the Iran-Iraq War, was running out of adult males for military service and started drafting teenage boys. "No one leaves home unless they love their children more than they love their own parents," Safi notes.

Immigrant culture presents interesting parallels with regard to the theme of community support and collective responsibility for the young. Both Griest and Moezzi write about a close-knit extended "family," not actual blood relations, who rallied around in times of need. Moezzi was raised by doting physician parents in a close-knit, affluent community of Iranian-American professionals in Dayton, Ohio; and Griest's IBM executive mother, Irene, drew support from her strong ties to the Mexican-American immigrant community in Corpus Christi, Texas.

In her essay, Moezzi recounts an incident when, as a child, she asked her parents who would take care of her if they were to die, and they answered without hesitation that the couple she grew up calling "uncle" and "aunt," who were not blood relations, would take her in and raise her with their children. Fortunately, in Melody's case, this scenario was never tested. But that is exactly what happened to Griest's mother and five siblings when they suddenly found themselves orphaned: they were immediately taken in, without question, by relations or friends of their parents whom they had grown up calling "Tio" and "Tia," without knowing, or caring, whether they were blood relations or not.

As Jaki Shelton Green says in her heart-wrenching poem "i want to undie you": "It took a village to raise you, and it takes a village to help you grow strong wings." In the absence of his mother, Randall Kenan was raised by a network of relatives headed by his great-aunt Mary, whom he called Mama. "The family originated from and lived in what local people referred to as 'The Quarters,' for upon the land where her home sat was where the enslaved people of the long-gone Chinquapin Plantation lived. Miss Viola had many children, so Clem had a vast arena of brothers and nephews and nieces and cousins galore. This was exactly the web of family into which I was born."

Safi recalls that their life in Iran was not as a nuclear family; there were hundreds of members of his parents' respective clans, and they were deeply embedded in that network. Many immigrants seek to recreate this social network in their new environment. As Moezzi puts it: "Such is the wonder and irony of networks in a diaspora: the farther we get from our original source, the stronger, tighter, and deeper our bonds grow."

That sense of community in diaspora operates in reverse as well, such as in expatriate American communities abroad, particularly among the Southern Baptist missionary community that Elaine Neil Orr describes. Wherever she traveled in Nigeria with her missionary parents, they could be assured of finding at day's end a warm welcome in the home of fellow missionaries whose lives paralleled their own: the accommodations, the food, the children's ages— everything would be familiar and reassuring.

## Strangers

If all our essayists found writing about their mother a soul-searching process of discovery, in some cases that process was particularly frustrating, not because the mother was secretive but because she was such an unreliable narrator. Daniel Wallace's mother, Joan, made the preposterous claim that she had eloped and contracted a secret marriage at the age of twelve, a wildly implausible claim given that she was the adored, only child of a thoroughly middle-class, strictly Presbyterian family in idyllic Edgewood, Alabama. By one account, her father, Weir, not only found out about the secret marriage but even built his child-bride daughter and her teenage husband a cabin in his backyard. Wallace protests: "He would never have built a house in his backyard for my mother and her husband: he would have shot him and built him a casket." To add to the mystery, there seemed to be no record whatsoever of the putative husband's name. In his essay, Wallace describes hiring a private detective to track down the elusive truth.

A different kind of dysfunctional mother-son relationship is examined from a threefold perspective by Philip Lopate, who recorded his mother's unreliable version of her life, including his own responses and questions, several years before her death. Twenty years later, he interrogates the subjectivity of the three points of view of that family history: his mother's, his own at the time, and his at present. "I suspect there is an emotional divide between women readers who will more readily sympathize with her, and men (or perhaps I should say men like myself) whose compassion keeps straying to the other side, do what we may to compensate for our gender bias. I wish there was a way to correct that astigmatic deviation and leap into her perspective with warmth and whole-heartedness, but my imagination will not take me that far," Lopate admits.

Secrets and lies complicate even the most devoted mother and child relationships. Sharon Swanson grew up believing that her mother had been hospitalized as a result of a nervous breakdown. "It would never have occurred to me to question my authoritarian father in the 1960s South. . . . And everyone in our little community knew the words he used to describe my mother's medical condition were the same ones used to encapsulate all kinds of crazy." Sharon, the oldest child, took on the anxious burden of watching her mother for signs of a relapse and helping her by looking after younger siblings. Only many years later, after her mother's death, does the adult Swanson realize the truth behind that dark secret.

Samia Serageldin's mother tried to protect her children from the desperate reality of their family's situation following Nasser's Socialist Decrees of the early 1960s in Egypt. "Overnight, my father's family and other politically prominent families like them were targeted by the regime for the confiscation . . . of every form of property. . . . Even worse, the 'dawn visitors,' as they were known, could come at any time to arbitrarily take away one of the men in the family, for a period of days or months." As a child, Samia could not but be aware of the overnight upheaval in the family's lifestyle and the pall of dread that pervaded the house. But she colluded with her mother's pretense of normality, sensing that the illusion was more for the adult's sake.

## The Last Word

There are many ways to lose a mother, and death is only one. Losing her to dementia is one of the cruelest. Jill McCorkle chronicles the frustration and grief of not knowing, when she enters her mother's room, if she will be met by a stranger who does not recognize her own daughter and who uses unconscionable language. But McCorkle realizes that, "if there is a sliver of grace to be pulled from the gnarled up tangle of dementia, it is that little bit of time given to loved ones to fully appreciate the scope of a whole life while the individual is still there and breathing and every now and then, for the briefest second, visible."

Equally cruel is an estrangement so implacable it persists even unto death, an estrangement forever beyond reconciliation, unspoken words that can never be spoken. Alan Shapiro's raw poem of remorse recalls being at his mother's deathbed, "not my lack of feeling but my flat refusal to pretend to feel, to play along (was that too much to ask?) and throw myself into the part so we could both, this once at least, rise to the occasion of what we never shared."

However cruel it is to lose a mother, it is in the natural order of things. A mother losing a child has no such consolation, no template to go by, no script to follow. Jaki Shelton Green's poem laments that her daughter's untimely death "is not even the theater you've dressed for."

## Legacies

One of the rewards for the reader of these essays is discovering how these exceptionally talented and creative writers were formed, and informed, by their mothers. Their legacies are big and small. Clyde Edgerton's fiction was inspired by his mother's idiom and life; Hal Crowther acknowledges a debt to his schoolteacher mother for his appreciation of poetry and sunsets; Michael Malone recognizes in himself his mother's optimism. Steven Petrow learned from his authority-questioning mother how to be proactive during her cancer treatment—just as she had been proactive when he himself had been treated for cancer at age twenty-six. Randall Kenan acknowledges his debt to the multiple women who raised him, especially his remarkable schoolteacher great-aunt, for his appreciation of books and of food. Belle Boggs recognizes an even more direct legacy, a unique relationship between her mother and her own toddler daughter, almost a reincarnation of the grandmother's spirit in the granddaughter.

The past is a foreign country, it has been said. In the process of exploring this treacherous territory, our contributors discovered much about their mothers, but perhaps even more about themselves. What sort of child were they? To what extent did they shape their mothers' lives, rather than the other way around? A cooperative, responsible, independent child empowers a mother to make choices quite differently from a demanding or a challenging child. Were they, willingly or unwillingly, their mother's confidante? Which parent did they identify with, whose side did they take in the family dynamics, and do they now see this alignment in a different light? Does their newly gained perspective help them reconcile themselves to their past? We invite you to accompany them on this fascinating journey.

PART I

*Angels*

# A Beautiful Mother

## — MARIANNE GINGHER —

MOTHER HAS BEEN at the hospital all day but, exhausted, goes home around midnight, leaving her oldest son to keep vigil at our father's bedside. Daddy has been in a coma for three days, and although death is thought imminent, no doctor or nurse is saying whether it will be hours or days.

At 3 A.M. a nurse nudges my brother awake and tells him it's over.

My parents, married forty-four years, had raised four headstrong children during the turbulent sixties. Mother was a homemaker; my father, a doctor. Their arrangement, traditional for the times, had pleased them both. Mother, a charming, witty, emotionally intelligent beauty, believed she'd done everything in the world that was worth doing as far as her own ambitions were concerned. She delighted in her marriage and her children, had devoted friends, and filled her leisure time with their company, with arts and crafts, voice lessons, cooking, garden and bridge clubs, and volunteer work, and she was always available to lend a sympathetic ear. If she'd had both opportunity and fire, she said, she might have been a torch singer, but *que será, será*. My father joked she would have made an excellent psychiatrist, had she been able to pass organic chemistry. "If I had *wanted* to pass organic chemistry, I would have," she retorted. In our family, she was the go-to person if you had a problem, and we children tended to tell her everything because she offered solid counsel. Throughout my girlhood she gave no indication of wanting to be anywhere other than in the briar patch of her family, which, from my perspective, suggested that she thrived on sacrifice.

Her only daughter, I was restless for more than keeping the home fires burning, and Mother was not my role model for career aspirations. Nobody in my family was. I was just born restless for something arty more. Mother might sit on the living room floor, drawing with her pastels while we renegades whooped all around her, but I was not my mother's daughter in that regard. I would have shooed us away. I would have shouted, "Pipe down! I need to concentrate!"

THE NIGHT MY FATHER DIES, I'm sleeping alone in the bed where both my sons were conceived. Their father is sleeping across the hall. We're in the throes of separation—the official documents have already been drawn up and signed. I've called my lawyer to okay inhabiting the house during my father's deathwatch. A separation agreement in North Carolina in 1990 requires from couples a year of zero cohabitation, and I've already moved out, staying with friends and family until more permanent arrangements are made. I'm nervous that moving back in might start the separation clock over, if my husband wants to make trouble. I suppose he has the right to make trouble. I'm the one who wants to leave the marriage.

My sons are with my in-laws. My three brothers are all piled up at my parents' townhouse a block away. I don't know why my almost-ex-husband hasn't joined our little boys at his parents' house, but he is the one whom the telephone rouses when the hospital rings at 3 A.M. He is the messenger, snapping on the overhead light, shaking my shoulder. "The hospital called. Your father died."

*No bedside manner whatsoever,* I hear my doctor father say in his newly acquired language of Angel-ish.

My husband does not accompany us to view my father's body. My brothers, my mother, and I ride in silence the few dark blocks to Moses Cone Memorial Hospital, where my father once strode the halls and commanded the diseases of others to shape up or ship out. I do not want to see him dead. He has been too much alive to ever be dead. I do not want to acknowledge the body without *his* distinct occupancy of it, whatever *his* means. It means nothing after death. The ability to possess no longer exists. One's essence, yearnings, talents, beliefs, the complications of being human—I'm about to gaze upon the ravaged lack of all that. My father's essence has been variously vibrant, endearing, irritating, meddlesome, generous, corny, laconic, garrulous, ferociously Republican, tender, merciful, loyal, impatient, opinionated, humane, stubborn—*complicated.*

Death *un*complicates. It takes a person's contradictions and complexities, the zigzags of life force and will, and flatlines it all.

There is the pale, untroubled face, superbleached under the florescent light of the hospital room. There is the frozen gape of the loved one's open mouth, evidence of a last gasp. Who could ever take a fish off a line again without remembering? But nothing is as disquieting as the absolute stillness of the body, its beyondness. All surrounding air turns to stone. The profound gravity of such stillness draws you like a sinkhole, even time collapsing into it.

We circle the bed as uncertainly as if viewing an imposter. He should be rearing up and telling us what to *do*.

I remember driving my mother home by myself in her parade float Chevrolet (the last car Daddy ever bought, I couldn't help thinking) while my brothers left together in a second car. She'd needed to sign some papers. She isn't feeling well, she says, slumping in the car seat. She feels strange. The black sky softens into lavender, and tentative birdsong floats through the open windows as if an orchestra is tuning up to play, as if nothing is wrong. We park in her driveway, but she makes no effort to get out of the car. She's still trying to absorb the finality of the ordeal. Sick as he was toward the end, she'd been able to give comfort, and my father had been able to receive it, to know she was with him. Her long days sitting bedside had united them in purpose the way their long marriage had. "I can't feel the left side of my face," she says to me. "I can't lift my left arm."

By 9:30 we are in the neurologist's office. My father has been dead less than seven hours.

They order a CAT scan. She's suffered a "warning" stroke, a mild TIA, or transient ischemic attack, they call it. The numbness in her arm and face begins to abate in the doctor's office, but she feels weak and nauseated. Rest, they say. Take aspirin. Return for a complete evaluation, an MRI. Oh yes, and avoid stress. On the way home she puts a hand on my arm. "I think your father is trying to take me with him," she says.

"We aren't going to let him," I say. "He had you long enough." But that isn't true. Nobody can have my mother long enough.

––––––––––

SHE'S SIXTY-SIX the night my father dies. Except for the TIA episode, she's in good health, mentally and physically. She gets on with her life, learning how to do the things for herself that Daddy had always managed: paying bills and puzzling out personal finances with the lawyers, brokers, insurance people my father had long trusted, calling repairmen, addressing the business side of life. She despises keeping track of money, but she's good at it, and she lives frugally. She takes out a long-term health care policy. She says she never wants to be a burden.

The first year after my father dies, I live with her. We are both in transition: she, adjusting to widowhood, and me, single with children. She gives me the master bedroom with its suite-size grandeur and bookcases and built-in desk and hires a carpenter to transform the spacious walk-in closet into a bedroom nook with bunk beds for my boys. She says she *prefers* to move into the guest room because it's sunnier. Sunny is good, as the gloom of winter approaches.

We are doing all right, cheering one another on. And then on Thanksgiving, as my brothers and sons and assorted relatives and friends gather around our table, I look down at the food on my plate and see that everything on it is beige.

Beige, the least robust of colors, the blandest, the most namby-pamby. "Namby-pamby" was my father's word for dullards with limp handshakes. There is dressing, brown rice, turkey, oyster casserole, bran rolls, and gravy. The skillet squash has cooked to a scorch-colored mush. Even the bing cherry salad is beige that year because we haven't put bings in the gelatin after all but canned Queen Annes, beige as oatmeal. What had we been thinking? *Were* we thinking? Where is the livid cranberry sauce? We have forgotten to make it. We forgot to make snap beans. The whole feast looks as if it has been prepared by dullards with limp hand shakes. Who are we fooling? We the resilient are muddling through at best.

The year is 1990. South Africa finally lets Nelson Mandela out of jail after more than twenty-seven years of incarceration. The first George Bush is still president, flanked by Vice-President Dan Quayle who everybody thinks is a dope. My sons are into the Teenage Mutant Ninja Turtles in a big way and, on television, *The Simpsons*, which my mother enjoys watching with them before *her* favorite show, *Seinfeld*, comes on. I've lucked into a visiting professor post, teaching writing at Hollins College near Roanoke that requires a weekly commute and would be impossible without Mother taking up the childcare slack.

Both boys are in elementary school, but they need afternoon supervision, a cozy supper, baths, and tucking in, and my divorce-pending husband and I have divided those responsibilities. They greatly need unrushed tenderness. In the first months following our separation, a large amount of that tenderness comes from my mother, their grandmother, who has always prioritized love over grief.

---

MORE THAN SIX YEARS LATER, I am in the little kitchen of my man friend's house making dinner. I am so much in love I'm whistling and dancing, pausing now and then to kiss my man, who sits on the countertop, grinning, watching, waiting for me to twirl by. My complicated life has turned fairy tale bright. What is going on in the world? Do I know? Do I care? The trouble with fairy tales is that they're fairy tales. The phone rings. My man answers it while I stir something on the stove. He listens, frowns, thrusts the phone at me.

It's October and Mother is away at her fifty-sixth high school reunion in Mount Vernon, Illinois. She got talked into it by her best old friend, and I egged her on. You are going to have some serious laughs and a really great time together, I told her. Two still-foxy seventy-something widows on a big nostalgia roll. But it's her first plane trip alone, since my father died, and she had been nervous about the trip. Her friend, Jayne, promised to meet her at the St. Louis airport and drive the two of them the hundred miles back to Mount Vernon.

"Hello, dear, it's Jayne," the caller says to me. "Something is going on with your mother."

When she puts Mother on the phone, I can't hear a word she's saying for all the sobbing. Jayne takes the phone back. "We went to the Mount Vernon cemetery this morning," Jayne says, "so your mother could visit her parents' graves."

"And?"

"She started feeling weird on the way home. I thought it was just emotional, you know? So I gave her a little glass of sherry and told her take a warm bath then, if she felt better, we'd go to the reunion cocktail party. She couldn't get out of the bath tub by herself."

My mother has regained enough control to tug the phone away from Jayne. "Um sluhwing muh woods," she says.

I ask her to put Jayne back on. "Call an ambulance," I tell Jayne. "She's having a stroke."

"She wants me to call the ambulance," Jayne tells my mother. My mother wails. "No! No ahmblunce!"

"She doesn't want me to call the ambulance," Jayne says, then, more softly, confidentially, "She doesn't want to make a scene. She doesn't want to ruin things."

"Thull ton on thuh suruns," my mother sobs.

"She doesn't want them to turn on the sirens, because it'll wake everybody in my neighborhood up," Jayne explains, as if it's a perfectly logical consideration.

They won't call the ambulance, no matter how strongly I beg. I hang up, call my oldest brother. He used to be a nurse, but he also has the ability to stand up to and commandeer our mother. Despite her stubborn, independent streak, Mother defers to men, especially if they are tall men, like my father was. My brother is tall enough, and he's also loud. My children call him Uncle Boom-Boom.

When he phones me back, he's grave. "I had to cuss at Jayne," he said. "It got ugly, but they finally called the ambulance."

Mother spends nearly two weeks in the Mount Vernon Hospital before she is stable enough to travel and we are able to charter a medically equipped plane to fly her back to North Carolina. She's suffered a stroke that leaves her physically disabled on her left side. Her arm and leg are most affected. She has no facial paralysis; her speech difficulties are improving. Her cognition and her wit remain intact. She's lucky, although until she gets out of rehab she won't believe that.

———

HOME AGAIN, her biggest complaint, besides the rehab exercises, is how to manage her hair. Since her forties, she has worn it in a bun or French twist. Sometimes she attaches a little wiglet to the back of her head and does a comb-over to help maximize the volume of her hairdo. Her trick for thickening her hair is to dust it all over with cornstarch. Hers is thin, fragile, spiderweb hair, the luminous see-through color of white wine. She will not take that hair to a beauty salon, never has. She has always tended to it herself, babying the ornery stuff, her lifelong cosmetic bane, because she doesn't believe there's a hair stylist on Earth patient enough to wrestle the mess into some temporary compliance, spinning its straw into gold. She has taught herself how to spin its pale threads into fool's gold, and that's good enough. People compliment her on her hair all the time, but if only they knew. But my mother has an entrenched sense of style. The upswept do, thickened by her remedy of cornstarch, gives her the look of having more hair. But it takes two hands to compose a French twist. Two hands to unfasten the container of cornstarch. Two hands to attach a wiglet if one wants a wiglet. It takes two hands to wrap up a bun and pin it into place on the nape of a neck, two hands to lasso a ponytail. My mother has one working hand.

The physical therapists cajole her; they tell her that vanity is an excellent motivator. If she wants to wear her hair in a distinctive style that only she can manage, then she's got to retrain her hand and arm to manage it. Her sons hover and check in, but they do not understand the necessity of getting the hair back on track. I try to coif it for her, but I bungle it. The hair, the hair. Once she is able to fix it to suit herself, that will mean as full a recovery as she might hope for.

By the time she leaves rehab, she is able, with exhausting effort, to wrangle her own little bun into a simple knot—without her favorite hair pins or combs, minus her treasured wiglet—with a clamp. She struggles to position the knot symmetrically on her head, and she succeeds where others have failed. It's a turning point. She can upsweep her own hair. Well enough. Not perfectly (and she has always been a fan of perfectly) but well enough.

SIX YEARS LATER, although she walks with a cane and has limited motion in her left arm, at age seventy-nine Mother is doing well. She still lives alone at her townhouse, still walks outside in the little back garden every night to bolt the gate against burglars—a task that requires her to go up and down the back porch steps. She stopped driving after her stroke, but occasionally she will accompany me to the grocery store to shop for her weekly groceries. Although she fusses about it, I make her push her own cart. All movement had gotten difficult for her, but she's still mobile and upright. I insist that exercise will keep her that way, but she's never been interested in exercise of any sort, except swimming. Two mornings a week she attends an elder class of water aerobics at the local YWCA. Her teacher is blind. The members of the class have assorted disabilities—from lameness to heart conditions—and come from all walks of life. Mother makes her first black friends. She loves this group, its solidarity of feisty slowpokes facing down the culture of rush, hence her determination to tug on a bathing suit with only one hand—not easy. After swimming, she wears the suit home because it will take her a good portion of the afternoon to remove it wet. It will have completely dried by the time she peels out of it.

Early spring 2004 I am introducing the writer Ellen Gilchrist, who has come to give a lecture at the University of North Carolina at Chapel Hill, where I teach. My mother is a devoted fan of Ellen Gilchrist's and has read everything Gilchrist ever wrote, so I strategize a way to transport her to campus from an hour away in Greensboro. A friend will drive her, but three problems remain. First, not only is her walking slow and uncertain, but she lacks stamina for maneuvering the considerable distance between parking facilities and the lecture hall. Second, the campus sidewalks are an obstacle course of uneven bricks, many of them humped up by tree roots or, occasionally, missing altogether. Hurrying to classes, I have fallen myself a time or two, tripping over bricks or the lack of bricks. The third problem has to do with mother's tenacious vanity. When I suggest that the friend who brings her should probably use a wheelchair, Mother balks. She will *not* appear at a public event as a handicapped person. *No.* She doesn't want to call attention to herself in that way. When a wheelchair appears, she says, all eyes fixate upon it. It's like sirens, albeit silent ones, *eye* sirens but sirens nonetheless. Out of the way, here comes a wheelchair! On top of that complication, she doesn't have anything nice to wear. Well, think about it. When was the last time a person who can't easily try on clothes went shopping for them? Then, there's her hair. There's the folderol of it all, so much preparation. She doesn't want the bother. She doesn't want to ruin things.

"You're doing fine with your hair," I tell her.

"It's never looked right since the stroke, and you know it," she argues. "Oh why do you keep pushing me to *do* things. I don't have to *see* Ellen Gilchrist to know she exists."

Nevertheless, the friend and I conspire to persuade her otherwise, and finally she relents. The thrill of meeting a literary hero is enough to overcome her obstinacy.

---

TWO PEOPLE FALL THAT NIGHT.

My mother, allowing but protesting the indignity of being transported in a wheelchair, afraid of being late to the lecture, urges her companion to hurry, to push the wheel chair at top speed. "Faster," Mother says. "On Dasher, on Dancer." They are laughing. Mother is enjoying the wind whistling past her ears so much that she's forgotten it might mess up her hair, dislodge a strand glued carefully in place with hair spray. Speeding across the main quad, one front wheel of the chair plunges into the small but significant abyss of a single missing brick, and the contraption flips and slings my mother forward and out. She lands somewhere near the flagpole in the center of the quad, flat on her back, looking up at the stars. Students and other bystanders gasp and gather around. "Don't move," they say. "Are you all right?" "Of course she's not all right." "Somebody call an ambulance."

"No," my mother says calmly. "Don't you dare call an ambulance."

She lies there for a few minutes, her companion hovering, asking her if she's okay, asking her who is the president of the United States. ("Willie Nelson," she says. It's her joke because she loves Willie Nelson and thinks he would make a good president.) "Actually it's George W. Bush, but I wish he weren't," my mother says. Finally, slowly, someone helps her sit up and she is lifted into her chair. "Is my hair messed up?" she asks.

For the lecture they've built a small step-up to the podium because Ellen Gilchrist is short and wanted a little riser to assist her in seeing over the lectern. Don't forget about the step, I'm told. Of course I won't forget. After delivering my introduction, and with my mother looking on—my mother who has never seen me give a presentation at the university—as the crowd explodes with enthusiastic applause for Ellen Gilchrist (and my splendidly prepared remarks, I am thinking), I step off the podium platform forgetting the step and into thin air. What law of physics turns a four-inch drop into an abyss for the unmindful? I plummet, collapsing behind the potted plants that decorate the stage. People who saw it say that first I was there, and then I wasn't—poof!—and then I popped up from nowhere land like Rumpelstiltskin's sister and limped to my chair, clutching my bun. "Are you all right?" Ellen Gilchrist asks me. I am all right, just shocked and rattled, just mortified in that pride-goeth-before-a-fall way. Is my hair messed up? I sit down and tend to the hairpins that have loosened and watch Ellen take the stage.

I do not know my mother has fallen earlier, but once I know, the symmetry of our accidents seems cosmically ordained. Both of us patting our mussed up hairdos back in place, both of us more embarrassed than hurt, both of us impetuous: either forgetful of hazard, like me, or simply relishing the sizzling glory of a speeding moment, like my mother, for whom the lit sparkler of reck-lessness is less and less an option. Brava, Mother!

After her lecture, I walk Ellen over to meet her. I notice that one of Mother's hairpins has risen from her little topknot like an antenna. Otherwise she looks in mint condition.

She takes Ellen's hand and beams; they confer a bit, out of my hearing. They make long, significant eye contact. They exchange the secret informa-tion that I like to imagine devoted fans and the writers who pause to deeply appreciate them are able to exchange, a wave length sparkling between them that would probably enable them under different circumstances to be great friends. Mother is not going to the reception afterward, so this is her audience with Ellen Gilchrist, and Gilchrist, bless her, takes her time about it.

"What was it like for you," Ellen asks me as we walk off toward the reception, "growing up with such a beautiful mother?"

---

NONE OF MY FRIENDS had a mother like mine. While many had dutiful mothers, reliable and well intentioned, and some might have called their moth-ers sweet, the sweetness was the insipid, Goody Two-shoes sort, and often the most dutiful mothers were humorless. Most other mothers *looked* like moth-ers, but my mother had style. She even spiffed up to go to the grocery store. Once, in the fifties, when she was shopping at Kroger, a stranger tried to pay her one hundred dollars as a reward for her neat and attractive appearance. She was funny, unpretentious, empathetic, and frank. She got a kick out of irony. She was tender more than she was sweet. She did not lord her adultness over us kids, did not deluge us with unsolicited advice. She was not judgmental, which brought out confession in all of us, and she was the best listener I have ever known. She smelled like Ponds cold cream and Jergen's almond-scented lotion, like Lustre-Creme shampoo, L'Air du Temps perfume, and Beech-Nut peppermint gum. As a kid, I always felt proud when she visited my school, that I belonged to her, that she was *mine*. My girlfriends loved her, too. She was easy to be with, did not interfere, wasn't a snoop, could keep a secret and offer practical suggestions for a way out of some emotional labyrinth in which we teenagers were often losing ourselves. She knew how to laugh at herself, and she could coax us to laugh at ourselves, too, when we were feeling most gloomy. I don't know how she did it. It was some inborn talent for believing in herself enough so that the overflow of that belief allowed her to be wise. Quite simply, she was my best friend, and when I confess this to other women my age, they tend to be incredulous.

------------

WHEN AT EIGHTY-THREE she gives up her townhouse and moves to Wellspring Retirement Community, she makes that decision herself. She has begun to fall again, and with such regularity that now she wears an amulet that summons help with the push of a button should she tumble. One evening, as I'm commuting home from work, I get a call from the alarm dispatcher, who tells me that she's fallen, and by the time I reach the townhouse I find her surrounded by four strapping firemen, a policeman, and a policewoman. They are trying to convince her to go to the hospital, but she won't budge. She had fallen into the bathtub leaning in to turn the faucet knobs and couldn't right herself. The first responders to arrive were the police, who accessed the townhouse not by breaking a window but by sticking hands through the front door mail slot and turning the big key on the interior side of the door. Now Mother will have the additional worry of how easily her house can be broken into.

------------

FOR A YEAR OR MORE she enjoys her life at Wellspring. A lot of her friends have moved there. She delights in the sunny privacy of her tiny assisted living apartment, the ease of not having to keep house or do laundry or cook. She likes the food: three hot meals a day served in a gracious dining room on linen tablecloths. There are cloth napkins and silverware and fresh flowers on the table. She signs up for art classes and goes swimming at the heated on-site pool. Then, one day, as she is taking her shower (she could have rung for assistance, but she didn't), she falls and cracks a vertebra in her neck.

She spends nearly three months in Wellspring's skilled rehab unit, recovering some degree of mobility. But by the time she's released, she's lost most of her ability to walk, to make wheelchair transfers without help, or to bathe or dress herself.

My brothers and I are summoned to a meeting with Mother and her resident health care providers, where we are all informed that she will be reassigned from her assisted living apartment to a room in skilled nursing. "It's the beginning of the end," she says grimly. "Nobody gets well from old age."

———————

MOTHER HATES HER big blank forehead. "Check out that gigantic forehead," she says, frowning into a mirror. "It looks like the Hoover Dam."

In her skilled nursing room at Wellspring where she now lives (she's taken to calling Wellspring "the Preservation"), she sorts through a sack hanging on a doorknob with her one functional hand and extracts a headband. "Color," she says, "covers a multitude of sins"—the sin being her forehead. Camouflaging it with a headband has become her new fashion statement, her "signature." Why stop accessorizing just because you're eighty-five, can't dress yourself anymore, and the medications you're on and your lack of exercise have made your figure balloon 40 pounds beyond its optimal, waist-cinched-by-a-belt 135 pounds? The first time she wears a headband into the Wellspring dining room, I hear some resident churl mutter, "Who's the hippie?" as we pass.

It takes courage to accept diminished life on the Preservation. With rueful acceptance, she has given up on cosmetics and beautiful clothes, no longer wears lipstick, rouge, eye makeup, her Grace Kelly bun, fashionable kicky shoes, skirts, pantyhose, jewelry. She's also given up her cherished privacy—an attendant is always bursting into her room for one purpose or another. Almost everything she wears now fastens with Velcro. She of the stylish fifties spike heels slips doggedly into her Crocs. We call them her "galumphers." She wears socks with bunnies and carrots on them. Who bought her such ridiculous socks? When she slides on the big beige Crocs, it looks like she's strapped on two fat loaves of bread. Whatever patchy outfit the nursing assistant dresses her in, she attempts to counter with her newfound self-differentiating accessory—headbands. The little knot of a ballerina's bun, that she'd worked so hard to upsweep herself, has become impossible for her to manage. Now a certified nursing assistant plaits what's left of her hair into a single braid the width of a shoestring. It's a stark look, made more stark by the Hoover. "Just look at that big old forehead," she says leaning into the mirror. "Do you think it's growing?"

"A high forehead means you have lots of brains," I say.

"Watch this." She tugs on one of the elasticized headbands she fancies. "Voila! Out, out, dam Hoover."

We study the effect. It's patterned like a bandana. She frowns. "Now I look like Willie Nelson," she says.

And, actually, she does.

"By the way," she says, "When I'm on my death bed, please play a Willie Nelson CD. Promise?"

"Oh for heaven's sake," I say. "Okay."

While we are eating lunch in the dining room, Jack McGinn shuffles up to our table to say hello. He's her contemporary, still dapper, trim, alert, fastidiously dressed in a brown tweed blazer, tortoise shell glasses. He has a small, neat white mustache. Even the way he maneuvers his walker seems debonair, as if he is driving the sports car of walkers. Mother can no longer use a walker. She rides the hallways in a motorized chair. Jack used to own Brownhill's, a posh women's apparel store, second only to Montaldo's when I was coming of age and paying attention to fashion. In the 1950s, her heyday of youthful beauty, Mother modeled Brownhill's fashions. Her photos were in the newspaper. It probably made her as nervous to model fashions for Brownhill's as it did to sing a solo in church. (She had a beautiful alto voice, but she trembled so nervously when she sang a solo that she had to take off her high heels and sing barefooted.) I have pictures of her modeling a sheath dress with a stole. She's wearing elbow-length gloves with it, spike heels. She's posed formally, feet splayed a certain way like they taught her to stand. Her face is sheer provincial innocence, an utterly guileless face that doesn't seem to recognize that she could have been a star.

"I like your head band, Betty Jane," Jack McGinn says, bless him.

———————

THEN, ON THE MORNING of 2 March 2012, the supervising nurse at her skilled care facility phones to tell me that when aides brought her breakfast tray to her that morning, she was unresponsive. I'd spoken to her by phone the night before when I got home from work. She was too tired, she said, for a long conversation, but she'd see me the next day and we'd catch up on the week. On my rush out the door, I see the camellias blooming. My father planted these bushes forty years ago or more. Before we sold Mother's townhouse, my youngest brother John had transplanted them from there to my backyard. They've grown tall and lush along the fence and, this year, are ultra-gussied-up with blooms. I pick a fistful to take with me. At her bedside, when I tell her I've brought her a bouquet of Daddy's camellias, her eyes flutter open and she smiles at me, at the flowers. "Oh," she says, with recognition and approval. "I love all of you so." I touch the blossoms against her cheeks, her forehead, her lips, and tell her they are Daddy's kisses. She nods, then she closes her eyes and begins to leave us, taking her time, waiting for the rest of our family to arrive. In one month she would turn eighty-eight, but she had never been someone who overstayed her welcome, had always believed it was best to leave a party with people begging her to stay.

We put on Willie Nelson that day, and ever since then, when I hear one of his songs, I think of her. Every time I make a pie crust, I summon her delight at teaching me how to do it when I was ten years old. Every time I put on lipstick I hear her instructions to start with a frosty basecoat, apply the darker shade, then blot. Headbands are in vogue again, and I can be any ordinary somewhere and feel her influence. I'm at the grocery store, browsing the navel oranges, and I think of her.

"Honey, if you were stuck on a desert island and could only eat one food, what food would it be?" she says.

"Chocolate."

"Chocolate won't sustain you. Choose either the potato or the orange."

"OK, orange."

"Good. Now you won't get scurvy. I'm going to choose the potato so that we'll have nearly a balanced diet. We'll catch fish for protein."

"I didn't realize that we'd be stranded on the same island, Mom."

"But wouldn't we have fun if we were?"

---

I HAVE A FRIEND who is currently undergoing a brutal regimen of chemotherapy, despite a less than ideal prognosis. I recently see her with her daughter at a local event. She looks frail but radiant. She wears a stylish blue cap to cover her baldness, a flowing linen tunic and long skirt. She looks younger somehow, fresh, elfin. It makes me feel happy to see her out, enjoying herself, with friends, her daughter hugging her close. "This is the first time we've ventured from the house to do something that isn't about cancer," the daughter tells me. "It's wonderful," she says, but she looks tired. I recognize in the daughter's face the strain of holding on to a beautiful mother for dear life. Such beauty is as delicate as bliss itself, like soap bubbles we carefree children blew into the sky. It's yet too early for her to know that her mother's gladness for life, her grace, humor, and dignity, have taught her everything she needs to know to be able to let go.

# The Imagined Sorrows of My Mother's Face

## — MICHAEL MALONE —

But one man loved the pilgrim soul in you,
And loved the sorrows of your changing face.

PHOTOS AND MOVIES are taken daily of my two-year-old granddaughter, Maisie, by her parents, relatives on both sides, family friends, nannies, playschool teachers. There are even close-up selfies that the toddler has snapped of herself on her own iPhone. She is nine hundred days old, and I suspect there now exist over ten thousand images of her.

I have only six photographs of my mother, frayed copies, none of them taken in her childhood. There are no digital shots, no Polaroids, no videos, nothing in color. Just these half-dozen black-and-whitish, sepia-stained "snapshots," most with scalloped edges. On the original backs of the pictures, in her fluid cursive script, the faded black ink rises in an optimistic diagonal, left to right, identifying relevant names, places, dates. Her own name, "Fay Jones" or later "Fay Jones Malone," arcing across the page like a swan dive into air.

When my mother was born, near the start of the twentieth century, and then well into its middle decades a photograph was a way of recording and thereby memorializing a particular occasion or location, or some important ceremonial gathering; a photo gave significance to meaningful moments in life. To photograph was not a primary method, as it is today, of making life *real* to the people in the pictures, people who may have often taken the pictures of themselves. Life was not defined by selfies of the self.

Two of my photographs of my mother were commemorative portraits made during her Trinity (Duke) college days. One is her senior class picture. The other is a studio shot of a young woman's social coming out: a small trim flapper poses in a beaded party dress with short blonde marcelled hair (a wave held in place by a beaded bobby pin). Her chin is raised expectantly at the future.

My mother was small; she was affectionately called "Runt" by her family. Had there been "petite" sizes for women, she would have worn them. Her older sister had died from influenza as a child, and their parents feared that my mother's smallness, her lack of sturdy bulk could cost them her life as well. Merchants of food by trade, Grandpa and Grandma were always feeding her from their bounty of produce and livestock. At Sunday dinners there might be as many as twenty dishes (from sweet pickles to a barbecued pigling) laid out on their long dining room table. On this diet of chickens, lambs, calves, country ham, potato salad, turnip greens, deviled eggs, cantaloupes, and pecan pie, Mama's brothers and sisters grew tall, large-boned, athletic—one of the brothers a golf pro, one a minor league outfielder, one of the sisters a national champion bowler and a tennis and golf player until shortly before her death.

But my mother was drawn to different talents and desires. In her youth, she sang, played the piano, danced. Then, after she went deaf, in her leisure she read. She had little instinct for sports or food and none for cigarettes and drink (except black coffee). Certainly, once married in Atlanta, she cared for none for the social climb of tennis and golf played at my father's country club. I always figured her indifference to society was one reason that he left her for the younger woman in whom he could instill such skills.

Among my half-dozen photos is a black-and-white group shot of my mother's family on their summer lawn. She stands, in her late twenties, second oldest and shortest, in a close-knit row of eight siblings (her three sisters, four brothers). The handsome healthy group stands in a row that rises to their parents together at its end. There my grandfather's long, lanky arm hangs easily over the shoulder of my tall, stout grandmother, who looks as strong as a pioneer woman wrestling a plow behind a lunging horse. My grandfather's black tie and my grandmother's black belt are distinctive—emphatic—against their starched white clothes. All ten of the Joneses, well dressed in summer outfits, stand easily together, lounging with casual familiarity in the wide, shady side yard.

My mother was herself a Christmas baby and loved the holiday. In another photo she bends beside a little table on which there's a small tree decorated with handmade ornaments and a shiny star on top; a few wrapped gifts are piled around a large seated white bear. The bear is nearly as big as the baby she's holding up like another gift. I'm the baby. I was born at Thanksgiving, so I'm a month old, and it's 1942. Mama (thirty-six then) and her sisters and sisters-in-law lived together in the big Jones house, for all their men had gone off

The Imagined Sorrows of My Mother's Face          27

to fight the Axis powers. This Christmas picture was taken, I imagine, to send to my father, stationed at Oak Ridge, Tennessee. He had missed my birth.

The photo that has the most effect on me is the most recent, taken back in the sixties, in the small messy living room of the last of many rental apartments in which we'd lived together once my mother brought us to North Carolina after our father left her. That happened when I was nine, and the youngest of us, our brother David, was a newborn. She was in the first round of a long fight with cancer. We had little money. Of our dozen rental homes, the only one I'd liked, and our briefest domicile, had been the largest, an old stucco place. It had more rooms than we had furniture for. I loved especially its big parlor, empty except for an upright piano. But the landlord would not renew our lease because my mother had challenged him over his diatribes against integration. She never raised her voice, but she never backed down. At the end of her life, she was back in a cramped, cluttered apartment—a far cry from either her parents' vast Victorian comfort or my father's Frank Lloyd Wright modernism.

My mother was not attentive to style; she never would have watched HGTV. Although she kept flowers everywhere, in broken-handled pitchers and old coffee cans, furnishings appeared to mean nothing to her. She threw random blankets over unmended couches, and she set the wobbly dinner table with mismatched plates and glasses. By the time this last photo of her was taken in the crowded apartment, she had half a year to live, and her clothes hung loosely on her. By then her hair was thin, silver-gray as a mouse; her once slender figure was distorted and scarred by surgery and radiation sores. Yet in this photograph, she posed in a comedic parody of a flamenco dancer—one hand held backward against her hip, the other hand raised flamboyantly high in air, miming clicking castanets. And she was laughing.

It was through studying this last image of her that I finally began to see her differently, and to see that the heart of the mother I'd felt from the first instant of my life to the last instant of hers was a comic heart, that for all her moral seriousness (because of it?) she was a *komodios*—a singer in the revels that affirm shared humanness. I had always held her up as an example of the best in human nature, firm in her principles, fair in her affections; I'd always believed that she was noble and just, despite a miserable, unlucky life. I had so ennobled her that I had missed the point. Although I had daily been its lucky recipient, I hadn't seen her quintessential quality: her joy.

This joy she shared easily. It was why people smiled back at her on the street, why relations and friends came to tell her their troubles. Why as adults my siblings and I each confessed to our spouses that we'd been always certain that our mother had loved us most. Why my little sister Sheila was so happily full of life that we called her "Sunshine." It was why my mother was fearless, though never fierce; why she cared so little for blame. She got angry, she never backed down, but she was never mean.

At the end of a novel of mine, *First Lady*, written many decades after she died, a young minister is asked following a rock star's concert to define the difference between stars and saints. I had the minister reply that stars draw all the light *to* them, whereas with saints, "the light just goes right through them to what they love so that we can see its beauty. They don't get in the way because they're looking too." That's how my mother saw life. When as a teenager I'd grouse that I disliked the smallness of our town, that I wanted to live in great cities, to see the whole world, she'd wave her arm and say, "The whole world's right here. Just look." Her attitude drove me crazy. But now, in each of those few old, cracked, smudged photographs, I can see that the lens she was looking through was grace. Her smile is absolute. Without tension in her eyes or mouth, she holds nothing back. Her look says she was happy. It says she felt lucky. I'd thought she was lying to me, if not herself. But she wasn't.

My mother would lose her hearing, a career in music, her husband, her health. Having grown up in harmonious ease, she died in her fifties, poor and in pain. Yet happiness stayed with her. And it was not innocent, not protected by lack of knowledge, lack of experience. She was a bright, insightful woman, well educated, with a passion for learning—more likely to forget to eat than forget to read. She was of the generation of the Great Depression and World War II, and never blind to the world's ugliness. Still, her faith was, "Life's a comedy, sweetheart. Life says 'yes.'"

Who I am, as a person and a writer, was nourished by that joy of hers. Yet only now, half a century after she died, now that I am nearly twenty years older than she was ever to become, do I daily bless the good fortune I always thought she was crazy to claim.

Only a few months after her death, I went north to graduate school. The stories I told of her while there always started with her illness: her horrific decades in the trench warfare that was breast cancer in the 1960s, botched surgeries, brutal chemotherapy, lethal radiation. Also, the fictional portraits of her I began to put into my stories and novels—few and far briefer than my portraits of my father (whom I'd rarely seen after the age of nine)—told a story of heroic endurance, of injustices suffered. In my narrative, her life was one long sorrowful progression of losses. I didn't yet hear her explaining to me that her losses were nothing compared to her gains. "Look out the window. That woman with the baby at the bus stop. Look at this book I'm reading. It's Jane Austen! Lucky me. Look at *you*. You're you! It's all gain to me, sweetheart. It's not loss. It's all yes."

From my childhood, in our important conversations, she held my face lightly in her hands. I habitually resisted until she let me go. She held me close because she was deaf and wanted to be sure she was reading my lips correctly. I pulled away because it so grieved me that she'd lost her hearing that I assumed it pained her even more, that she too thought her going deaf was another of life's injustices.

Now I didn't have to make up fictions to claim that her life had had—for a twentieth-century, middle-class American—serious losses:

As a toddler, she fell into a fire of sidewalk leaves, was badly burned, and might have died had it not been for a stranger's rescue. She carried the scars all her life.

As a child, she lost a beloved older sister in an influenza epidemic.

In her midtwenties, while a graduate student in piano at Peabody Conservatory in Baltimore, she'd gone suddenly deaf. In a matter of days. Bacterial meningitis. No doubt today the right antibiotic could have stopped the damage. She told me, when I was in my early twenties and fretting about a future career, that her hearing loss had done two good things for her: one, enabled her to raise four children alone in a small apartment while reading Jane Austen in the still center of cacophony; and two, spared her the knowledge that (while still pretty good at playing songs for parties) by temperament and talent she would never have succeeded as a professional pianist.

At the time, I resisted both her laughing at calamity and her acceptance of such negative self-appraisal. Now, in life, and in my fiction, I at least try to rely on what was instinctive to her. Now—like Raleigh Hayes in my novel *Handling Sin* (who took as long to learn the lesson as I did)—I know laughter is a prayer and that self-appraisal is the start of salvation.

After a hospitalization failed to repair my mother's sudden hearing loss, two of her brothers brought her home from Baltimore to the large house in the Carolina Piedmont where they'd grown up together in a big, good-natured family. And where, cheerful despite their eventual loss of limbs, speech, loved ones, the whole family met regularly for dinner until they all died, usually of diabetes or heart attacks, usually in their forties or fifties. They are the family in that novel of mine, *Handling Sin*—their characters based not on the facts of their lives but on their philosophy of life: That laughter is a prayer. That life is just a bowl of cherries. That they were sitting on top of the world. That when you're smiling, the whole world smiles with you. They were an easy sentimental version of my mother's joy. They were less literate disciples of American happiness, without her lifetime of Shakespeare, Austen, Flaubert, Balzac, without her lost Chopin and Bach, without her capaciousness. A number of them thought she was a communist because of her admiration for Martin Luther King, bless her heart.

Back home, she trained for and went to teach in an elementary school. Able to understand others by lip reading and by bone conduction of sounds through a clumsy hearing device, she could communicate. At the time, American know-how was fast moving, but when she started teaching, the hearing-aid battery she carried was still the shape and size of a shoeshine box. She set it on her desk in a fourth-grade classroom at a public school in a low-rent neighborhood of mill and factory workers. She rode to the school daily first on a trolley and later on a bus. Never in her life did she drive a car. But some of her friends did, and she apparently had a whole gang of friends.

While in her twenties and thirties, my mother traveled often with groups of girlfriends. They rode donkeys down trails into the Grand Canyon, made a laughing chorus line of linked arms and raised legs at the surf's edge of a Florida beach, waved at the camera from the observation deck of the new Empire State Building. One of her life's regrets (or one of the few she mentioned) was that she had missed her trip to Europe, although she and her friends held tickets for the *Queen Mary*'s scheduled departure from a New York City pier in September 1939. But England suddenly declared war on Germany; their crossing was abruptly canceled, and the *Queen Mary* was sent to dry dock. Mama kept her ticket in her purse for years, hoping to use it after the war.

What she did when she came home surprised everyone, herself most of all. She broke off an engagement to a fine man she'd known since childhood because she'd fallen in love with a younger brother's college friend. Her family had taken him into their home because he was so far from his own; because, although a Yankee and even a Catholic, they felt sorry for him. They called him Tommy even when they hated him for leaving my mother with four children— the oldest (me) nine, the youngest (my brother David) a newborn. "Tommy" was bright and good looking and had a beautiful Irish tenor voice.

He claimed to be from the west coast of Connemara but apparently wasn't. Still my mother, in love not just with him but also with Ireland, started spending her evenings listening to his sad stories and accompanying on her piano the soulful Irish songs he sang. My father said he had grown up in an impoverished coal-mining Pennsylvania town. He said that as a child he'd had to steal coal from slag heaps to keep the family's tenement home heated. He said he'd sold newspapers outside the 30th Street Station in Philadelphia to buy food. Mama had to have known that Mahanoy City, where he lived, was on the other side of Pennsylvania, so his claim probably wasn't true. He lied habitually, as though being Irish depended on it.

My mother eloped with him, had two children (the first one, me, at thirty-six), used her job, her savings, and the sale of her Steinway grand to get him through a Ph.D. in psychology and an M.D. in psychiatry, moved with him to Atlanta, had two more children. Somewhere along the way, she quit teaching.

Because of my father's frequent cheating on my mother, I hadn't trusted him since I was eight—when I'd figured it out, though I assumed she hadn't. My rebuff was not just to decline to take part in the circuses he created, which I loved, but to remove my brother and sister, then six and three, from his circus employ as well. I packed the two of them in a red wagon with cheese crackers and my Hopalong Cassidy pistol and headed out of the neighborhood, toward downtown Atlanta. We got no farther than a small local park with a playground. My mother, in a police car, found us.

One December, after ten years of marriage, my father walked out on my mother and her four children. The baby, David, had probably been home from the hospital for a few weeks by then, but in my memory and in my stories, my father drove both mother and baby home the day after David's birth and then moved out. While he was packing, I crawled up a tree in the backyard and refused—despite my mother's plea—to climb down to say goodbye. I resisted for the rest of her life her efforts to persuade me not to repudiate my father. From my point of view, I was making sacrifices for her, by acts of Galahad-like gallantry. From North Carolina, I returned the best gifts he sent me—always great temptations, like a boxed set of LPs of Beethoven's nine symphonies, for he knew what gifts to give. By the divorce decree, I was sent to Atlanta to visit him. At eleven I robbed him, somehow got to a train station, somehow got someone to buy me a ticket, and rode the train up to North Carolina. I walked home from the station and was shocked when my frantic mother didn't run to me in delight, like Melanie to Ashley, back from war, but angrily shook me. It was the only time she did that. It was the first time I realized how weakened she already was from treatment for the cancer that had just been diagnosed.

Tommy was a very charming and handsome and successful man. In my early childhood he was magic to me, the one who sang, the one who put on the circuses. As an adult I discovered he was also a deeply sad, uncertain man. My mother never lost hope or faith either, not even in her dying.

I read two Yeats poems at her funeral service. Her siblings thought an Irish poet like "Yeets" was a bad thing to pick. One of her sisters told me, "You should have read an American poem. Tommy was the worst thing ever happened to Fay. Till Tommy got hold of her with all that 'Danny Boy' boo-hoo bull, she was a good American. Well, except for being a commie."

Reluctantly I admitted, "She never stopped loving him."

"She was a fool for love. Oh, Sweet Bug, I am gonna miss her so so much. Check my mascara! Do I look like a raccoon? Don't answer!"

One of her brothers said, "We might as well have hauled a ten-foot copperhead into our house as let Tommy move in with us."

She'd been divorced for more than a decade when she died. Her family had never seen the perfidious "Tommy" again, but he was still part of their evening conversations on the big wraparound porch of the home where he'd been a guest boarder for years. They retold endlessly how he'd stolen her away from the good southern man to whom she'd been engaged, how she'd run away with a Yankee twelve years her junior. How I was born (eight months later) and had almost killed her in the process. "The doctors told her, it was her or the baby. That it was too much for her at her age. And your mama squeezed the doctor's hand so hard, she left her nail prints in it. And she said, 'You are *not* going to lose me *or* my baby. You are not gonna dare!' Honey, you weighed eight pounds, fifteen ounces, and you know how petite your mama was."

"I weighed eight pounds, fifteen ounces at eight months?"

"You did. When she got her mind set on something, you know how she was."

Her siblings talked on the porch year after year of how grief over my father's infidelities had given their sister the cancer that was to kill her. It was if he had savagely driven a car right over her body only a few days before her funeral. Tommy was one of the few individuals in the world in whom my mother's family could see no value. Their prejudices—and they had many—were general: un-American Americans, Yankee snoots, foreigners who wouldn't learn English, arrogant blacks and the long-hair crowd and feminists who caused trouble, the "light in the loafers" crowd. But frankly I never saw the *individual* they could resist—white, black, long-haired. A gay from New York with a Spanish accent they would invite to dinner after an hour of conversation on a plane. They couldn't resist individuals. But Tommy they never forgave.

And none of them seemed to question the sudden recklessness that might have given my mother pause. None wondered why she hadn't fought to keep her marriage together for her children, or fought in the divorce settlement for enough money to live on without working jobs, like stuffing envelopes or being a seasonal sales clerk. They believed she had run off with her baby brother's best friend because he had literally bewitched her with his Irish singing and his "Yeets" poetry, the kind of poetry I should *not* be reading at her funeral. But I didn't know whether my father had even liked Yeats. These two poems were my mother's favorites.

One was Yeats's bittersweet address to Maud Gonne, the Irish revolutionary:

"When You Are Old," a translation of Ronsard's "Quand vous serez bien vieille." Two lines of this poem were to form the mantra for the mournful portrait of my mother that I would paint for years to come:

> But one man loved the pilgrim soul in you,
> And loved the sorrows of your changing face.

The lines were rosary beads on which I began, reciting it at her funeral, to count the sorrows of my mother's unfortunate life. But her siblings wanted a different kind of poetry at her grave. Songs. "We will meet, but we will miss her. There will be an empty chair." My mother had predicted that her sisters would sing this country tune at her graveside. They did.

The other Yeats poem I read was "The Lake Isle of Innisfree." She had first read it to me shortly after her second surgery for cancer. She'd read from a large anthology she'd brought to the hospital titled *A Thousand Years of Irish Poetry*.

Half a century later, I have that anthology in my study. Looking at it, I can hear her soft southern voice reading to me in that sterile hospital room.

> I will arise and go now, and go to Innisfree . . . .
> And I shall have some peace there, for peace comes dropping slow . . . .
> I will arise and go now, for always night and day
> I hear lake water lapping with low sounds by the shore;
> While I stand on the roadway, or on the pavements grey,
> I hear it in the deep heart's core.

Reading that poem now, I can see my mother propped on thin white pillows, beside her one of the most familiar objects of my childhood: her hearing device, a headband attached by tangled wire to a battery box.

Both of my parents have novels of mine dedicated to them. My father's dedication came first, in *Handling Sin* (1986), an expansive comedy with joyful characters: "To my father. Thank you for the gift."

All I can conclude is "the gift" was an unconscious reference to those unacknowledged presents from him that I had always returned. Or maybe because he was always the artistic one—he sang songs, wrote poems, painted pictures, made furniture, published books. I probably assumed any literary gift I had must have been inherited from him.

My mother's dedication was for the novel I wrote next, *Time's Witness* (1989), a novel with my favorite hero, Cuddy Mangum, a novel about a capital punishment case, about white supremacists—neo-Nazis and the Klan—and about how powerful conservative business and political leaders in North Carolina manipulated their racism and nativism for their own agendas.

In memory of my mother, Faylene Jones Malone, a Southern school-teacher who taught that justice is everyone's right and everyone's responsibility.

*Time's Witness* rightly belonged to her. But I know now that so did *Handling Sin*. That the gift was hers. She didn't live to know that all of her children would live useful lives and would marry, stay married, stay in touch, have children, have grandchildren, make contributions to their worlds. She never knew I'd become a novelist. But she would have predicted all these futures.

She would have been happy that finally I was able to stop disavowing my father and admit that I loved him. She would have been glad I'd sat by his deathbed and to know that when, demented, he asked who I was, I talked a little about the book I was writing and he told me, "My eldest son is an excellent novelist." She would have liked that.

My father mentioned my mother to me only once. When I was in my forties, he'd shown up, a surprise knock at the door, at my house in Philadelphia where my family and I lived. He'd come there, he said, to see his brother. I had no idea he had a brother in Philadelphia. After an awkward evening of the long silences that had always filled our time together, I asked him, "If you had to say one thing about my mother, what would you say?"

He didn't hesitate. He said, "She was the only person I ever met in my whole life who never once forgot the person for their function. She always saw the person."

I used to wish I could have told her that he realized that truth about her, but now I suspect she knew it.

In a photograph, my mother is carrying my brother Patrick. He would have been a year or so old. I'm a toddler, about two and a half. It's spring or summer. We're all dressed up and walking in a garden or a park. I'm impatiently pulling on her free hand, trying to tug her forward, clearly feeling she was too slow, she was slowing me down on my way to the great world.

I now know why she's smiling so beautifully in that picture. It's because it gives her joy for me to be moving ahead, hurrying into life.

As she was dying, on the last of many hospital beds where I sat beside her, her last words to me were, "Honey, you have to let go of my hand."

And so, now, I do. And I thank her for the gift.

# You Dumb Bell

## — JAMES SEAY —

THE GREETING on the face of the valentine, "You Dumb Bell," says more about my mother than about the recipient: my father, the putative "dumb bell" in question. The valentine is in the shape of a dumbbell, the weight used for exercise and made popular during the time my mother gave the valentine to my father, the early 1930s, before they married. When opened, the little dumbbell carries the jussive: "Get Onto The Fact That I'd Like To Be Your Valentine." Above that directive float two hearts, a single arrow piercing them both.

My father, though, needed little assurance that Lucie Belle Page was his valentine. Already during their closely supervised courtship he had lifted his cigarette—remember, no romantic movie of that era lacked a cigarette—and spelled out "I love you" in the air of the Page living room in Como, Mississippi. They were not allowed to sit together on the settee during his visits. My mother's older brother, Damon, a Puritan of the first water, was in the adjacent room, alert to any threat to his notion of purity. You will recall the Puritans who interrupted the nuptial party in Hawthorne's "The May-Pole of Merry Mount." They shot the dancing bear and cropped the locks of the bridegroom who had danced with and then wed the Lady of the May. Breaks your heart. Puritans bent on killing any merriment. Damon would have been in their front ranks.

When I say that the valentine reveals more about my mother's sensibility than my father's, I do not mean that he was without a sense of levity, as evidenced in his amorous smoke signal sent across the room in secret. But my mother had an impulsiveness and whimsy that he lacked. I have a photograph of her around age seventeen in a neighbor's lily pond. She wears a one-piece bathing suit of black wool jersey, and she is standing among the lily pads with one hand on the concrete lip of the small pond. The waterline is at her breasts, and white lily blossoms surround her. She is smiling, as if to say, "Look at me now. I've snuck out and jumped into Vashti Lewis's lily pond. And Damon can't do anything about it."

My father, on the other hand, while capable of the "I love you" sent in wisps of smoke, would sit and talk of Caterpillar bulldozers or recite to her the mnemonic "Washington And Jefferson Made Many A Joke." W-A-J-M-M-A-J: Washington, Adams, Jefferson, Madison, Monroe, Adams, Jackson. "Van Buren Had To Pay, Taylor's Frying Pan Broke. Lincoln Just Gasped, 'Heaven Guard America!'" He could take it all the way to FDR, who was president at the time.

The Depression did not need a Wall Street crash to enter the Deep South. Hard times had been a way of life for most people in the South forever, and FDR's New Deal, while a grand effort and a success, by and large, had a limited effect in some areas. My mother's family in Mississippi played the economic hand they were dealt with remarkable skill and decidedness. They tended a large vegetable garden in season, cultivated pecan and fruit trees, raised chickens, and had cows for milk, cream, and butter.

Butter was on the table every day. My mother did the churning. She was instructed by her mother, though, not ever to straddle the churn. That would be vulgar. The churning was to be done sidesaddle, so to speak. But when her mother left the room, my mother straddled the churn, pumping the dasher like a wanton, intent on getting the butter to the top as soon as possible. To churn to the side, her body twisted, was much more physically demanding. And slower. There were lily ponds out there waiting to be jumped into.

And there was sweet sorghum cane to be had for peeling and chewing. My mother's father had a sorghum field and a small mill for making sorghum syrup—imagine an earthy, mild caramel flavor—which was put up in jars for the winter cupboard. His mule Thunder, named for unceasing flatulence, was harnessed to a long pole attached to the sorghum mill. Thunder plodded in a circle to put in motion the gears that governed the crushing mechanism. Sorghum cane was fed into the mill, and the juice that flowed from it was soon in the settling tank and then into copper pans for stirring and evaporation over the wood fire until it arrived at proper consistency.

My mother went one day to the field to fetch canes of sorghum for her and her siblings. Thunder was given a rest, and my mother's father collected choice stalks for her to deliver to the house. There Damon would cut the cane into sections and apportion them to his siblings.

As she made her way up the dirt road through the field, my mother stopped and put one of the canes beneath her heel. She didn't have a knife, but she was determined to get into the sweetness of the sorghum before her brother had a chance to use it as demand for payment on indulgences from his papacy. As she pulled up on one end of the cane, the section beneath her heel split, forming a razor-sharp edge along both sides of the separation. When she released the end of the cane, it sought its natural bind and caught a portion of flesh in its vise, cutting deeply into her heel. My mother began hopping around and kicking to free herself. When liberated from the cane, her heel was bleeding profusely into the dust of the road.

Perhaps as a reaction to the trauma—or perhaps just coincidence, the cut and a natural onset—her menses began. Blood trickled down her thighs and joined that issuing from the cut in her heel. She did not know which was which in the confluence that soaked into the dust, nor did she know what was wound and what was not. But the dust helped stanch the flow from her heel, and she gathered herself for the delivery of the sweet cane to the house. There in a bedroom her mother explained to her what one realm of her life was now given over to.

I never knew of any of this until, in her late years, my mother showed me the scar on her heel and told me of its source. Though she did not provide all of the details in my narrative, I summon them to make her story more vivid and at the same time mysterious and elusive to me. I do not want her generic or sentimentalized. I want her to be somewhere between the girl surrounded by white blossoms in a lily pond and the young woman bleeding in the cane field with a lone scar in the making and her womb opened to the world. I want her also in fixed defiance of her brother Damon and what he stands for.

That is not to say that Damon was an evil person. In adulthood he was a hardworking man, decent enough. But he retained the rigidity and intense censoriousness of his earlier years. When my mother's mother had her sixth and final child, Joe David Page, Damon left the house in a fury and moved into the barn. He told his parents that they could barely feed the children they had and now they were bringing another mouth to the table. I can find empathy for him, however, in the humiliation he suffered at the hands of a man who sold him a baby coffin when he was a young boy. Damon passed by the hardware store in town and saw in the window what he took to be a little boat. He wanted to float in the little boat past the bluffs on the river nearby. He saved his money and took it to the man, who assured him that he could float past the bluffs in it. When Damon brought his little boat home, his father told him it was a baby coffin.

It's possible also that I can find feeling for him in his marriage. He married a woman, Jennie Ruth Hay, who had just been married for two days to a Mr. Sweat from Arkansas. (I am told that she was particularly insistent that her family pronounce his last name properly: "Sweet.") After her one-night honeymoon, she returned to her parents' home, and the next morning Mr. Sweat had left her trousseau luggage on the front porch. Soon after that, Jennie Ruth married Damon. She was the bane of our Sunday visits to their home, especially with her unrelenting reminders that she was a member of the Daughters of the

American Revolution. Nothing we could do or say escaped her judgment. My mother despised her but instructed my sisters and me to mind our manners. At some point before Jennie Ruth died, she stipulated that there be no birth date on her gravestone, only the year of her death. Vain into eternity, she waited there to be joined by the finally hapless Damon. In the months before his death he claimed that the nurses at the assisted-care center were "having their way" with him. When my sisters were clearing out his house to settle his estate, they discovered *Playboy* magazines in his closet. I'm confident that he found more release there than any he found with the one-night honeymooner Jennie Ruth.

I was living in the south of France in 1990 when word came from my sisters in Mississippi that they had taken my mother to the hospital in Memphis. Given the cost of last-minute transatlantic airfares, they suggested that I remain in France until they could advise me further about her condition. After their call, I went to a restaurant near Place Masséna in Nice called Spaghettisimo or some such. I've Googled and Binged for current restaurants there but cannot find a Spaghettisimo. I wanted to verify its name so as to re-create in sum that fraught moment in my life. I recall distinctly the uncertainty, the dread of guilt should I not go to my mother in an hour of need, the vacancy that I would feel if she died while I was in France.

When I had finished my pasta, I walked to a promontory overlooking the Mediterranean. The sun was behind a bank of clouds. As I looked into the sky, the sun broke from the clouds and cast a soft brilliance across the surface of the sea and spilled onto the city. It was a gift of light from my mother. Lucie, *lux*, light. *I am okay*, she said, *go back and have some espresso. Stay there until I need you. I've survived Damon, open bleeding in a sorghum cane field, and, who knows, possible drowning in a lily pond.*

The last words my mother spoke to me were, "You feel warm." It was 1992, two years after the sun broke from the clouds over the water and brought my mother across the ocean to me. She was in the hospital in Memphis again, and she would die there, but I did not know that. My sisters assured me that they would watch over her and get her home when she recovered. I had to get back to my work in North Carolina. I leaned over to hug and kiss my mother good-bye, and she commented on my warmth. "You feel warm." What she meant was that I felt as though I had a fever and she needed to get up and tend to me. Put a flannel cloth with Vicks VapoRub on my chest. Read *The Adventures of Tom Sawyer* out loud. Fix me some cream of tomato soup and a grilled cheese sandwich. Tell me Little Moron jokes and why the chicken crossed the road. To get to the other side.

Ah, Lucie, you dumb bell.

# From Tehran to Florida

## Pouri joon's Fierce Love

— OMID SAFI —

WHEN I STARTED as a freshman at Duke, the university had invited the famed author Maya Angelou to offer words of wisdom and inspiration to the incoming first-year student class. I remember only one thing she told us: in the middle of her speech, she pointed in her inimitable, dramatic way to the crowd and thundered, *"You have been paid for."*

We were thousands crammed into the chapel, but somehow I felt like she was looking at me. It was as if Maya Angelou's loving, wise glance reached right to me. *"You have been paid for."*

Maya Angelou *saw* me. She saw my family. She saw my mother, Pouri joon. She saw our sacrifice. She saw our struggle. She saw our humanity. I had been *paid for*. I didn't know fully what that meant. That language, though, resonated deeply.

I have been paid for through the blood, sweat, and tears of my parents. I was paid for. I was paid for, not in heaven but right here on Earth. My own education, my life, was paid for.

Almost every piece of writing about Muslim mothers features a saying of the Prophet: "Paradise lies beneath the feet of mothers." The saying states that, in the sight of God, the status of mothers is so elevated that they are too good, too sublime, for paradise. So God has no choice but to position them above Paradise. They are above Paradise; Paradise is under their feet.

There is much that is made of motherhood, love, and sacrifice. I know the critique, how the ideal of sacrifice takes away from women's own sense of destiny and selfhood, how the burden of maternal sacrifice lets others (namely men) off the hook. What am I to do, when the mother I've been blessed with is a living model of love and sacrifice?

I am who I am because Pouri joon loved me.

I am who I am because I have been loved into my bones.

I am who I am because, thanks to her love, I have never wondered for my own sense of self-worth.

My mom's name, Pouran, is always abbreviated to Pouri. *Joon* is the intensely more intimate version of *jaan*, the Persian word that means "soul" or "life force." As an honorific, it is added to the name of people so dear to you it is as if they are your own soul, as if they are the life force through whom you live. Never in my life have I called my mother "Pouran" or "Pouri." It's always *Pouri joon*. "Soul-Mother." Pouri joon, who is as dear to me as my own life.

## First Memories

The earliest memory I have of my mother is of a night, a feverish night. I must have been around four years old. I ran the kind of high fever that children run. I have seen my own children with that kind of fever—102, 103. These little bodies seem like they are burning up. My own fever ran so high that I slipped in and out of consciousness. Each time I came back into consciousness, there was my mother by my bed, keeping a night vigil. Prayers, smiles, and holding my hand. There was Pouri joon, staring into my eyes, her mouth whispering a prayer whose words were known only to her and to God.

She taught me that night that keeping nighttime vigil by your children is a prayer. You look at God by looking at your children.

## Leaving Iran

Our life in Iran was not as a nuclear family. There were hundreds of members of the Safi family (my Baba's side) and the Ashtari side (my Mom's). Every Friday we went to Pouri joon's parents' house, where we would be with grandparents, aunts, and cousins. The family felt like a starry night with so many constellations. My parents were the moon, but there were always stars.

Both my Baba and Pouri joon were deeply embedded in this large network of love. It may take a village to raise a child, and this was our village. In 1985, six years after the Iranian revolution and five years after the start of the war, my parents decided to leave home, leave Iran, leave the family, leave the village. It was not a decision they reached casually or easily.

When the revolution happened and most Iranians who could afford to left Iran, my parents said, "You don't leave your home because of a little revolution." When the next year Saddam Hussein invaded Iran (supported by both the United States and almost all of the Arab countries), my parents said, "You don't leave your home because of a little war." When the war was not such a little war, and Saddam started bombing Iranian cities with both missiles and planes, they said, "You don't leave home because of a little bombing." By 1985 the Iranian regime, like the Iraqis, was running out of men, and it started to draft high school students. The government started a policy that ensured all high school students were prohibited from leaving the country until they had fulfilled their almost surely fatal military service, and it was then that my parents said, "*Now* is the time to leave your homeland."

And leave we did. Six of us—two parents and four children—left Iran with two suitcases. We left everything else behind. We left our home, our cars, our families, my parents' recognition and standing in society. We were not refugees, but we had this in common with the refugees that would follow from Iraq, Bosnia, Syria, and elsewhere: no one leaves home unless they love their children more than they love their own parents. I remember the haunting lines from the great poet Warsan Shire:

> no one leaves home unless
> home is the mouth of a shark
> you have to understand,
> that no one puts their children in a boat
> unless the water is safer than the land

When we were deciding to leave, Pouri joon knew her own father was dying. This man, this kind and gentle and devastatingly handsome, generous man was my rock, her rock. He was a loving man who would tear up each time he saw me, his first grandchild. He was more dignified than a movie star, and he had the kind of warm fleshy hug that exuded deep love. Pouri joon loved him so, and she had to choose between staying with him and getting her children to safety. She chose her children. She chose life for us. I can never imagine having to make that kind of a choice, and I pray no one may ever have to do so. Knowing that she did makes me love her oh so much more. I cannot pay her back. I can only hope that, if called upon, I'd be able to save both my children and my parents.

A few months after we arrived in America, my grandfather, my loving Baba Ashtari, Pouri joon's beautiful father, passed away. Pouri joon knew he would when we left Iran. She was unable to be there for her own father's funeral, or to visit his gravesite for many years.

Pouri joon wept.

# Pouri joon's Tears

Moving from Iran was a humbling experience for us. We moved into a tiny townhouse, and my Baba who had been the dean of a medical school in Iran was made to take the American medical board exams once more, some decades after he had last studied for medical school, and this time in a new language. Money was extremely tight, but our love was tighter. We kids knew our job: get into the best college we could. And get a scholarship.

I am not sure we were ever teenagers. There was none of the cosmic moping, brooding, and sitting in our bedrooms. We spent time together as a family, and then we studied. And then we studied some more.

After three years of studying, learning a new language, and studying some more came the big answer: college acceptance. I had long dreamed of getting into an Ivy League school, and I was so thrilled to receive the fat envelope from Yale. The night before I was to mail my acceptance letter, Pouri joon had what I refer to as the Storm of Tears. Yale was too far from Florida. She could not have her firstborn go that far away. I begged and pleaded, saying that I would call every night. Nope. She insisted that even on the phone she would know that I would be a thousand miles away. So we compromised on Duke, a school I had never seen, in North Carolina, a state I had never set foot in.

So off to Duke I went. Pouri joon and Baba joon came to drop me off, and for the first night in my life I slept under a roof that was not either their home or the home of a family member. I still remember that night, staring at the ceiling and listening to the snoring of my roommate.

The highways from North Carolina to Florida are not the most scenic ones. You take I-40 from Durham to Raleigh, continue past the Raleigh beltway on I-40, and then drive for seven hours on I-95. I learned later that when Baba and Pouri joon were driving home, they were shedding so many tears that twice they went all the way around the Raleigh Beltway. Through her tears, Pouri joon laughingly teased my Baba: "Ali jan, I think we've seen these buildings before."

God works through human beings. And in particular, through my Momma.

I went to Duke to study medicine. In my career there, I met a few amazing teachers and had a change of heart. I turned down medical school in favor of an academic career in Islamic studies. Now I am a writer, a professor of religion, and a blogger. I am who I am, and I do what I do, because my Momma had the Storm of Tears. If she hadn't cried, I would have gone to Yale and probably become a doctor. God works in mysterious ways, including through my Momma's tears.

I am the eldest of Pouri joon's four children. Four times she has had to take the children she gave birth to, put them in a car, drive with them to their university, and leave them. Four times she has wept, sobbed, and returned to a home without all of her children. But she was not done being a mother when her babies went to college. She stayed up late at night praying for her children, and when my sister, Farnaz, went to the Caribbean for medical school before coming back to New York, Mom flew down with a suitcase filled with her alchemical food. She kept Farnaz company for the stressful exam period, and on the day of the exam, Pouri joon sat outside the door of the exam room and said her most special prayers for my sister.

God hears the prayers of a Momma.

## Pouri joon's Cooking

When people speak of my mom, they often speak of her cooking. It's not food, really. It's more like alchemy. Persian cooking is considered refined in a part of the world where there is much refined cooking: Lebanese cuisine, Egyptian cuisine, Afghan cuisine, Turkish cuisine, Indian cuisine, Armenian cuisine, and so on . . . I won't tempt the gods by elevating one of these above the others. So let me just say that Persian cuisine has a special magic. It is not as spicy as Indian cuisine, nor is it as meat centered as some of the other cuisines. Rather, it shines through subtle flavors that mingle through hours and hours of slow cooking in which beans, dried fruit, vegetables, spices, and meats gradually come together.

Some of the Persian dishes, like *qormeh sabzi, qaymeh, albalo polo,* and *fesenjoon*, are legendary. *Qormeh sabzi* features every vegetable known to man or woman, kidney beans, and small cuts of choice meat. My mother's *qormeh sabzi* is so delightful that other amazing cooks have retired their dishes. It's not modesty; it is the look of knowing when one has seen the divine archetype of a masterpiece. *Qaymeh* includes yellow lentils, dried lemons, tomato paste and onion, and chunks of meats. *Albaalo polo* has sour cherries and meatballs. Sour cherries! Really, how many cuisines feature cooked sour cherries? And *fesenjoon*—oh my goodness! Pomegranates, walnuts, and chicken/pheasant/duck slow cooked to sheer perfection . . . if Pouri joon's dishes are not in heaven, I may ask to be excused.

My mom is also one of the hardest people in the world to learn cooking from. She has so internalized the recipes that there is no measurement. No tablespoons, no teaspoons, no cups. It's "a little bit of cinnamon," a pinch of that, "just enough of this," "not too much of that." Like many great cooks, she does not cook from a cookbook. I don't think I have seen her open a cookbook in decades. The recipes come from her—well, her heart. To watch her in a kitchen is like watching the union of a dancer and a symphony conductor. Everything is graceful, everything is purposeful and beautiful. How at ease she is.

There is a secret ingredient, too. It's her love that she puts into the cooking because her love is too intense, too much to fit into words. So she whips up her alchemy every day. When we visit my parents in Florida, we go for weeks without ever eating out. Why would we go to a restaurant? It never tastes as good, is never as good for you, and never has Pouri joon's magical ingredient, love.

Our family gatherings look like *My Big Fat Greek Wedding*, where laughter, joy, love, and stories all mingle. A few years ago we decided that the burden of cooking for eighteen people under one roof was too much for Pouri joon, and like dutiful children we decided to take turns. Pouri joon would cook one night, followed by each of the children. Or so we thought. She tasted her children's cooking and told us in that truthful way that only she is allowed to speak: "Thank you for trying. Now, get out of my kitchen."

In the presence of a queen, you know to get out of her throne room.

## Momma Was Right

One of the challenges of life with Momma is that Momma is a tiger. She is fierce, her emotions passionate. She loves her children more than life itself, and so the people who have dared to love her children always have to meet her high standards.

I was twenty-five when I met my future wife. It was an insane, crazy, irrational love. Or lust. We had nothing in common, aside from being young people in love with the romance of it all—us against the world. Us against our parents. Her parents asked how many camels my parents would expect for the wedding. They knew nothing about the world my parents came from, with no interest in learning about it. My parents saw how little we had in common and were dead set against the relationship. When we got engaged, they were against that engagement. And when we told them that we would get married, they were against the marriage.

Mom and Baba are quite different. They both love immensely. My Baba's love is gentle, like a stream that flows under your feet. My Momma's love is like a fierce raging fire, a lightning bolt. Baba and Momma were both agreed that they would not come to the wedding. But their way of voicing their disapproval was different. Baba called every day, he begged, he pleaded, he reasoned. "Precious one of my heart, please don't do this. You don't have anything in common. You will find real love, be patient, trust me." Three days before the wedding, Baba said that he would, reluctantly, come to the wedding. Not happily. But come he did. He came, he sat sad and brokenhearted, and he held my hand.

Pouri joon did not come. And to make sure that she would not change her mind last minute, Pouri joon went overseas. She took my brothers and went to Iran. One of the last things Momma said to my then-wife was, "You and Omid are not right for each other. You'll be together for twenty years, and then you'll be divorced. As God is my witness, mark my words."

Momma was right.

We were together for twenty years, and we were divorced. Almost exactly as she had predicted. We had nothing in common, and we drifted apart as she said we would. I fought harder than I have for anything in my life to keep the marriage together, but eventually, after some bitter and painful betrayals, we parted ways.

Momma was right, but she took no pleasure at having been right. When I finally told her about the divorce, the only thing she said was, "It has hurt us so much to see you for the last twenty years try again and again and again to keep this marriage together. You deserve better, so much better. We just want to see you have true happiness in life."

I made a choice to never tell her about how hard, how devastating, how broken the two decades had been. I am not sure I had to. Pouri joon knew without me saying. That's the thing about Mom. Pouri joon always knows.

After the divorce, Pouri joon was kind and cordial to my ex-wife. As I knew she would be. She might be a tiger, but she is a loving tiger.

## Pouri joon's Happiness

There is an amazing quality to life, how light and love can enter through wounds. There is a great truth that both Rumi and Leonard Cohen have written about:

> There is a crack in everything
> That's how the light gets in

That wounded, painful relationship that Momma disapproved of also led to the birth of her first grandchild, and in many ways the perfect love of her life. Her granddaughter Roya, my love Roya, is the spitting image of Pouri joon. There are times that I look at pictures of the two of them, and it is hard to imagine Roya as anything but Pouri joon's spirit reborn. Their love for each other is joyous, fierce, and absolutely, unquestionably unconditional.

Moving from Iran, leaving her family behind, leaving behind the life of riches, dignity, and prestige, coming to a country when they had to learn a new language, raising four children through the culture clash of migration, it all took a toll on Pouri joon. She gave and gave and sacrificed. And the years of building up a life were hard years, challenging years. But when Roya was born, there was joy. Here was this child that God sprinkled just a little extra *something* on. Roya was, and is, gorgeous, beyond words. She was a little doll as a newborn and a toddler, and my mother absolutely adored her. She would giggle as she held Roya, whispering *jaaaaaan-am* ("my soul," "my life force").

And I saw something amazing, unexpected, looking not at my child, my love, my own adored heart beating outside of my chest, but at my mother looking at her. There is joy, real joy, for Pouri joon in beholding Roya, in loving Roya, in being with Roya. And I took pleasure from Pouri joon's pleasure. For us immigrants, so much of life is about survival. Struggle to be, to make it, to have stability. And it was in my child that I saw Pouri joon experience real, lasting, enduring joy.

Mom calls my daughter "Spoily girl," and Roya jokingly calls my Mom, Pouri joon, "PJ." No one else dares do that, no one else would dare do that, but Roya is not everyone else. And Mom loves it. Roya loves to be loved by my mom, the adorer and adored, mirror to mirror, as if they come from a medieval Persian love story. And to see that my mom can love without bounds, fiercely, purely, this beautiful mirror image of herself . . . it brings me joy beyond words.

Roya would not be her last joy. I'd have more children, Amir and Layla. My brother Farshid has two beautiful children, Neema and Neeka. My younger brother, Farzad, has two beautiful children, Cyrus and Maryam. Each time, I have seen Pouri joon's heart get bigger to love each new grandchild as much as the ones before. (Well, Roya remains her favorite.) It's the amazing thing about a heart: it expands to make room for new arrivals.

And I've learned to love again. I met my beautiful partner Corina, who adores Pouri joon and is loved by her. To see the two of them share in their love—there is peace, there is joy, there is harmony. Life feels good, feels complete. *Alhamdulilah.* God be praised.

## Paying Pouri joon's Love Back/Forward

No, I could never, and I cannot now, pay my Pouri joon back. But I can pay it forward. So now, as I look upon my own children, and my own (God willing) as-of-yet unborn grandchildren, I want them to know that they are paid for.

And so it goes. We are paid for and must pay it forward.

There is a circle of life. And there are circles of love. Circles of sacrifice. It is a circle because it has no beginning and no end.

I am are here because Pouri joon loved me.

I am here because Pouri joon sacrificed for me.

I am here because Pouri joon paid for me.

There is no way to thank her. All I can do is to pay it forward.

# i want to undie you

## —JAKI SHELTON GREEN—

*i want to undie you*


1

i have come to this new place whose trees have no medicine
barren ground that has never tasted a thimble of blood
where birds fly backwards and sky is afraid of falling
it is here that I say goodbye to my woman-child who is remembering her true
name and searching for the river where her story was born

the woman-child climbs hills that scratch her without mercy
she becomes the balm for the angry ground that refuses to see her
she is without country so she becomes the map of all her ages
she is without eyes so she becomes the compass of her own heart

i hear her offering sacrifices to the ocean the wind
to the fires of her uncertainty
*not now spirit wails*
*not now*

spirit carves patience grace tenderness inside her palms
between her ribs
the lost ones wait for her
the ones she's been waiting for
pale ghosts running from their own shadows
she is the one they've been waiting for

death is not enough for you my woman-child
it will not feed the dry season in your throat
it will not water the parched soles of the ones who came before you
it is not even the theater you've dressed for

the trees cry out for your medicine
this earth does not need your breath
the earth needs your hands planting and watering new seeds

this place needs the medicine inside your hands

your clan waits for the feast you have prepared for this season of harvest
choose red vibrant pulsating knives that go gently into your bread of life

the trees have no song
muted by ghosts who trod dragging skeletons
dragging undergrowth dragging swords of a sun-bleached confederacy

2

any road traveled any room any door any window courting the wafting breeze
of lemon balm jasmine rosemary cypress all lead back to you sweet woman-
child first born first death of your mother's heart
the hands of a village draw invisible smoke circles of myrrh frankincense cedar
around the hospice house this sweet house wrapping you in new skin for new
dreams that weave new story

we gather with open unclenched palms we gather all the markings of your tribe
who you were before you were born and who you are now becoming as you
once again travel towards the river where blood is born

it took a village to raise you, and it takes a village to help you grow strong wings
of flight and tenderness for this unknown sky
the spirits of mothers grandmothers fathers and grandfathers spoke to you
through the last rain you'd ever smell hear feel

JAKI SHELTON GREEN

the hands of our womb tribe gently caressed your skin still warm
it contained another breath that we felt under our hands as we washed your
body oiled your crevices valleys your cheeks flushed with smile


the people of many villages gathered to hold me
they came with food flowers holy water words open hearts
unnamed strangers gathered at your gravesite unnamed faces and familial faces
cried a river of tears into a double rainbow as we gently unraveled the strings of
our hearts that released you and your new wings into a new sky


3

people bring stories of you to me written on linen rags befitting for your nights
of rescuing lost desperate souls your nights of sharing food offering a bed offering a sanctuary for affirmation


people bring stories of you to me written inside the coat sleeves of a battered
coat that is so alive with the language of sorrow you can hear the coat whispering a coat that used to be purple is covered with dirty grease and the colors of
nights gone bad nights without light or shadows


people bring stories of you to me wrapped with sharp precision inside blank
envelopes that tremble with all the stories they've carried these stories wet with
the breath of rivers where you've jumped in to save the teenage girl when other
suicides weren't enough for her


people bring stories of you to me in shiny glass bottles where you live as their
genies of hope but they've forgotten the magic words that might bring you
back they hold on to the bottles where you've helped them tuck their dreams
for safe passage


people bring stories of you to me in bright colored pyrex dishes steaming hot
with their memories of your own open festive table brimming with soulful

vibrant food that fed their souls deeper than their bellies your recipes of ancient healing crawling inside shattered spines crushed limbs reviving diseased hearts

people bring their stories of you to me inside baskets woven so tight they hold the tears of four generations of torn women their skirts stained with ancestral trauma they bring stories of your arrival to their village no secret potions no magical creams or oils only you with wide open face wide open spirit and the needles of sisterhood helping them stitch the shawls of balm for their unborn generations

4

*i want you to un-die. come back said the mother.*

i want you to undie. i want the dust of you un-scattered. i want the hush of you un-hushed. i want the cries for you un-cried. i want you to un-die. i want the tomb of you un-tombed. i want the dirge of you un-sung. i want the grief of you un-grieved. i want you to un-die.
the clock of you un-stopped. the length of you un-folded. i want the scars of you un-scarred. i want the road of you un-traveled. i want the fret of you un-fretted. the loss of you un-lost. the prayers of you un-prayed.
i want the scream of you un-screamed. i want you to un-die.
i want the verb of you un-verbed. i want the slumber of you un-slept.
i want the shroud of you un-shrouded. i want the earth of you un-broken. the river of you un-flowed. the desert of you un-barren. i want to un-morning that morning. i want to un-break the broken of you. i want to un-confuse the confusion of you. un-diagnose the diagnosis of you. un-steal the stolen of you. un-murder the murdered of you. un-butcher the butchered of you. un-wound the wounded of you. un-bound the bondage of you. un-sterilize the sterility of you. un-deny a life denied to you. un-seal the sealed of you. un-mask the masks of you. un-veil the veils of you.
un-expose the exposed of you. un-sacrifice the sacrifice of you. un-erase the erasure of you. un-lock the locked of you. un-take the taking of you. un-still the stillness of you

for several hours i watch a straight beam of light crossing a closing day
it becomes appendage pointing never quivering completely straight
in your dreams now you chase dragonflies
pattern your wings from their colors
pretend you are a mother
once you were a mother to a sweet dog

at least i want to believe that you dream because i can't un-die you.
i can't un-die the width length breath of you. i want to un-die the color of you
the shadow fire smoke blood and water of you. i want to undie the sharp wet
smooth ice of you. i want you to un-die. your hair head eyes mouth teeth neck
shoulders arms elbows hands breasts belly thighs hips legs knees ribs ankles
feet of you. i want to un-die you. i want to undie your heat your wounds your
cries hugs screams whispers. i want to un-die the house bowl cup sip swallow
bite of you. i want to un-die you. un-die the silk wool nappy coarse sexy round
and long of you. un-die your words your songs your dance the very crawl of you

*it's what a mother does.* she un-dies your blood the colors of your birth and the
colors of your death. she un-dies every crumb of you she undies your smell
your touch your taste she un-dies your heart. your touch your taste. she un-
dies your heart. she becomes a ghost forensic inside a tangled lullaby. you live
there now in the upper crust of my heart trespassing all the barbed wires elec-
tric fences in its basin where you once built delicate tattered houses fragments
of leftover storms. left over childhoods. leftover deaths. you arrived spirit-
hungry with journeying midwives carolina moons and false indigo smeared
across your windows waiting to be lifted

*we are raw thrust. i wake up with the kinky salt of you burning my mouth. black-
ness comes apart like corners becoming tops becoming sides.*
*salt burned. kinky mouth exploding ripping off shark heads. this ocean we swim
becomes death trap. penalty to breathe. vigilante of privilege. why is this culture of
the personal so hard to bear*

*her tongue has forgotten the currency of okra. the language of paw paw fruit burns*
*like december ice under her fingernails.*
*i have traveled to the priestess who barters for johnny walker red.*
*twelve gutted and cleaned drum fish. seventy-four american dollars for*
*the wise one in her gap-toothed regalness*

## dusk

all the pieces of my heart slather long rays of sunlight. dance over fruit that a
heart refuses. a heart cut open into perfect sections. one for the mother one for
the father one for the son two for the daughter. enough fruit. enough light for
the bees that gather to sting light into flowers

i've only visited your grave once before at dusk for i believe it to be your quiet
time. your time to visit with granddaddy great-grandmother great-grandfather
great-aunts great-uncles cousins

in the silver air i heard you turn to listen to footsteps of a long lost friend who
trekked the skies from california searching for your grave in the dark
*dusk* i find him there walking sideways with grief. holding flowers

*dusk* what do you call your mornings your noondays your evenings of moon-
less sky winter grace and summer frill.
what do you drink at dusk from the hands of a lost angel

8

from somewhere far beneath the hearts that love you the memory of you
dances across a threshold of stardust. your heart sings forth a new face.
how does a mother continue to sing

how does a mother continue to whisper the story of a daughter's death
why does the night bring me over and over again to this river

with deaf hands a tongue learns to swim across continents undressing mute
men in holy robes holy cloth


tongues become dances inside an opera of revolution rebellion
daughters offer open legs for the storage of gunpowder blades bullets
while grandmothers become live spittoons for the sharpening of
hidden machetes buried deep under rotten sugar cane
this is the march for water
this is song for the thirst of newborns dry breasts and dry bread
the elegy of the two-legged ones who come to battle without one god in sight


9

who will count the children carrying alphabets of memory beneath collapsing
chins. it is this language of water that does not translate beyond its own reflection. who will decoy the forever promises we made to each other


have mercy upon him whose capital is hope and whose weapon is fear. we bring
the soil. it is such a poetic gesture for your journey through an ocean of sky.
i've still not named you. new star. body of my body. body of my breath. citizen
of my womb. i have been waiting for your face to open beneath this ground
and pour out seven nations. seven generations. seven rivers. fire of my hair . . .
crackling like bluebirds in the farkleberries


### woman-child is born to the woman-child

*it is this one a.m. slow dance across the floors of my mind. disco. apartheid. harlem
drive. bruised ankles of a shackled dancer. chasing unicorns around the hudson
river. on sundays everything tastes like rain. chinese-cuban take-out reminds me
that my mouth is an un-claimed foreign country with poppies growing along the
borders. brown bag ecstasy. hartford connecticut bourgeois deception. secrets. illegal mind weapons. poems that slide off rooftops when your father's fingers foreplay
the german bass violin. sundays that never promised anything beyond blue black
welts hiding beneath all the colors of the artist's wand. you were born inside a room
of turkish smoke. swaddled in opaque blush linen. i become the mother who has
forgotten who she is. who she might me. the women chant story songs about mothers they never knew. your father's father brings white lilies. your other grandfather*

i want to undie you

*stretches deeper in his grave. you are born on the first anniversary of his death. he is waiting. knowing you will recognize him on the other side. she is the you. you and i become more of me. you will call on your grandfather to guide you beyond the stars. it is enough to be born in a windowless room. walls perspiring with the heaviness of rose water cinnabar rosemary. it is enough to recognize your own shadow in the middle of a hailstorm. our shadows are ghosts in a holy city. mother. daughter. forever locked inside the belly of the woman with knives.*

## now

*i write books. store grief upside down on the top pantry shelf where seldom used wedding gifts rest beside oversized serving platters the antique tea service and those tacky fake porcelain teacups i can't bear to toss. in the books there is no grief. only food sex sultry winter music and the teeth of clowns. the genetic complexities of your death bear roots. unravel. implode. graft themselves into continents oceans volcanoes of blood-stained bones that will not un-die.*

— PART II —

Strangers

# Are You My Mother?

## — JILL McCORKLE —

*Are you my mother?*
*I'm your daughter.*
*Daughter? I have a daughter?*
*You have two.*
*Am I married?*
*Yes.*
*Thank the Lord!*

Many of my conversations with my mother begin this way and have for several years now. She has dementia, and we are never sure what a visit will bring: a groggy inwardly turned old woman who will not hold her head up, or a lively fast-talking hall monitor greeting everyone who passes, usually with the exuberant kindness she would have dispensed in the vestibule of the First Baptist Church a decade ago and the many years prior to that—*Hello, sweetie, how are you today?* Then, just as easily, she will slip into another realm that is common in this new existence but completely foreign to her old one. *Where did you get such a big tail? God, I'd do something about that. And look at that one!*

I often think of those old topsy/turvy dolls with her changing moods, one minute smiling and cheerful and the next angry and saying things she never would have uttered in her *other* life. Sometimes I am a long dead cousin or her grandmother; sometimes I am even myself, but more and more our roles are reversed, and I have found that the easiest thing to do is walk in and adjust to wherever she is.

*Mama?*
*Yes.*
*Your name is S-H-I-T.* (She often spells things.)
*You must be thinking of someone else.*
*Well then, I'll call you Cooter or Crocker.*

*Okay.*
*Who named you Cooter?*
*You did, I guess. You're my mother.*

Sometimes in the midst of some kind of nonsensical banter, it is as if a shade lifts and for a split second she is there, the woman who would have *only* spelled an expletive and then *only* when pushed to the very limit of tolerance. Like her mother before her, you knew she was at the end of her rope if you heard something like *Jesus, God, Jesus.* Invoking greater powers when not in church or saying the blessing meant you better scatter until it passed or you would be out at the ligustrum bush picking your own switch. Sometimes the shade lifts: *I wouldn't name a child Cooter,* and we laugh.

*Men don't last long. Every woman I know who had one had him die. A sorry one might last longer than a good one, but I don't know.*

My mother was born in 1929 in Lumberton, North Carolina, as was my dad. They grew up just blocks from one another, and though they didn't begin dating until they were sixteen, were always in school together and friends. In fact, they often told how on the first day of first grade their mothers walked together to take them to school; then at the end of the day, Melba (my mother) was crying because she couldn't remember her way and my dad told her he knew where her home was and he would help her get there. He liked to say he had been doing that ever since, but the truth is they took turns finding the best way home.

*Did your Daddy die?*
*Yes.*
*Oh no. What happened?*
*Lung cancer.*
*Was I there?*
*Every minute. All the way to the end.*

I've often thought that if there is a sliver of grace to be pulled from that gnarled up tangle of dementia, it is that little bit of time given to loved ones to fully appreciate the scope of a whole life while the individual is still there and breathing and every now and then, for the briefest second, visible.

*Do you know who I am?*
*Of course. You're my daughter, Jill.*
*I am and I am so proud of you.*
*Why?*

*You're a really good mother.*
*Oh I'm so glad to hear that. I wanted to be.*

My mother was what she called the knee baby and spoke often of all the work that she did around the house as a child. Her younger brother, Joe, had a lot of problems, and her parents did all that they could to help him. It's quite possible that these days someone would have recognized this or that learning disability early on, mental illness manifesting in his adolescence in ways that today might lead to a diagnosis of schizophrenia. At that time, my grandmother was told many things, including that he was "just mean." My mother felt the responsibility for him early in life and helped my grandmother finally get him the right help, and when my grandmother could no longer be in charge, my mother was caretaker and advocate for them both, along with a great-aunt and a distant cousin who had no one. She was there for all of them, my dad supportive of her, generous with all they had.

My mother worked a forty-hour week as a secretary to a pediatric group for over thirty years, and she also managed to assist with the lives of all these other people. When other mothers were staying home and baking cookies and doing the June Cleaver thing, my mother was at work, and the phone number to the Lumberton Children's Clinic is forever burned into my brain because my sister and I called it a million times; I often called as tattletale to say it was my turn to sit in the big chair or that my sister said I had to hang out the clothes by myself. "Don't make me come home," she would say, "I mean it." Now, I look back and marvel at all she was juggling and how terribly annoying we were. Then, it never occurred to us that she had no choice *but* to work the hours that she did. We never felt slighted in the least. In fact, our cousin, Jennifer, was jealous of our freedom and showed up early all those summer mornings we were home alone to see what we were watching on TV and if we had any good snacks. We always did.

*I want to make vegetable soup like grandma made. Can you help me?*
*Sure. Get a big ham bone and boil it a long time.*
*Okay. Great. And then what?*
*And then just go around your house and throw whatever trinkets you find into the pot.*

My dad struggled with clinical depression at a time when people didn't talk about it. I think many viewed it as a weakness and something that a person could just buck up and handle. The young me has memories of us visiting my dad in the hospital on an Easter Sunday. Someone had offered to drive us, and my sister and I were all dressed up. Our dad came out onto the lawn in his robe with a card he had bought for us there in the hospital gift shop. I remember running up and down a hill, getting hot and sweaty, and at the end of it all being told to wave goodbye and counting up the floors on the brick building to where my dad waved from a window covered in wire mesh. I don't recall many specifics of that time. I know my mother told me that I focused and worried in ways that prompted her to talk to a psychiatrist.

Apparently I had heard her tell my sister she didn't have her lunch money for school (meaning the correct change) and I interpreted it to mean we had no money at all. One of the doctors my mom worked for suggested she go to the bank and get lots of change, fill her purse with it all, and then send me to get something for her. I have no memory of the ecstasy she described to me. What I remember is her *telling* me the story with great pride and ending with "it worked." In fact she teased that it might have worked too well because I was not a very good saver. But what I marvel at looking back is all that she was able to manage at that time; she was the one working and she was the one maintaining the home and she was the one who noticed a problem that needed attention.

> *You're way too old to wear your hair that way.*
> *Well I like it.*
> *I like your hair real, real short.*
> *I know you do.*
> *Do you really think it looks good that way?*

I think many women of my mother's generation thought it was a bad thing to compliment your children. I'm not sure why praise was not the first card drawn—why wouldn't it be? But perhaps it was all tied up with pride and how that *goeth before falls* and all kinds of Bible-speak my mother and I disagreed on fairly early, though I was careful not to say too much. One of my earliest reckonings of our differences was knowing that I needed to hide little things important to me that I didn't want thrown or given away (she could guilt you in a second to give your things to those less fortunate) and figuring out ways to get out of going to things like training union, which I found so depressing. I hated church clothes—the starch and the itch and hard shoes—and I remember being all but stripped down to a pair of Buster Brown underwear in the back seat on the way home, barefooted and relieved to get away from all of that. I remember promising myself that I would never make my children do that and I would never switch them or make them wash their mouths out with soap.

I wondered at the time if I would have felt differently if I had had ribbons and bows, sashes and lace, which I really wanted at one time, something other than the practical hand-me-downs of my sister and cousins; I was the bottom of the food chain and got things third or fourth. I wanted a long ponytail or a French braid, anything other than the utilitarian prince cut my mother kept me in. She did it herself in those early years, often saying "my Daddy was a barber" as if this automatically gave her the skill. Once she skinned a couple of kids in the neighborhood, too (their mothers had agreed), and they went home crying. I probably would have, too, but I *was* home and I was used to it. Maybe short hair was easier, but long hair became for me a great symbol of independence.

The other parts of my physical appearance studied and questioned were, "Where did you get those feet?" and "Where did you get that rear end?" My mother is a tiny little thing, one of those women who just gained a speck while pregnant, just needed to unbutton that top skirt button. Narrow little feet and petite clothes, what she clearly thought was the ideal.

I was long legged and swaybacked and wore a size nine shoe. I remember the first time I ever saw *Our Town* and was struck with great recognition when Emily asks her mother if she is pretty and her mother replies, "Pretty enough for all practical purposes." *Pretty is as pretty does.* And so on. Of course what I also took from that play—knowledge that grows stronger and clearer with each passing day—is the comfort and joy to be found within daily life, as well as the recognition of hardships you didn't see at the time.

*Where did you get those shoes?*
*Do you like them?*
*Maybe. But what size are they?*

My mother had been a majorette in high school and also at Mars Hill College the one year she attended taking some business courses. She often would come out into the front yard where we were all playing and twirl. She could toss it way up and catch it behind her back. She still had her white boots with tassels. She loved to roller skate and play hopscotch and would get out in the street with us to play. She liked to whistle and sing and could play the piano by ear. All you had to do was hum something and she could play and improvise. She wanted a piano. She wanted a bicycle. She wanted a screened-in porch. She got a bike for her fiftieth birthday. She finally got a piano in her fifties as well. She never got the screened-in porch; it was something she talked about in those years after my dad died and she moved to a condo. She did a lot of things in those years—church trips to places she had always wanted to see: the Grand Canyon and Hawaii.

She came quite a few times to visit me in Boston, where I was living at the time, visits that my children and I enjoyed, visits where many of her sentences began with, "Poor thing, I know if you only had more time you would" and then fill in the blank: clean the refrigerator, rake your yard, sweep the driveway, go through the children's closets to get rid of things, get a haircut, go to church. . . . Her favorite thing was to look at shoes, and there were so *many* places to go in Boston. I will never forget, after a long afternoon of browsing, a salesclerk in Macy's hearing us talk and asking where we were from.

My mother said: "Lumberton."

I added: "North Carolina."

She said, "I bet you've heard all about our county."

That was one of those moments I fully realized the scope of her life; it was like seeing her whole world from a different angle. It was also during this time I began to notice a lot of repetition and frustration. "Let me tell you what happened!" Oh. We just talked about that. The last time she visited me there, I got permission to walk her to her gate at the airport. "I'm still in charge," she always liked to say, a reference to what my grandmother, her mother, had said often in her later years.

> *Do you have to tell everything you know? Do you want the neighbors to*
> *hear you?*
> *You care more about the neighbors than you care about me!*
> *I'll show you who cares.*

Sometimes, my mother has loud days, streams of what sounds like another language rolling out of her, sometimes peppered with words she never would have *really* said. I sometimes tell her we're in church and she stops. "We are?" Though the last time I tried this little trick, she said, "So what?" She once let loose a string of what sounded like Latin gibberish only to learn that she had actually called someone an ear infection as she sought the right words, and all I could picture was her at her desk at the Children's Clinic, fingers typing a mile a minute while listening to the Dictaphone reel off some diagnosis and also answering whatever question I had popped in to ask—"Mama, can I" and fill in the blank: have some money, go to the beach, drive the car?

> *Does your car run on gas?*
> *Yes.*
> *Mine runs on a monogram.*
> *Really?*
> *Yes. It works very well, too.*

My mother once gave a speech in front of the church board asking that they allow the teenagers to dance in the youth building when they came to training union on Sunday nights. "Better to dance at the church than go who knows where."

My mother once asked me if I thought my cousin would be getting married. I said not unless some serious laws changed that would allow her to marry her partner of many years. "Well then, I think I should give them a Christmas present that is equivalent to what you were given for a wedding gift."

My mother liked to dress up like a clown on Halloween and hand out candy to the children in the waiting room. On several occasions she answered the phone in her nursing facility, "Lumberton Children's Clinic."

*May I help you?*
*Do you know who I am?*
*Well, I know I've known you for a very long time.*
*My whole life.*
*How about that. I knew that.*

My sister and I marvel at how our parents did it. A secretary and a postal worker who owned a home and sent two children to college and faithfully tithed to the church where she had been in the cradle roll. And they were generous to others, always, without question. Of course the answer to that question is that they did without a lot for themselves. It's the kind of knowledge that is absolutely heartbreaking, and yet it also fills me with a great sense of pride. I wish I could go back and give my dad more time in those later, much happier years and that I could give her some softer, easier days when she wasn't feeling the burdens she was feeling as a young woman. And I marvel at the wit and sense of humor that survived such difficult times.

———

YEARS AGO, long before any glimpse of the approaching dementia, my mother called me to say that someone living in the mountains had called to tell her there was a wonderful photo of me in their paper. The woman had said: "Melba, I had no idea you had such a pretty daughter." My mother said, "and Jill, it's true. It is the best picture I've ever seen of you!"

I had no idea what she was talking about and asked her to send it to me. It was a picture of the lovely writer, Julia Alvarez, with my name under it. We had both spoken in the same series, and they had mixed up the photos. I immediately called my mother, laughing hysterically but also in complete disbelief. I said, "That's not me!"

She said: "Well, it says it's you."

I think that perhaps that very concrete nature is what enabled her survival;

she could compartmentalize and work through just about anything. She would get the occasional migraine (what people then called a sick headache), sleep it all off, and then start over. I really don't recall her being sick for more than one day at a time, and I only saw her completely lose it and cry and scream a couple of times. Once we were at the beach and she walked way down to the point and stood and screamed and screamed, her whole body shaking. I was in junior high and had followed behind her and witnessed it, knowing that she would never have wanted to be seen.

The circumstances were simple enough. Some kids no one had expected or invited piled in and started eating a lot of food that she had prepared for the week. My sister didn't know they were coming and did her best to get rid of them, but by then the order had been shaken. My mother returned, pleasant enough, and the week went on with her reading the kind of book my dad teased her about—*The Flame and the Flower* (one title that comes to mind), frying her pale freckled skin (she used QT, turning herself orange, and even once wore pantyhose under shorts, which all the kids still laugh about), looking at flip-flops for sale, and collecting tiny shells with holes in them that she liked to string into necklaces, something she had done since we were little.

*Mama, don't leave me.*
*I won't.*
*Will you be at my school party?*
*Yes. Of course I will.*

When my sister and I were little, she would have us build frog houses, patting the sand all over our foot and then gently pulling it out to leave a little cave. Then, while we swam or walked, she put shells, maybe a quarter, inside for us to find. She and my Dad liked to say that they had seen the frogs come by, and they would describe what they were wearing.

*Mama, is that the dog that vomits right before somebody dies?*
*Gosh, I hope not.*
*Well, me too! Make him leave before he does it.*

I sometimes imagine who my mother would have been in a simpler, easier life—the sharp wit and eagerness for fun, her talent for playing the piano or for sketching and coloring, which she also loved to do. She always liked to say that she was a Saturday's child and "works hard for a living." And I think that the same little girl who cared for and protected her brother put on the caretaker hat early in life and wore it all the way through. One of my earliest memories of going to school was her stressing that you should always keep an eye on the people who don't get chosen and that, when in a position to pick, to remember and try to include those who usually got left out. This was one of her greatest strengths, and something she always did; I think I see now that it probably grew out of her own insecurities and perhaps her desire to have been acknowledged and included in ways she had felt left out. There is grace in connecting the dots and seeing the whole pattern of a life and understanding how someone became the person she is.

*Where is your daddy?*
*I was going to ask you.*
*I think he's here, but I'm not sure. Do you think he's here?*
*Yes. Yes I do.*

In those later years she relaxed. She stopped worrying as much. And now, in this alternate universe, she really doesn't care what the neighbors hear, and she says exactly what she thinks in the moment she thinks it. Much of the time she is so complimentary, praising those who pass up and down the hall; she tells people she loves them. And occasionally she comments on feet and butts and hair but almost always in ways that makes whoever is hearing laugh.

*God, who is that old man?*
*I don't know.*
*But did you see him? God he's a mess! And old!*

I like to think that those times we witness the curtain lift, she feels it as well, that she feels a very real connection of love and acceptance. Sometimes I will say "802" and she will quickly say: "East Second Street." That's her childhood address, the one my dad helped her find all those years ago, and she follows with something like "my mother is there." Then I say "240" and she says "River-wood," which is the house where I grew up.

*Riverwood. That's our house.*
*Yes.*
*That's where we are.*
*Yes.*
*We're here at home.*
*Yes we are.*

# Child Bride

— DANIEL WALLACE —

—an essay about my mother—

1

## True

My mother was twelve years old the first time she got married; her husband, seventeen. This is how she told it, anyway, over and over again, how she was married when she was twelve, and her husband's name was John Stephens, and they ran off together to Columbiana, Alabama, where they found a judge who would marry them. Her maiden name was Joan Rangeley Pedigo. She was born in 1931, so this would have made it the summer of 1943, right in the middle of World War II. My mother was living with her parents, of course— she was, after all, twelve years old—so they couldn't and didn't know about the engagement, which occurred about 11 A.M., and the ceremony, which was around 3 P.M.

The journey to Columbiana began in Edgewood, Alabama, about thirty miles away. That summer my mother went to the community swimming pool almost every day, a vast rectangular tub of water, cloudy with chlorine. Swimming pools were the only escape from the weather. Very few homes were outfitted with air conditioners, and Alabama summers are cruelly hot and muggy. To have a pool full of tepid water, as chemically repellent as it must have been by July, was a godsend. My grandmother, Eva Pedigo, would drop Joan off in the morning with a sack lunch and a towel and not have to pick her up until later that afternoon. The lifeguard was the babysitter of hundreds of young children. But they weren't all children: John Stephens was there too, and he was seventeen years old.

"We'd been going out for some time by then," my mother always said when she told this story. I never followed up with her about this, or took time to really think about what "going out" could possibly mean to a twelve-year-old and a teenager. Going out was impossible. They could only see each other in public spaces like the pool, and at school. She'd hang out by his car in the parking lot. She'd get in the car with him. They wouldn't "do" anything, she said, not then, but John, she said, was intent upon it. And eventually so was she.

And yet the relationship was kept a secret, from everybody, from her friends and from his, and, of course from their parents. Edgewood, Alabama, where my mother grew up, was a quiet, solidly middle-class neighborhood, as it is to this day. It's on the outskirts of Birmingham and, in every way, practically idyllic. There are a lot of neighborhoods like this in Birmingham—Edgewood, Home-wood, Mountain Brook, Crestline—that are really beautiful, clean, and safe, great places to raise your kids. Her father was a food distributor; her mother worked part-time for him as his secretary and bookkeeper. One day he would become wealthy enough to buy a twenty-acre farm, with cows and horses on it. He later installed his own par three golf course, but that was a disaster: the cows trampled the greens. He also built a tiny chapel, a little bit bigger than an outhouse, beside the pool. There was a miniature organ inside of it, a cross, and a beechwood kneeler covered in velvet. My grandparents were serious Presbyterians.

As she told it, nobody knew they were anything other than friends, if they knew anything at all. A friendship of any kind between a girl and a boy with that age difference doesn't seem right. They were just two people who went to the same school together and swam in the same community pool, along with a lot of other kids. To hear my mother tell it, boys were always drawn to her; she said she couldn't help it, and I believed her. I had seen plenty of evidence by the time I was old enough to see and understand what was going on in her adult world, and yes, men were drawn to her then as well. She was pretty, smart, sexy, and, even when she was married to my father somehow made herself seem available. And then later, when she was older and had dementia, she imagined that all men wanted her, oh how they wished they could have her. Men, she said, were animals.

My grandfather adored my mother. When she was a child they would go on walks together down Edgewood's sun-dappled streets, and when cars stopped at a sign or a light he told her they were stopping to look at her, because she was the prettiest girl in the world.

My grandmother, Eva, took a different tack. She sensed in my mother her burgeoning womanhood, and it scared her. My mother was maturing much too quickly. And not just her body, but her way of being in the world, and how the world saw her in it. Like Eula Varner in Faulkner's *The Hamlet*, "as soon as she passes anything in long pants she begins to give off something. You can smell it!" Her mother could smell it too.

This is how, inadvertently, my grandmother encouraged my mother to marry.

"I would rather stand over your grave," she told her, "than to learn you had sex out of wedlock."

I imagine my mother in bed, covers pulled up to her chin, wheels turning, my sweet grandmother towering above her, glowering in the shadowed light.

So this, she said, is how it happened.

They were at the Edgewood Community Pool, John and Joan. It was a Tuesday. And let's say, with the crazy logic of two kids who were in love and in the grip of some uncontrollable hormones—trying to find any way to be together, to have sex with each other and make it right, make it okay somehow—they decided to get married. And they decided to get married that very day. Still in their bathing suits, John drove them to the Shelby County Courthouse in Columbiana and stood before a probate (or whomever one stands before when a seventeen-year-old man is marrying a twelve-year-old girl), and they took their vows, my mother still dripping in her suit. Standing in one place long enough to lie about her age and sign her marriage license, a small pool of chlorinated water puddled at her feet. So, barefoot and newly married, Joan set out, not to live as man and wife with John, because that wasn't going to happen, but to have sex as a newly married couple might: with a feral eagerness. But *legally*, and with the unintentional blessing of her mother. Where they had sex is unclear to me—my mother just said "everywhere they could"—and they continued thusly until somehow my grandparents found out about it and had the marriage annulled. "It was a summer marriage," she said.

———

THIS ISN'T CLASSIFIED information or a dark family secret I'm sharing with the world because I'm a writer and it makes a good story (though I am, and it does). If she were alive, she would tell you. She told just about anybody. She told my younger sister on her twenty-first birthday, because, she said, "we're friends now, not mother and daughter." Within hours of meeting Laura—my girlfriend at the time, now my wife—she told her this story. Laura thought it was alarming, first impressions being what they are, that this is what my mother would want to lead with. On the other hand, it was the perfect story because it cut to the chase of the kind of woman my mother was, and who she always had been: defiant, sexual, shocking.

So everyone knew about it. It was her great tale of youthful misadventure. She was an open book like this. She would talk about anything, tell you about anything, the more outrageous the better. If you had a scandalous story to tell she would love to hear it, but she would have a better one, like this one, and yours would pale in comparison. "Married when I was twelve years old: beat that." She had too much fun telling the story and spared no details. If oversharing is something everyone in my family does (it is), we definitely got it from her.

She was a great storyteller, and much more creative than I ever gave her credit for. Because what I came to learn, after a little bit of sleuthing, is that it wasn't really true, this story she told. It didn't happen like this at all.

## 2

### *If Only Helen Were Alive (or Carol or Sally)! She Would Know*

It's something you hear a lot when you start digging into the past of someone older, even the relatively recent past. There is always someone who knows what you want to know, but they're dead, alas, and now no one knows what really happened. The part of that life you want to know about now is unknowable. Time disappears, is erased. Death precludes the future, corrodes the past. Without a witness it's all hearsay, a story.

Joanie S. was one of my mother's best friends. She and my mother knew each other for decades. They became Buddhists together and went to northern Alabama and Florida on Buddhist retreats. She was my mother's best friend, even though my mother had "broken up" with her not long before she died. In her last years my mother took umbrage easily. She could be your pal on Wednesday and freeze you out on Thursday, a loving mother this week and a dragon lady the next, and it might not be for some time before you realized what she thought you'd done. Eventually she'd come around, everyone would be friends again, but she never had a chance to make up with Joanie because my mother fell, broke her neck, and died before she could. But other than Joanie there was really no one else for me to talk to.

Luckily, she said she knew what happened. Everything, pretty much. She knew the story because one day she was hanging out with my mother while she was cleaning out some drawers in a side table in her living room. This is when my mother was forty-eight years old, her second marriage (to my father) almost over. In a drawer were a lot of old photographs, and one of them caught Joanie's eye.

"That's John Stephens," Joanie said. A small black-and-white photo of a young handsome man. "Why do you have a picture of John Stephens? He was two years behind me in high school. I didn't even know you ever knew him."

"Oh, I knew him," my mother said, off-handedly. "He was my first husband."

This is when she told Joanie the story, the story she told me and everyone else, how when she was twelve and he was seventeen they left the pool and drove down to Columbiana in their bathing suits, and still dripping in the courtroom the judge signed the papers, and it was official, they were married.

"That's what she told me," I said.

"But there was no way she could have been twelve years old: she was thirteen at least and he was at most *sixteen*, because John was two years behind me in school. So I don't know where your mother got that," she said. "But maybe I'm wrong because she said it was true. She said it was in the law books as the earliest marriage ever performed in Alabama."

Then she told me this: "When Weir [her father] found out about her getting hitched he was not happy about it, as you can imagine. But even so, he wanted her to be happy, so he built a small house for them in the backyard, and she and John lived there until they went to Auburn, where they broke up and got divorced. And then of course she met your father, so."

"Wait. What? He built a *house* for them?"

"In the backyard." She shrugged. She was shrugging because it was a fact and if I didn't believe her that was up to me. "That's what she told me."

"I don't know, Joanie," I said. "I don't know how that could have worked."

Because that would mean a twelve-year-old and a seventeen-year-old—or a thirteen-year-old and a sixteen-year-old, as Joanie said, high school students; or actually, in the case of my mother, one just leaving middle school—lived in my grandparents' backyard as husband and wife, having sex with each other. The idea of her having sex even once with this adult man is chilling; sex that was sanctioned by her parents is grotesque and obviously child abuse. And how could she not have become pregnant if she did in fact live there until she went to college?

He would never have built a house in his backyard for my mother and her husband: he would have shot him and built him a casket. Joanie didn't know about any of that. She was just repeating what she'd been told. "John Stephens was gorgeous," she said. "I will say that. His father was a tree man, though, and looked like a monkey."

I'd never heard about this house in the backyard. My mother never told this part of the story to me or my sisters. (There were no offspring from her first marriage, thank God.) We are all from her second, and last, marriage, to my father. She was relatively ancient by the time she met and married him— eighteen years of age. And for the second time in her life she eloped.

There's a photo of the two of them "chained" (tied by a string) to a pole outside Toomer's Drug Store in Auburn, with a sign that says "Just Married. G.I. Bill won't pay for hotel room. Need $10 for night."

They are both heartbreakingly young. My father is smiling like a guy who just bluffed his way to a win in a high-stakes poker game. My mother's face is so sweet, seraphic, unblemished, like a girl who has only heard stories about what it might be like to be married, to be with a man. It doesn't look like this is her second time around, that long before she met my father she'd been married to another man. I don't know if he ever knew.

I'm beginning to understand that I don't even know what I know. The backyard-home story is impossible. But Joanie was one of my mother's best friends: why would she tell her this? And yet clearly it's not a credible story. Now I don't know what else was made up, or if all of it was, or why this fictional creation of self, of a controversial and even tragic past that never happened, was necessary. Maybe she just loved how the story, like a car wreck, got your attention and made it impossible to look away. The sex part, of course, she loved. And the fact that it was against the law, even in Alabama, only made it better. She lied about her age to the judge and got away with it, and she loved that. The judge never even asked to see proof. She loved that, too. Apparently no one asked to see proof of anything, ever. Until I did.

Nothing intimate in their relation at all? Well, I doubt that. And you might well ask, why do I even care? But that's not the question. The question is, why did *she* care? Why did she lie about it the way she did? That's the most intriguing part of it all to me. Because what really happened is only important to the degree that it differs from the story she told, and the story she told is the more important one. We learn more about people through the lies they tell than we do from the truths they share. I think this is why I became a fiction writer in the first place. It's how I was raised.

### 3

*May I Speak to Mr. Stephens?*

One reason I write fiction, as opposed to nonfiction, is the freedom the form allows me, which is almost total. I'm free to write the story I want to write, the way I want to write it, and if something displeases me or doesn't work I can delete a word, a paragraph, or much, much more—all from the comfort of my office, couch, or king-size bed. The only conflict I experience is on the page.

I've never been much for research, or being investigative, asking questions, insinuating myself into the real lives of other people. Who knows what might happen if I did? The conflict could get very real. But worse than that, it's limiting: the more facts I have, the less latitude I have to make things up. I get hamstrung by the truth.

After Joanie, though, I knew I needed to talk to John Stephens, though the events in question happened over sixty years ago, and he may well have forgotten them, the bones of that memory covered by the sands of time. To hear from me, the son of the girl he once loved, could be, to say the least, jarring.

But there he was—his telephone number, online where anyone could see it. His address was there as well. He still lived in Edgewood! This was all too wonderful, and yet a little unnerving. How would he react when I told him who I was? And when is the last time he'd even thought of her? Would he hang up on me, or have a heart attack and die midsentence? Or would he just tell me the story I'd been hoping to hear?

So I dialed him up, and it rang two or three times. He didn't answer, though—a woman did. It was, I assumed, his wife—his second wife. I asked for Mr. Stephens in my brightest voice.

"Oh," she said. "I'm sorry. Mr. Stephens died three years ago. This is Estelle Stephens, his widow. Is there anything I can help you with?"

She had a sweet, deeply southern voice. And an old one: she had to have been eighty years old at least.

"Well," I said. "Yes. Possibly you can." I had not thought this through. I had no plan for Mrs. Stephens—what to ask her, to ask her anything at all. But I had to make a plan now, what to do, right now. And so I did. "My name is Daniel Wallace," I said. "My mother's maiden name was Joan Pedigo. I don't know if you knew her."

There was a short pause, or maybe not even a pause at all. Maybe I misinterpreted it, or my fictional inclinations were adding it there for effect. Maybe she was taking a sip of water, or was distracted by a cardinal on the red berry bush outside her window. "Of course I remember Joan Pedigo," she said. "She and John were . . . an item. In high school."

An item. An item! I should say so.

I soldiered on.

"Well, that's what my mother told me." I was trying to sound as breezy as possible about it all, but she must have been wondering why Joan Pedigo's son was calling her. "She's passed on as well."

"She lived right down the street from where my house is now," she said. "My best friend lives in the house next door so I see it all the time."

"Oh," I said. "Well, the reason I'm calling"—and here is where I begin to stutter, not really knowing what the next words out of my mouth were going to be—"there was a story I'd heard, and maybe not even a story, but, I don't know what you would call it, something that had come up at some point or another and I was wondering, and I was going to ask him, your husband, because what I might have heard was something about how he and my mother got married. In high school. Just briefly. Really, just for the summer."

And this time there was a long thoughtful silence.

"That's odd," she said. "Well. They *were* an item." And she laughed a little laugh. "But nothing like that ever happened. I can tell you that. I can tell you that for certain. We were married for nearly sixty years. In all that time I think something would have come up about it, once or twice, don't you?"

She was so sweet about this, and so sure of things. It was refreshing.

"Yes!" I said, as quickly as I possibly could. "Of course. I didn't think it happened. It sounded so farfetched. But I didn't know who else to call. I'm sorry I bothered you, but it was something I just needed to clear up. For myself."

"I understand," she said.

"Thank you."

I was ready to hang up, but she went on.

"The timing doesn't work out," she said. "Because we were married right after high school. And I definitely think someone would have brought it to my attention."

"Exactly. Clearly, it never happened. And I'm sorry—"

"And when did you hear this?"

"I don't even know," I said. I felt like I was chipping away at her life, little by little, that I might be changing the way she thought about her husband forever. "At some point my mother brought it up. But my mother said a lot of things about a lot of things, and a lot of them weren't necessarily true."

"Joan Pedigo was a firecracker," she said. "That's for sure."

That's for sure. Firecracker or not, though, my mother had never been married to John Stephens. I believed Estelle completely. I had brought my mother's lies into an old widow's life, a good woman, probably, and I felt as if I'd done something terribly wrong. I wondered if my mother had ever married *anybody*, if she had ever been a child bride at all, if the whole thing had been her fiction, just a way of getting attention, of celebrating her indifference to convention.

Yet I couldn't stop thinking about it: maybe Estelle *didn't* know. Maybe they'd been crafty enough to hide it from everybody.

Within a week I found someone to do some digging, a sort of private investigator. And it turns out, yes, she did get married, she was a child bride, but not to a man named John Stephens, and not when she was twelve.

The man she married was named John Sorsby, a man I'd never heard of in my life, and she was fifteen years old.

# 4

## *Nothing but the Facts*

Ric Dice—that is his real name—is a writer living in Alabama, and he knows how to solve mysteries. We've never met or even spoken on the phone. Jeannie Thompson, who runs the Alabama Writer's Network, is a mutual friend, and she heard me telling this story about my mother, the one I just told you, and she mentioned Ric, how he'd learned some investigative tricks researching a mystery in his own family, that he knows how to find the paper trail.

Being a writer myself, I might should have known this, or hoped for it at the very least, that it would all come down to paper. After all, has anything happened in the last few hundred years that hasn't left a paper trail behind it? And paper gets the last word. Contracts, electricity and telephone bills, notes, diaries—these are the things that tell our stories. Memories are faulty, people die, and the living ones are often averse to the truth, but at the end of the day if there's a piece of paper you can hold up and say, "This is true, this is what happened, this is where he was on the day in question," the mystery will be a mystery no more. This story I'm telling you now, for instance, though it's full of inaccuracies and conjecture, will end up being the last word on the subject. No one is coming after me to adjust or correct it. This is what will be known as history. "What you don't know could fill a book," my father used to tell me. But he underestimated me: I have actually filled six books so far with what I don't know, and I am working on the seventh.

Ric said he would be happy to help me. All I had to do was give him a name and a birth date. So I told him: Joan Pedigo. And he did it. This man I'd never met found the paper I needed.

Joan Pedigo, he told me, married my father on 27 October 1950, when they were both students at Auburn. This I knew.

"But a Joan Pedigo *also* marries on 29 July 29 1947. She would've been fifteen. And the man she married," he told me, "wasn't named John Stephens: his name was John R. Sorsby. I'm guessing the marriage was annulled, because she's back in high school in fall 1949 and her name is Joan Pedigo, and not Joan Sorsby."

Not twelve years old, fifteen; and not John Stephens, John Sorsby.

Well, this didn't make sense at all.

Why would my mother have lied about how old she was when she first got married? Or, if there was going to be a lie, wouldn't she have lied in the other direction? If you were married at the indecently young age of twelve, wouldn't you want to bump it up a little and say, possibly, fifteen? Fifteen is young, really young to be married, but not really that rare a thing in Alabama in the forties. She may have known other girls who were married at fifteen. But twelve? Who gets married when they're twelve? No one. No one but Joan Pedigo. "The earliest marriage ever performed in the history of Alabama." Not one of the youngest—*the* youngest. She had distinguished herself early on; maybe that's what she was trying to get at: that of the wild, she was the wildest.

But who is this Sorsby? Why would she lie about his name? And how does it even make sense: no one had ever mentioned a John Sorsby, while it had been established that John Stephens was very real. Joanie had even known him, had seen his picture in my mother's drawer. And his widow had known Joan Pedigo, knew her husband had dated her, but were never, ever married . . .

I didn't really believe Mrs. Stephens when I spoke to her, when she denied this first marriage. I thought that somehow her husband of half a century had hidden the fact from her all these years. But she was right. It wasn't Stephens, it was Sorsby.

All I needed to know now is whether John Sorsby was still alive, because I wanted to talk with him if he was. Ric promised to find out for me.

It took only two days.

"You were asking about Sorsby and if he might be alive," he wrote. "The John Sorbsy who appears to have married your mother was born April or May 1929, the son of John Sorsby and a woman named Vernelle Pilkington. Then he seems to disappear—until he marries your mom. Then he seems to disappear *again*. He doesn't appear in any city directory, doesn't pay a power bill or a phone bill, doesn't register to vote or serve in the military. He's off the grid. But Pilkington. Vernelle Pilkington. I realized I'd seen that name before."

And so Ric proceeds to unravel the story of my mother's first husband's name. Vernelle Pilkington's husband was John Sorsby, and they had a son together, also named John. But then they were divorced, and she later married a man named Aubry Beck Stephens; he became John Sorsby's stepdad. And so John changed his name to Stephens. John Stephens.

"See? John Stephens and John Sorsby are one in the same. John Sorsby was born April 1929, and so was John Stephens. And they both died on 25 April 2010. So." I could almost hear him smiling on the other end of this e-mail, having figured all this stuff out, from top to bottom.

She did marry John Stephens, but that summer day they married in the small courthouse in the middle of Alabama, he must have still been John Sorsby.

And so, just like that, in a matter of days the mystery of a lifetime was solved. I have it all on paper now: the original marriage license and the annulment. Every historical date, every indisputable fact.

But it's more than paper. Nestled within what is supposed to be a bloodless legal document, there's a hidden narrative.

The marriage wasn't discovered (I don't know how it finally was) until an entire year had passed, a year in which my mother lived at home and appeared to be dating John, while he was in fact her husband. Once discovered, though, my grandfather moved quickly to have it annulled, which means that, legally at least, the marriage almost never happened at all.

The annulment document contains three testimonies: one from my mother, one from John Sorsby, and one from my grandfather. In his testimony my grandfather says that "John had called on my daughter since the alleged marriage, and I have seen no difference in their relation. They have acted toward each other the whole time like kid sweethearts usually do. There has been nothing intimate in their relation."

And John Sorsby: "Last July it occurred to me that if we would go through with a marriage ceremony that it would prevent her from going out with other boys, and, being somewhat jealous . . . we drove to Columbiana. Neither of us had any intention of considering this any more than a binding engagement . . . and our relations have been nothing other than that of fiancé and fiancée."

Finally, it's my mother's turn. She says she and John "have been friends for quite a while and we had discussed getting married in the future for some time. Last July . . . he suggested that we could go to a county seat and get married, and that it would have the effect of an engagement, and we could later remarry. . . . [Neither] he or I in any way treated our relation as husband and wife."

*They acted toward each other the whole time like kid sweethearts usually do,* my grandfather said. *There was nothing intimate in their relation at all.*

Nothing intimate in their relations at all? Well, maybe, maybe not. But then I don't know what he knew, either—if he thought that what he was saying was true, or that what they were saying was true, or if he, like her, like me, was only telling a story.

Nothing intimate in their relation at all? Well, I doubt that. And you might well ask, why do I even care? But that's not the question. The question is, why did *she* care? Why did she lie about it the way she did? That's the most intriguing part of it all to me. Because what really happened is only important to the degree it differs from the story she told, and the story she told is the more important one. We learn more about people through the lies they tell than we do from the truths they share. I think this is why I became a fiction writer in the first place. It's how I was raised.

# Settling into Marriage

## — PHILLIP LOPATE —

"WHAT WAS IT LIKE when you got back from your honeymoon?"

"We got married on the eleventh of June, so we rented an apartment as of the first of June. Up until the eleventh, I spent that time fixing it up. As soon as the couch was delivered, and the radio was delivered, Mr. Lopate stretched out and did not get up. I climbed up on the ladder; I put up the window shades, the hooks, and the curtain rods. I learned how to do a lot of things by myself. I would ask for help and never got it. It was unbelievable! I don't know how many times those first couple of months I would say, 'What am I doing here? Why am I going through this?' And it all came down to the same thing: 'You're doing it because he's the only one you know who has a steady job, and it's Depression time.' I'm being honest. Never mind the commitment, never mind the possibility of love afterwards. I knew there was no love. I knew there would never be love. But I tried. I hoped it would work. I hoped he would change. I hoped he would be—a good husband. I found he was not. I took my chances: It's like gambling. You put your money down. If it comes up red, fine. If it comes up black, you're shit out of luck."

"I have a feeling a lot of men at that time didn't do housework," I said.

"Yes, it was partly that generation of men. But by that time, the change was already starting. Husbands were already starting to wheel baby carriages, starting to be proud of their children. My husband never took my children to the park in a baby carriage. I don't know why, but . . . Did he ever take you to the park? Did he ever spend time with you?"

"He did spend some time with us, yes."

"All right—did he ever spend the time you would expect of a father? I used to hear, 'Hey, Fran, the baby's crying.' As if I couldn't hear the baby crying. However, some of the changes were really distressing. The first couple of weeks, I would look out the window and see him coming from the bus. And a block before, he would start running, really anxious to get home. And there

79

would be a tub of water ready for him, and he would jump in as soon as he got home. Because he would come home from that factory job with collars of black dirt on his legs and arms that I couldn't stand. And he would get into the tub every night when he came home. For about a week. Afterwards, he would not bother to get into the tub. The water would stand there every night, and he wouldn't bathe. Every night he would come home dirtier and dirtier and dirtier. He couldn't understand why I didn't want him near me. And it got so that I had to reject him—constantly. He smelled. His teeth, his mouth, his legs. It hurts to say these things. It hurts me to say them because I had to tolerate him, and it hurts me to say them because I did tolerate him. He had no idea how tempting it was to bed somebody else. To be able to have someone that I could enjoy, without that awful smell. I guess my getting pregnant was an excuse to have him stay away. And I was able to live without him for a long time, when I was pregnant. It was wonderful. I couldn't understand why he felt the need— what was he holding on to all that dirt for? So much about him I couldn't understand. The way he would come home and listen to the radio. It was always sports, a basketball game, or a football game. That hasn't changed over the years. I even had to absorb it: I watch and I know a little bit about sports, from the process of osmosis. But it wasn't pleasant to constantly be a maid. And then of course when Lenny was born, he still wouldn't help me, absolutely wouldn't wash a dish, wouldn't take the laundry over to the launderette. He did nothing! My legs were swollen three times the size of normal, I had such edema it was unbelievable. And the doctor said, 'You must stay with your feet elevated.' You know what my husband did? He brought me a high stool from the factory, so that I should be able to sit and wash the dishes. That's consideration of a sort. But he wouldn't wash the dishes himself."

It's starting to sound like *Sons and Lovers*. When I read that great D. H. Lawrence novel, I thought: okay, I'm not alone, here again is the middle-class woman horrified by her dirty working-class husband, and the sensitive son going back and forth between the two. Except my father was not only a working-class brute but an autodidact semi-intellectual who read Kafka and Dostoevsky. I could imagine him coming home exhausted from the physically draining day at factory work, the sole financial support of his expanding family, wanting only to zone out with a ballgame, and there was his wife, who wasn't working, expecting him to help around the house and do the dishes, and who wouldn't go near him unless he took a bath, proof in his mind that she did not love him, did not care for him enough to embrace him as he was, so out of stubbornness and resentment at being rejected he did not take a bath, and the situation worsened.

PHILLIP LOPATE

Of course in looking at it in this way, I am maximizing sympathy for my father as a generic working-class guy at this stage in history, worn down by labor on the one hand and the complex demands of domestic life, for which he was ill-prepared, on the other. All of which may be true, but what I am not acknowledging sufficiently is that my father was peculiar, hermetic, weirdly silent, and withdrawn, especially when he felt himself under attack. Increasingly mocked by us for his morose antisocial manner, he became isolated in his head, expecting not to be understood, and hopeless to reach.

I am well aware that I am not succeeding in making my father come alive on the page, turning him into a three-dimensional character or simply giving a proper account of the man. In part it's because the focus of this book is my mother and her point of view, and in part because I've already written a long personal essay about him ("The Story of My Father," published previously)— though that's hardly a valid excuse. The main reason is that he was so remote and shadowlike in life that I find it difficult to describe him, much less understand him.

In any case, who can blame my mother for being repulsed when he smelled and wouldn't wash? What was that all about? I don't share his need to hold on to body dirt. As for the rest, I too drift into silence at times, and my own family berates me for not being livelier and more present at the breakfast table. I tell myself it's because I'm a writer, and writers are always going off into interior space, writing in their heads. What is more likely is that I'm my father's son, and would have inherited this peculiarly quiet, watchful, impassive way regardless of what career path I followed. In short, it's not a professional deformation, it's genetic. So if I cut my father slack for his introverted oddities, it's probably because I want the same type of slack cut for myself.

"Were you working at the time?" I asked.

"I had quit all my jobs. I had quit everything."

"Well, what did you do in the house when you were alone?"

"While I was pregnant, there was no problem. I used to go to the movies a lot. Once the housework was done I walked out of the house. But I always managed to have a meal on the table. I'd go to the movies. I saw all the musicals. I didn't like the Westerns, but Dick Powell, when he sang—I liked all those big Goldwyn musicals, Busby Berkeley, they were terrific. I liked The Thin Man, and the mysteries. The matinee idols I liked were William Powell, Clark Gable, Melvyn Douglas, and of course Leslie Howard. I think I saw *Romeo and Juliet*, with Leslie Howard and cross-eyed Norma Shearer, two or three times. I had a crush on James Mason when I saw him in *The Seventh Veil*. I think every woman sees an unobtainable man that she wants to tame and obtain for herself. And in that picture he was the unapproachable man who was finally won by young innocent girl. Every time it's on television I watch it. I don't care if there's a ballgame on or not, I have my rights.

"So, besides going to the movies, I'd stop by Butch's gas station and he would take me home in his car. After I had Lenny, I would sometimes bring the baby carriage over to Butch's to visit, and he would put the carriage in the back of his car and drive me home, and always he would say: 'Why can't you lose that guy and come with me? How can you live with him? He's dull, he's terrible. How can you live that way?' It didn't make any impression on me. I didn't leave Daddy, I just wanted a ride home.

"Everything was fine. There was no problem before the babies were born, because there was not a lot of work to do. But once the babies were there, once Lenny was born, forget it! I had my hands full and I had no one to turn to. I remember Al's cousin Suzanne walked into our house one time when Lenny was an infant. She asked me if we were moving. Every stitch was out of the closet, every dish was in the sink, because I hadn't gotten around to doing the dishes. I couldn't do it all. I was not an organized person. I never had the experience, I never had the training. I never had anyone teach me how to do it. I was just a kid! Okay, so I was twenty-one years old—that's not a kid, really. But in my head I was a kid. I didn't know anything. But I had a man who was eight years older than I, who at least should have helped. No, nothing. If you're doing childcare, and you have nobody to help you with the other things like housekeeping, it's rough for a kid who never had to do it."

All very true, to which must be added that my mother was a dreadful housekeeper. Her resentment at having to clean without my father's assistance, combined with a certain inability to organize and simplify the piles that accumulated everywhere around us, led to our living in what she termed "a pigsty," long after she had left her twenties behind her.

I am still struggling to adjudicate in my mind my mother's claims of being mistreated in the early stage of her marriage with her testimony that she went to the movies regularly and dropped in on her friend Butch who had a crush on her, while my father was working long hours in a factory. Do I sound naïve by saying it doesn't seem such a bad deal? Being a cinephile myself, I can never fault her going to the movies: it was a great period for American sound pictures, and who could resist Clark Gable, James Mason, and Busby Berkeley musicals? Intellectually, I can grasp the "diary of a mad housewife" scenario and the basic injustice of a sexist social structure that could leave a young wife feeling bereft and adrift. But I suspect there is an emotional divide between women readers who will more readily sympathize with her, and men (or perhaps I should say men like myself) whose compassion keeps straying to the other side, do what we may to compensate for our gender bias. I wish there was a way to correct that astigmatic deviation and leap into her perspective with warmth and whole-heartedness, but my imagination will not take me that far. Such are the limits of a feminist-friendly male, which I consider myself to be, who is nevertheless—a male. What I cannot seem to do is bluff an empathy I do not feel. Instead I keep wanting to convince her to go easier on the guy. Try talking more honestly or less accusatorily; maybe go to a sex therapist. These sorts of remedies occurred to me when I heard them arguing and they still occur to me, even after they are both cremated ashes. It was always too late for reconciliation: the possibility had closed down before I was even born. But the son in me could never stop myself from hoping for a more rational solution or a miracle, some magic transformation of antagonism into affection.

# Encore

## — ALAN SHAPIRO —

Cold, that's how I was. I couldn't shake it off, especially
those last days and nights doing all the right things
in the wrong spirit, in the antithesis of spirit, more
machine of son than son, mechanical, efficient, wiping
and cleaning and so having to see and touch what it would have
sickened me to touch and look at if I hadn't left my body
to the automatic pilot of its own devices so I could do
what needed doing inside the deprivation chamber of this final
chapter, which the TV looked out on glumly through game·
show, soap, old sappy black-and-white unmastered films.

I was cold all the time, I couldn't shake it off till
I was free of her, however briefly, in the parking lot
or at home for a quick drink or toke, anything
to draw some vestige of fellow feeling out of hiding—the
hiding deer-like in a clearing at the end of hunting season,
starved but fearful, warily sniffing the scentless air,
breathing in the fresh absence of her scent too new
too sudden not to be another trap—you're dutiful,
she'd say when I'd come back, as always, I'll give you that.

And I *was* cold: I couldn't help feel there was something
scripted and too rehearsed even about her dying,
laid on too thickly, like a role that every book club
romance, soap, musical, and greeting card had been
a training for, role of a lifetime, role "to die for"
and O how she would have played it to the hilt
if not for the cold I couldn't shake—which must have so

enraged her—not my lack of feeling but my flat refusal
to pretend to feel, to play along (was that too much to ask?)
and throw myself into the part so we could both, this once
at least, rise to the occasion of what we never shared.

That final day, for instance, the way the Fighting Sullivans on TV
seemed to watch us watch them as a taunt or dare parade their
small town big war grieving fanfare across the screen,
the five sons killed in battle, only the old man holding back,
not crying when he's told the news, not breaking down or
even touching the wife he still calls mother, a stoicism fraught
with all the feeling he stuffs back down inside him as he grabs
his lunch pail, heads to work, just as he would on any other day,
the only hint of sorrow the salute he gives as the train chugs past
the water tower on the top of which the apparitions of his boys
stand waving calling out goodbye pop, see you round pop—

and as the credits roll she's asking if there's anything, anything
at all about the past, the family, her childhood that I'd like to
hear about before she dies, her voice decked out so gaudily
in matriarchal sweetness that I freeze, I shake my head, say,
no, ma, no, I'm good. And just like that the scene is over,
the sweetness vanishes into the air, into thin air, like the
baseless fabric of the mawkish film, an insubstantial pageant
faded as she nods and grimaces and turns away
relieved (it almost seemed) that that was that. Was us. Was me.
The role that I was born for, and she was done with now.

And yet it's never done, is it. The pageant's never faded.
Shake off the cold and it gets colder. There's just no end
to how cold the cold can get, not even on the coldest nights,
not even if I throw the windows open wide and turn
the ceiling fan on high and lie in bed, uncovered,
naked, shivering inward back into myself as if to draw
the cold in with me deeper, down to the icy center stage
where I will always find her frozen in the act of turning from me
while I in turn stand freezing in the act of saying no, I'm good.

# —PART III—
# Manners and Mores

# Frankye

## — FRANCES MAYES —

MY MOTHER WAS forty-seven when her husband was laid beside his mother under marble slabs at Evergreen Cemetery. She thought she was still young. At fourteen, I did not think she was young, but I was about to notice that, although she was full of high spirits and wants, she was—to my astonishment—utterly helpless. Not that she didn't warn me. *You think I'm made of iron. I am not made of iron*, she repeated over and over again. What was she made of?

Without either the high drama of her entanglement with my father in his swaggering days, or the day-and-night vigil over his decline into brave-and-sweet ghost of himself, she emerged like a spooky velvet-winged spectral moth that flaps toward porch lights.

As for him, she didn't know which to prefer—the hand pouring the Southern Comfort over ice, or the hand weak and bony on the bedspread, constantly reaching out to us as we walked by his bed. Arrogant (*You low-down pissant*) or pitiful (*I'll be dead and you'll be fastening those pearls*, and he yanks off the pearls, sending them scurrying all over the kitchen floor). Raging big boss (*I want it yesterday*) or supplicant (*Please, darlin', some chipped ice*). Wild (roaring into the driveway at dawn) or snagged (pus-stained bandages over wounds).

In the first winter of our loss, Frankye found that we had no money. The mill check came, even when Daddy came home sick, but when he died, nothing. Mayes Manufacturing had long since sold to New York owners, and Daddy was their manager, while Daddy Jack, my grandfather, sat on the money. There must have been health insurance then, but we didn't have it. My parents had neglected to pay the installments on the life insurance policy; they simply forgot. The life insurance would have made all the difference in our lives. When I asked why, she replied, *You have no idea what I go through*. Months in the Atlanta hospital, operations, nurses, medicines, doctors; the costs never were mentioned but must have been staggering. When all the medical bills were paid, the First National Bank statement said one thousand dollars.

BECAUSE I AM four years under eighteen, she can apply for government aid for minors. When the first check arrives, she looks at it incredulously. I can tell she's concentrating hard from the way she works her bottom lip back and forth, as when she focuses on spreading hot peanut brittle fast across the porcelain-topped kitchen table.

"Don't do that with your lip," I complain.

"Do what?"

"That sticking out your bottom lip. It looks stupid."

"You don't know what you're talking about."

"I do too."

"You certainly do not. You think you know so much."

I drop it with *I know more than you* on the brink of my sassy lips.

She lets the check float to the floor. "You can have these. They're useless to me. Use them to buy clothes. Use them to light fires." The sum is around two hundred dollars a month. At today's value, a thousand dollars or more.

Out of instinct, I begin to call her Frankye instead of Mammy or Mother. I sense that the mother role is now in question. I open a checking account and buy anything I want. A nice pleated wool skirt costs fifteen dollars, a cashmere sweater about twenty-five. I collect Capezios, which, via an ad in *Mademoiselle*, I order all the way from New Rochelle, New York. Pink ballet flats, pointed-toe loafers in red alligator, blue sandals with ankle straps, suede pumps with kitten heels, fur-cuffed little boots—my closet floor is littered with shoes. Miss Leila, our neighbor, sews Capri pants in pink linen, a yellow dress with silver-dollar-sized buttons down the front, a hydrangea-printed organdy formal dress, strapless and with a trailing purple ribbon at the waist.

A local florist asked my mother to help him out a few days a week, since she was a founder of the Magnolia Garden Club and known for flower arrangements. She went to his greenhouse a few times then decided that she didn't want to. The humidity made her hair sticky. Then there was something about the owner's bad taste—red anthuriums and screaming red ribbons—and not being able to stand looking at his mossy teeth. She bought a typewriter and enrolled in an English course at a college thirty miles away. To get there, she had to get up at seven, even before Willie Bell, our housekeeper, arrived. She lasted a few weeks, and then gave the typewriter to me and I used it all through high school and college. I brightly suggested that we move to Atlanta, where my sister and her husband lived. Surely there was a job she'd like in Atlanta. "What do you expect me to do, clerk in a store?"

They'd always tipped the bottle. Now Frankye sometimes drank a bit in the daytime. After school, I'd find her at the kitchen table with a gin and tonic, not even looking at a magazine. What was she to do? She always wanted to go somewhere, anywhere. She had the vibrancy, the looks, the determined helplessness that made you step forth to take over, even if you were eight or nine years old. She had nowhere to go. I watched her energy start to fizzle. Neither my sisters, who were nowhere near, nor I, knew depression; we knew bad mood. We didn't know drinking as disease, but as character flaw. Weakness. We didn't know "dysfunctional," but we lived it. We knew that if you were miserable, you brought it on yourself. She taught us.

She gazes in the mirror of her dresser, with two side mirrors reflecting her three-quarter profile. She is multiplied, faceted, broken into aspects. I look at her with blame. When I mention a job, she stares at me as though I'd suggested she walk the streets. Work is not going to work out. She becomes interested in competitive bridge. Unlikely as it is, she's an excellent bridge player and begins to accumulate master's points. When Daddy Jack says she can go on a duplicate bridge cruise in the Caribbean, she has several linen sundresses made, packs her bags, and leaves.

Bridge was the focus of the trip but I knew my mother hoped to meet someone exciting. She'd already surveyed Fitzgerald and found no one presentable. Or, instead, just found no one. During Daddy's illness, when he still had the wherewithal to drink bourbon, gin, and vodka, I overheard him say, "You'll be remarried before I'm cold in the grave." She did not dispute that.

--------

DURING THE DAY while Frankye cruises, Willie Bell tends to the house and I get myself to school. I'd started driving when I was nine. By twelve, while they were away at the hospital in Atlanta, I'd back out of the driveway then speed back in, over and over. I still can back up as well as I can drive forward. By fifteen, I drive everywhere. After school, my friends and I "ride around." Up Lee, down Pine, out the ten-mile stretch where I floor the blue Buick and see how fast it speeds up to 110 mph. At night, I read *The Foxes of Harrow* and other Frank Yerby novels one after another, although the librarian had called my mother to report that I was reading "unsuitable" books. (Yerby was a mulatto.) Reading omnivorously across the library, I by fluke choose Jane Austen, Hamilton Basso, Willa Cather, Flaubert, Hemingway, Thoreau, Fitzgerald, Dreiser, Steinbeck, and Turgenev. (I know this because I still have the blue Reading Log I kept for fifteen years.) Propped in my white spool bed, a tin of cheese straws within reach, a stack of library books on the table, the house quiet, protective. I am perfectly happy. Imagine, writing a book. What else could you do with your life that could compare with that? I began to keep lists of good words and quotes, to underline sentences I liked, and write notes in margins. Carson McCullers, from right over in Columbus, how did she do it? "In the town there were two mutes, and they were always together." You can begin a book like that, and, yes, the heart is a lonely hunter.

Every day Willie Bell leaves a pan of chicken and some deviled eggs, or a pot roast and a plate of icebox cookies. I spend some nights at friends' houses, sometimes one of them stays with me, and once or twice I stay at Daddy Jack's, but usually during the two weeks Frankye is gone, I am alone. No one seems to think this odd, so I don't either. We never locked our doors. I read late, listening to LPs that I ordered from a record club. Often they sent the wrong choice so I ended up hearing Rachmaninoff, Tchaikovsky, and Concierto de Aranjuez and Boléro. My favorite is a dramatic reading of "John Brown's Body" by Stephen Vincent Benét. The spinning rhythms and haunting repetitions of the story of the War between the States expressed my sense of the land I lived on. I underlined "the old wise dog with Autumn in his eyes," and descriptions that named my feelings.

With the lights out in my room, I listen as the lively voice reads to me, imprinting the Old South myth. What if you could write something that sings? I know the breeze does not smell of warm peaches, but it seems as though it does. And the Lost Cause, that's a subject still reverberating. It had occurred to me that there was another side to the whole story but at that time I was like the Mayas, who used the wheel in toys but never made the leap to chariots and carts. A couple of postcards arrive. One day in Barbados, natives who shouted *Yankee, go home* pelted the cruise group with rotten fruit as they walked around the port buying straw bags. The card, a view of the harbor, said how insulting to be called a Yankee when she was with Southerners and Canadians and that her turquoise linen dress was ruined.

When Frankye returned, she confessed that she'd been quite taken with a man from Vancouver. His name, Cliff, caused me to imagine my mother in the arms of Montgomery Clift, leaning into his kiss on the top deck of a ship sailing farther and farther south, as south as you could go. Cliff, slick black hair I saw in the snapshot, was not Montgomery Clift by any stretch. Instead, the word "swarthy" came to mind, and I hoped I never had to move to Canada (the moon) because of him. He escorted her on the day trips, she said, had been a grand dance partner, and my daddy would never dance. A few days later, I asked if she'd heard from Cliff. Then she admitted that she found on checking out the last morning that the bar tabs he'd signed for all the lovely rum drinks they'd shared while the moon rose over the water, he'd signed in her name and room number. He was off the boat by then. Was it then that she realized that her flamboyant college romance days were not going to reappear? That all the men who flattered her when she was married (sending Daddy into apoplexy) somehow had fast-faded into the background? *John Brown's body lies a-mouldering in the grave . . .*

# Shut Up!
# We're Going to the Masters

— MARSHALL CHAPMAN —

WHEN I WAS ABOUT six years old, I announced to my mother that I wasn't going to have children. "Really?" she said. "So what are you going to have?

"Colts," I said.

I was serious. And I truly believed that one day I could spread my legs and bam! Out would pop a baby horse. And that that horse would one day grow up so I could put a saddle on it and ride off into the world. Like the boy in those Black Stallion novels by Walter Farley that I loved so much.

Somehow, I instinctively knew that if I had a baby human child, that child would one day grow up and put a saddle on *me* . . . then ride my ass into the ground.

Naturally, I got my views on motherhood from observing my own mother. And by the time I was six, I knew that on some level she wasn't crazy about the reality of motherhood. She and my father liked the *idea* of having children, so they had four. They originally planned to have six, but after four they realized enough was enough.

Their first child, a girl, was born in 1946. That was my sister Mary. Two years later I came along. Then three years after that, my sister Dorothy was born. So basically my mother kept having daughters until she at last fulfilled the great expectation of her life—that of producing a male heir. He arrived in the form of James Alfred Chapman IV, on October 7, 1955. And from that day until his death from AIDS forty years later, my sisters and I pretty much fended for ourselves. At least emotionally.

I remember the first time I spoke with Mother after Jamie's death. ("Jamie" is what everybody called my brother.) It was a revelation. Our conversation was pleasant. She was present and caring. Nonjudgmental. I kept waiting for the other shoe to drop, but it never did. My sisters were having the same experience. One of them called. "Have you talked to Mother?" she said. "Can you believe it!" As the three of us compared notes, we came to the great realization that our brother, from the day he was born until the day he died, had required *every ounce of maternal strength* our mother had.

I was forty-seven when my brother died. By then I'd undergone a lot of therapy and been treated for depression. So to have my mother back at this later stage in life was an unexpected gift.

But back to Mother and the pressure to produce a male heir. You have to understand, this was 1950s Spartanburg, South Carolina. White male imperialism was in its heyday.

To understand my mother, you have to understand her mother—my grandmother, Mama Cloud. Mama Cloud was a terror. We grandchildren were taught to fear her. It's my personal belief she was on a dry drunk her entire life. She was born into Birmingham society. Then, while a student at Converse College, she met a dashing engineering major from Georgia Tech named Fayette Cloud. After graduation, she and Fayette married and moved to North Carolina, where they settled into a house on the edge of a sand and gravel pit out in the middle of nowhere near Lilesville (population small). They immediately began having children. Mother was their firstborn, born nine months to the day after their wedding—a honeymoon baby.

After their fourth child—my Uncle Pete—was born, Mother was sent off to Birmingham to live with her maternal grandmother. The way I heard it, Mama Cloud decided she simply had too many children to deal with. Also, she thought Mother would get a better education in Birmingham than in the one-room schoolhouse in Lilesville. Mother was only seven years old when this happened. She lived in Birmingham for eight years, then went off to Converse College at age fifteen. I didn't find out about this until I'd just been released from treatment (for depression) when I was thirty-nine. As for Uncle Pete, who was always Mama Cloud's favorite, he never married and ended up blowing his brains out with a shotgun somewhere down in Florida when he was thirty-six.

One more thing: when Mother married my father, after the preacher said, "I now pronounce you man and wife," Mother turned to her mother (Mama Cloud) and said, "I hate you."

After I was born in January 1949, Mother went into a postpartum depression so severe, she left our home to go home to Mama Cloud, the one and only time in her adult life she ever did this. I always figured her depression stemmed from her inability to produce a male heir. Let's face it, I was supposed to be a boy. Mary was their firstborn, and they were happy to have her. But after that it was time for a boy, and Mama had failed. Years later, I had the opportunity to ask

Mother about this—why she had gone home to Mama Cloud when she hated her so much. "Well," she said, "that just shows you how depressed I was."

Mother may not have been the nurturing type, but she had a great sense of adventure. One time she piled the four of us children into her station wagon and drove us to Fort Lauderdale, Florida. I was a second grader at Pine Street Elementary School. This was not spring break (or Christmas). This was mid-February. School was in session, but Mama didn't care. She took us out of school and we just . . . took off!

Once when I was in the third grade at Pine Street, I heard Mama's high heels clicking purposefully down the echoey hallway outside my classroom. Without knocking or anything, she just marched in while class was in session and whispered something into Mrs. Simkins's ear. (Mrs. Simkins was my third-grade teacher.) Then she walked over to my desk and grabbed me by the arm. Once we were out in the hallway, I began to protest. "Mama?" I said. "I'm not sick."

"Shut up!" Mama said. "We're going to the Masters."

This was April 2, 1959. Arnold Palmer was the defending champion, and a nineteen-year-old Jack Nicklaus was making his Masters debut. But Mother, as always, insisted we follow Ben Hogan because he was "the best player from tee to green."

Mother taught me to drive a car. And to swim. And play golf. And on school nights she'd take us to baseball games at Duncan Park (where the Philadelphia Phillies had a farm league team). And Mother would, on occasion, read to us. *Charlotte's Web* and *Now We Are Six* are two books I remember from when we were young. Then later came *Heidi* and *The Hound of the Baskervilles*. One moving passage in *Heidi* had Mother in tears. It was the first time, and one of only three times, I ever saw her cry.

Mother was outspoken and opinionated. Her lack of a filter combined sometimes with alcohol occasionally caused her to say cruel things. And because she was smart as a whip, she could be *really* cruel.

I have always had an athletic walk. One time when I was about seven, Mother told me I walked funny. "You walk funny," she said. "Like you've got something between your legs." Of course, I had no idea what she was talking about. But this was mild shame compared to some other things she said. Things that, when told to seasoned therapists, caused their jaws to drop.

When I was seventeen, I picked up the phrase "Be real" from my best friend's older brother. "Be real," he'd say in his James Dean way. So I began saying that to Mother whenever she'd start acting like she thought Mrs. James A. Chapman Jr. was supposed to act. "Be REAL," I'd say. And boy, would that piss her off.

Another time, when I just couldn't take it any more, I told Mother I hated her.

"I *hate* you," I said.

"You can't hate me," she said. "I'm your mother."

"Well, if you weren't my mother, you wouldn't be my friend."

When I was in my thirties in the mid-1980s, Mother and I didn't speak for about three years. Looking back on it, it was a necessary break. But the drought came to an end when I called her out of the blue after I'd finished writing a song called "Goodbye Little Rock and Roller."

The song tells the story of a young girl who painfully leaves home to become a rock and roll star. After she crashes and burns, she rises again to find serenity and true love. Then she has a baby girl she names Lucille. Things come full circle when Lucille leaves her to go out into the world.

I've often wondered if it was coincidence or serendipity that I finished the song on Mother's Day, which is when I wrote the last two verses:

> She rocked Lucille to sleep each night
> Then sang her lullabies she'd write
> She thought her heart would break in two
> The first time she heard "Mom, I love you"
> Then one day her baby girl
> Walked outside to find her world
> She never dreamed she'd see the day
> She'd be fighting back the tears to say
> Goodbye little rock and roller
> Gee it sure was good to know you
> Goodbye my little rock and roller
> Goodbye

I was crying my eyeballs out writing some of those lines. And after it was all finished and done, like something in a dream, I reached for the phone and began dialing. Then I heard my mother's voice.

"Hello," she said.

"Hey Mama, listen to this," I said, as I set the phone's receiver down. I began to sing,

> Once there was a little girl
> Unlike any in the world
> One night she looked inside her soul
> And all she saw was rock and roll,

and kept on singing until the song was finished. As the last note faded, I was fully prepared to hear a dial tone. Instead, I heard silence.

"So what do you think?" I asked.

"That's fine and well," Mama said. "Now when are you coming home for Christmas?"

My sister Dorothy once said, "Our mother was a terrible mother, but a great person." And that's a pretty fair assessment. And I've always thought there were two Mothers at play: the real, authentic one and the one that hid behind the mantle of being Mrs. James A. Chapman Jr. But the great thing about Mother is she became a better and better person as she got older. She became more and more real, more Martha and less Mrs. James A. Chapman Jr.

Life has a way of seasoning us. And as far as I can tell, two things happened that caused profound change in my mother. The first was divorce.

After my father died (at age sixty-two) in 1983, Mother married a man from North Carolina none of us knew. He was as headstrong as Mother and had a temper. She stayed with him seven years before filing for divorce. This must've been a hard thing for her to do, because Mother had always thought people who got divorced were morally deficient. So basically, she had to eat a lot of crow. Years later, I asked her when she knew her marriage to this man was over.

"I knew it was over after four months," she said. "But pride made me hang on another seven years."

Then four years after her divorce, Jamie died. Her only son. James Alfred Chapman IV. King James. The heir apparent.

So with my father and brother both gone, our family became a family of women. Four women. Mother, Mary, me, and Dorothy. All of us six feet tall. Daddy once referred to us as "twenty-four feet of women."

It was one Christmas holiday in the late 1960s. He was escorting the four of us into the Piedmont Club in Spartanburg. Dorothy and I were home from college on Christmas break. Mary was home from New York, which is where she moved after college. Anyway, we were all dressed up in our winter coats—looking good, I might add. And when Daddy threw open the front door to the Piedmont Club, we were enveloped by the sounds and smells of Christmas: the holiday music, laughter, ice cubes clinking against crystal, the crackling of a roaring fire in the fireplace, and so on. These were all friends of my parents. And as they turned to smile and call out greetings, Daddy was the first to enter, followed by Mother and us three daughters. "Y'all better back up," he shouted out. "I'm coming through here with twenty-four feet of women!"

I was always a daddy's girl, and I loved our original family of six. But this new family of four—all women—well, it took some adjusting, but over time the four of us became something special.

As I mentioned earlier, I was forty-seven when Jamie died. Mother was seventy-three. Mary was forty-nine, and Dorothy, forty-four. It sounds strange, but with no more Daddy and no more Jamie, the four of us became incredibly supportive of one another. Mary developed into a world-class flower arranger and had a few short stories published. Dorothy became serious about her painting and had a few shows. I continued to do my music and started writing my first book. We all began to thrive as artists. There was no competition or jealousy, only support and encouragement. It was a great time.

Once while on a book tour—this was in the spring of 2004; I was fifty-five and Mother was eighty-two—anyway, I was passing through Spartanburg on my way to a literary event in Atlanta. So I called Mother just to check in.

"Where are you?" she said.

"I'm in the parking lot at the Skillet."

"I'm a block away. I'll meet you there."

I explained how our visit would have to be short, as I had to be in Atlanta in a few hours. She seemed fine with that. "I just want to see you," she said.

In less than a minute, I saw her Prius pulling into the Skillet parking lot. So I got out of my car and got in hers. "Hi, Mama," I said. I was tired from the road, so without any further ado, I stretched out across the console between our seats and rested my head in her lap. Mother didn't say anything either. She just sat there like having my head in her lap in a public parking lot in Spartanburg was an everyday occurrence.

After a while, I said, "Mama, the world's so scary. Sometimes I wish I could just crawl back up inside your womb."

There was a momentary pause. Then . . .

"You can't," she deadpanned. "You're too big. You wouldn't fit."

During this same period, I once heard Mother say, "I can't believe it. Y'all are all so *talented*. Mary can do anything, and Dorothy with her art, and you with your music . . . and Jamie was so creative. *Where* did y'all come from? I was just a vessel! Just a *vessel!*"

"Mama," I said, laughing. "Get a grip. And go look in the mirror. Are you kidding? We're all just watered-down versions of you. You're the mother lode."

My mother was born Martha LeNoir Cloud in Lilesville, North Carolina, on September 28, 1922. She died in Spartanburg, South Carolina, on October 22, 2014, less than a month after turning ninety-two. The year before, Mother could, on a bet, stand on her head at a Spartanburg cocktail party, dressed to the nines in an outfit that included a girdle and high heels. But in the summer of 2014, she contracted a bad infection that had her bedridden and barely able to move. After five weeks at a rehab hospital, after it became apparent that no progress had been made, she was moved to the regional hospice home. Her body had simply given out. But her mind remained sharp until the very end.

When the head doctor at the rehab hospital realized he would be the one giving Mother "the talk," that is to say, inform her that they were moving her to the hospice home, he admitted he felt a little trepidation, since my mother was a known force to be reckoned with. Talks of that nature are often difficult, but Mother made it easy.

"So when are you planning to move me?" she asked.

"This Wednesday," replied the doctor.

"I can't do it then," she said. "I have a tennis lesson."

Her memorial service was at the First Presbyterian Church in Spartanburg. The sanctuary was packed, which is remarkable considering Mother had outlived all but two of her friends. My two sisters spoke, the four granddaughters read scripture, and I sang. But before launching into my song "Happy Childhood," I looked out at the nearly nine hundred who had gathered and thanked them for being there.

"You know the great thing about our mothers is this," I said. "We wouldn't be who we are without them. And right now, I feel like I'm the luckiest girl in the world."

# Helen of Marion,
# the Woman behind the Velvet Mask

— E. C. HANES —

I RECENTLY LEARNED with the births of my most recent grandbabies that human children are born without knee caps, that these are formed over a number of years—three or four, to be exact. In the world of revelations, this one falls in the interesting but so-what category. However, as I thought about my kneecapless grandchildren, something occurred to me of greater importance: babies are also born without that most essential thing they'll need as adults— a mask or, more accurately, masks. This is not a tangible organic body part; rather, it is the amorphous shield that all humans develop to protect or hide their soul.

On 2 October 1917, Helen Greever Copenhaver, my mother, came into this world. She was the daughter of Margaret and Eldridge Copenhaver, a housewife and a Lutheran minister, respectively, who made their home in a small, comfortable town in southwest Virginia called Marion. I was never told, and never thought to ask, whether mother was born in a hospital or at home, but whether hospital or home, I know that her father, Eldridge, was in the room when she took her first breath.

I don't know why she was given the name Helen. Perhaps there was a Helen somewhere in the limbs of the Greever or Copenhaver family trees, or perhaps it was inspired by Helen of Troy, the legendary Homeric beauty. Why not? Mother was a beautiful woman: tall, dark hair, well formed, and blessed with a smile capable of launching, if not thousands, at least dozens of ships.

———

REGARDLESS, at some point in her youth, probably in college, she acquired the nickname by which she was known for the rest of her life: Copey, a shortened version of Copenhaver.

Helen must have sensed that Copey's future did not lie along the shady streets and neighborhoods of Marion where she grew up but somewhere new, somewhere that awaited a woman named Copey, an artist, a singer, an actress, a leader, a wife and mother, and a traveler of the world.

Of course no one in Marion ever called her Copey. To them she was Helen and always would be. We knew that when someone asked for Helen they were either from Marion or Burkes Garden, Virginia, her mother's home.

Whether Copey or Helen, I believe the soul behind her mask was that of a preacher's daughter from a small, close-knit, deeply religious, mountain community, and whenever it felt she was wandering from that place it would pull her back home.

---

ONE DAY SHE PICKED me and my sister, Drewry, up from grade school in Winston-Salem. On our way home, we saw a truck with fresh produce parked on the side of the road. Mother stopped to buy something from the old gentleman standing beside his truck, and he happened to notice some branches with berries on them in the back of our car, pyracantha berries I think. He looked at mother and said, "Them shore is pretty berries, ain't they." She said without any hesitation, "Ain't they."

Drewry and I broke out laughing when we got back in the car, and for the next five obnoxious minutes kept saying to each other, "Ain't they." This was not the kind of thing that Copey Hanes, an English major and a woman who corrected our every utterance, would say, but it was exactly the kind of thing that Helen Copenhaver from Marion, Virginia, would say.

---

IT IS SAID, usually by vegetarians or their more zealous cousins, the vegans, that we are what we eat. (This may be true, though I suspect it's not, but if it is then I'm part steak, part fish, a large part fowl, and a mess of collard greens, all swimming in a broth of aged single-malt whiskey and southern iced tea.) My own theory is that we're first and foremost the result of how we're raised, or to put it in southern terms, "Don't git beyond your raise'ns."

Who was your daddy and momma? Where'd you come from? Where'd you go to school? What church you belong to? These are the questions southern folk ask when trying to see behind your mask, and for those who sought the woman behind Copey's mask, they needed only look to the people and small towns in southwest Virginia that raised her.

ELDRIDGE COPENHAVER graduated from Roanoke College and got his divinity degree from Moody Bible College in Chicago. In addition to being the pastor of the Ebenezer Lutheran church, he was also the president of Marion College, a small junior college for women.

Marion College no longer exists, having been sized out of business by much richer and more established institutions, but in its day it provided an education for a lot of women who were usually the first in their family to attend college and certainly the first woman in the family.

He enjoyed his job as a minister on Sunday and a junior college president on Monday, and I am told that he was good at it. He was forty-five years old when Helen was born and forty-three when her sister Margaret Sue was born. I was named Eldridge after him since my older brother, Jim, had inherited the primogenitor title, James G. Hanes III. I consoled myself by being a "first."

I never really knew Eldridge Copenhaver, since he died when I was seven years old, but I heard stories from my mother, my aunt Margaret Sue, and assorted friends of the family. The postmaster of Marion is reported to have said that when he saw Eldridge Copenhaver walking down the streets of Marion it was like watching Jesus walk past. So what would it have been like to have your report card signed by Jesus?

I once asked mom what her father was like, and her answer, unsurprisingly, was that he was a man of unquestioning faith and integrity, a man admired by all and with few faults; in short, he was her ideal male figure, then and always. When I asked whether he was a hard man, a stern man, she replied that, while serious, he also loved to laugh, though I imagine the humor in Marion was somewhat more restrained than that in Winston-Salem, or at least what passed for humor among the rowdy Hanes family into which she was to marry.

I also learned that at some point Eldridge was removed from the presidency of Marion College by a group of church elders. I don't recall the who, what, how, and why's, but I do recall the unquenched anger of his daughter at the evil men who crucified Marion's Jesus.

Margaret Greever, Helen's mother, was from a small community called Burkes Garden, Virginia, a paradise if there ever was one. Located an hour or so from Marion, the valley is covered with centuries-old oak trees and sugar maples that stand like sentinels in pastures so thick with blue grass that one can hardly walk through them during the summer. Cattle, sheep, and horses fatten. In the fall, buckets are hung from taps on the sugar maple trees and the mills flow syrup in amber cascades.

It has always seemed ironic that Burkes Garden, like Marion, was included in what outsiders call Appalachia. College-educated, devout, prosperous farmers and professionals had lived in this valley since before the Revolutionary War. In fact, Philip Greever Sr. is said to have fired the first shot at the battle of King's Mountain. His grandson, John Dudley Greever, my mother's grandfather, fought under the command of General Lee in the Army of Northern Virginia. He was at Chancellorsville, Gettysburg, and the Wilderness and was a prisoner of war in Maryland.

Helen finished high school in Marion, graduated from Wittenberg College in Ohio, and was accepted in the graduate dramatic arts program at the University of North Carolina in Chapel Hill. After only a year, she was offered a job at Salem Academy in Winston-Salem teaching drama and voice. While she never received her master's degree, she did, as a result of taking the job at Salem, receive an invitation of marriage from her future husband of fifty-five years, James Gordon Hanes Jr., known as Gordon.

The story goes that Gordon's grandmother, Anna Hodgin Hanes, volunteered him to pay the salary for the new soloist at Centenary Methodist Church in Winston. It turned out that the soloist in question was one Helen Greever Copenhaver, known as Copey. Apparently, for Gordon, it was love at first sight. Copey said that she needed more looks.

———

THE HANES FAMILY, like the Copenhavers and Greevers, started out as farmers and soldiers, but after the Civil War the Haneses decided that business was the more desirable career. The Hanes name has been sewn into more pairs of sleepwear, underwear, hosiery, and socks than almost any other. The worlds of finance, banking, and medicine, both in North Carolina and in the entire country, were all pursued with equal success. It was into this world that Helen, now Copey, married. So how does a young woman, wearing a mask molded in a furnace of deep faith, modest means, and rural expanses, fit into a family of outspoken overachievers and political leaders?

Warily.

Soon after they were married, Gordon and Copey moved to Wheeling, West Virginia. Gordon had tried to enlist in the navy at the start of the war but was turned down because he couldn't pass the physical as a result of kidney problems. He then tried to get into any service that would have him, including those of Canada and Great Britain, but they too turned him down. Having no luck getting into a military service, he got a job working at a munitions factory in Wheeling making guns for naval ships. I think that moving to Wheeling was the best thing that could have happened to the young couple because it gave them time to get to know each other away from Winston and the pressure of being in a city where every other park, school, and factory was named for some member of the Hanes family.

Copey and Gordon settled into their life in Winston with seeming ease, but then what would I, as a young boy, know about the underlying pressures of life or relationships? I do know that as far back as I can remember our household was one of peace and love. I don't recall a fight or yelling match between my parents, ever. I'm sure there were differences between them, but if so, they hid them well.

Copey wore many hats. She was an attentive mother, a community volunteer, a gardener, a fishing enthusiast, a hunter, and the wearer of a dozen other hats. But she was first and foremost the loving companion and partner of a man who needed and cherished the family he never had growing up.

Gordon's mother had died in childbirth. His father, Jim Hanes, was crushed. It was not something he was prepared for, so his brother Fred and Fred's wife, Betty, volunteered to help raise Gordon. Eventually Jim remarried, but his new wife, Molly, was not exactly the motherly type.

––––––––––

FAST-FORWARD to the days when children no longer simply accept parents as necessary evils and realize that they are individuals with their own peculiarities and problems. I don't recall the exact point when I realized that we are rarely privy to what lies behind another's mask, even a parent's. All we can do is distill what we are told with what we observe.

My distillation of the woman behind Copey's mask yields a woman who carried a sense of guilt for years. Why did she have so much while her sister had so little? Margaret Sue never married, probably was never asked, so she went back to Marion to take care of her parents when they got older. She never let Helen forget it, and while she held her Marion, devout, Christian mask up for the world to see, the woman behind Margaret's mask would make digs at her sister, nieces, and nephews. She would of course never acknowledge that these remarks were meant to be mean.

Copey had on occasion the same tendency, but her mask would say that she was just making a joke: "Everybody else can make a joke so why can't I?" Because, mother, it wasn't meant as a joke—how many times have I heard this line? One of my biggest failings was to not confront mother when she aimed one of her "jokes" at my wife, Jane.

When we swapped houses with mother and dad in the late eighties, Jane wanted to make our new house—mother's old house—more personal, more "our house." When we changed the lighting fixtures in the front hall, instead of saying how pretty they were, mother said: "They're very nice. Much fancier and more expensive than ours, but more you." It was not a big thing, but also not the kind of thing that a kind, Christian, Marion girl would have said, and especially not one who had hired one of the most renowned decorators in New York to design her living room in that very house. I didn't say anything, and perhaps this was cowardice, or perhaps it was a fear of damaging a relationship with a woman whom I deeply loved.

One of our ministers at Centenary Church once said, "Sometimes silence isn't golden, it's just yellow." I have been yellow on occasion.

———————

A GLIMPSE BEHIND another's mask is most frightening when it reminds us of what lies behind our own. This is the reason that, as a schoolmate once cautioned me, I try to judge people for what they are, not what they aren't, and what Helen "Copey" Hanes was, was a woman of extraordinary generosity and kindness, with a wonderful sense of humor. The number of people whose lives she positively affected are too numerous to count.

For her ninetieth birthday she said she didn't want anyone to give her a party; rather, she wanted to throw a party for the community. She asked the Winston-Salem Symphony to invite Van Cliburn to come and perform; she would pay for the whole thing as her present to the city and the symphony that she had loved for so many years. It was, quite simply, a magnificent gesture and typical of both the woman and the woman behind the velvet mask. Van Cliburn presented her with a mass of birthday roses at the reception following his concert and for her birthday every year from then onward until he died.

———————

HER HUMOR comes through in a letter she sent to me and my siblings some-time in the 1960's. It was written on a single piece of Lufthansa stationary as she was flying to Europe.

Dearest Redge [my nickname],

I've written Drewry and Jim and I'm sure each of you will laugh like hell over what I have to say. I loathe flying and naturally assume on every trip I'll never see you again. I need to say I love you more than all the world and please don't fight when I'm gone!!! Make your beds, pick up your clothes, write your thank you's, be loving to shut ins, remember peoples' birthdays, don't say shit at parties, divide the pictures evenly, DON'T FIGHT—HELP ONE ANOTHER!!!

Meet us if we come home

Mom

---

WHEN DAD DIED IN 1995, mother was seventy-eight years old. She never remarried or, to my knowledge, even had dinner with a man alone. Her own mother died just two years after Eldridge passed away, and I thought this might be mother's fate, but Helen lived to be ninety-six.

While she had a very productive and outwardly happy life after dad died, she grew tired and regretful. She had regrets about her loyalty to her parents, her relationship with her sister, and eventually portions of her life with dad. This is not to say that she ever regretted being with him—quite the contrary. Her bedroom was a temple to him, with pictures of him everywhere, but she kept saying "if only . . ." and "why didn't I . . ."

At ninety-five she had a small stroke that, while leaving her functional, took away many of the things she enjoyed. She couldn't drive, she needed help using the bathroom, and she needed round-the-clock assistance in her house. She got more and more agitated. On Christmas Eve at my sister's house she had a massive stroke from which she never woke. We took turns sitting with her in the hospital and later at hospice. Drewry and one of her daughters spent the first days in the hospital, Jim took over at hospice, and then it was my turn.

I wiped her forehead and patted her arm while speaking to her as if she would answer back. I imagined that she did. She was at peace and was, as she had been ninety-six years before, sweet, clean, and sinless. At some point early in the morning I sat up from my recliner because her breathing had become barely audible. I walked over to the bed and stood by her when her breathing stopped. I said, "Momma, you still here?" She wasn't, 'cause she'd gone home. She went to be with Gordon, the love of her life, as a woman with no regrets and no mask.

Selfishly, I hope she also went knowing that, just as when she took her first breath, when she took her last, Eldridge Copenhaver was at her side.

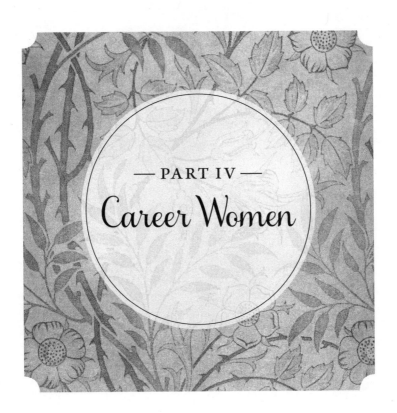

— PART IV —

Career Women

# Estate Sale

— SALLY GREENE —

MORNINGS ARE THE BEST time of day here. Still on eastern time, I am up by six, cup of French roast in hand. I sit on the sofa in my mother's living room, surrounded by familiar objects of her life, sorted and recombined into unfamiliar arrangements. It's quiet and still dark.

It is Thursday, 21 January. Only three more mornings like this remain before I head back to North Carolina. Having entrusted my mother, who can no longer live alone, to the care of others several years ago, I now leave her house in the hands of capable women, the women from Dallas that we've hired to manage her estate sale. The next time I see this house it will be empty, its contents scattered to the four winds.

As Sunday approaches, I wonder: what's the proper ritual for the last hours alone in your mother's house? There's no Book of Common Prayer at hand, only Methodist hymnals. Online, I find a supplement to the prayer book containing prayers for occasional events, among them the establishment of a new home:

> Let the mighty power of the Holy God be present in this place to banish from it every unclean spirit, to cleanse it from every residue of evil, and to make it a secure habitation for those who dwell in it.
>
> Sovereign Lord, you are Alpha and Omega, the beginning and the end: Send your servants out from this place on many errands, be their constant companion in the way, and welcome them upon their return, so that coming and going they may be sustained by your presence, O Christ our Lord.
>
> The effect of righteousness will be peace, and the result of righteousness tranquility and trust for ever. My people will abide in secure dwellings and in quiet resting places.

So many errands did Sarah Greene run out of this place! How many times did these walls embrace her comings and goings, her return from places as far as China and as dear as North Carolina.

This small split-level house, with its vaulted-ceiling living room that feels at once enfolding and spacious, this house surrounded by woods in a mostly treeless subdivision—this was her refuge, her secure habitation, her quiet resting place. All of these blessings were hers, but they speak to beginnings. What speaks to the end, to leaving the last house behind?

In the foyer hangs a small European needlework framed with the legend "Peace to all who enter here." Let me hold on, then, to a prayer for peace, for this was no trifling sentiment.

This house is not the one I grew up in. It's the house she designed for herself, over thirty years ago, as she emerged from a bitter divorce. The story of the dissolution of my parents' marriage is a tragedy, one that to my lasting regret I observed mostly from afar (while my younger brother, Russ, not only witnessed it but suffered much in the process). I had moved to Washington, D.C. by then and was launched, working full time by day and going to law school by night. My world was all before me, while my mother's was coming apart.

In a tall stack of court papers from the divorce, found hiding in plain sight against the wall of the loft room, a four-page answer to interrogatories, pages that I had never seen, brings it into focus:

> At some point, the worry over his drinking problem, and my inability to communicate with him, or to get him to pay any attention to my worries and dissatisfaction with his job performance, crossed the line that really did make living together insupportable.

His drinking on the job, while at a remote printing plant waiting for the paper to be printed,

> became a weekly source of anxiety and constituted a kind of mental cruelty peculiar to the weekly newspaper business.
>
> I was trying very hard to hold the marriage together, but this was mainly because of the effect I feared a divorce would have on the business. The marriage had obviously lost any personal value for me . . . , but I was so concerned about Russ that I simply couldn't face the volcanic explosion I feared would result if I didn't keep Ray pacified.

I did, at least, attend the trial. I can still see my father on the witness stand, testifying that alcohol "came upon" him, overpowered him. I would like to say that I went to him, for he is my father, and told him that I loved him. But I did not. He died without ever seeing me again. How do you ask forgiveness of a dead man? This is the question I have been asking for thirty years, my remorse without resolution, my own part in the tragedy, and this is why the prayer for peace must abide.

---

FRIDAY MORNING, 22 January. Something I loved discovering about this house when it was new was the way my mother had taken tired old items from the house she had left and put them in surprising juxtapositions. A metal piggy bank with garish red eyes, a sand dollar, an old plastic fan, and a pair of tiny ceramic Dutch clogs combine with a small French tray to make an artful, whimsical vignette in a shuttered wooden cabinet, hung above a toilet. In such ways did objects that I might have cast aside gain new luster for being loved again.

So it wasn't a clean break that she had made, but an evolution. This is how she lived, taking what good fortune had given her (or the hand she was dealt) and, with creativity and hard work, spinning it into gold. Immersed as I am here in the material relics of her life, I've come to see more fully, for example, how in so many ways her interests built upon those of her mother.

She followed her mother into the newspaper profession, taking her place as copublisher (with my father), just as her mother had done (with her husband). Thus the ownership of the *Gilmer Mirror,* beginning with her grandfather George Tucker's purchase of it in 1915, extended through the matrilineal line to the third generation. I can't reflect on the course of her life without asking, and not for the first time, why I did not follow the same path.

Plenty of reasons come to mind, and it's far too late for the question to make any sense. But, surrounded by so many indicia of the rootedness of my mother's life, its interconnectedness with the lives of her parents and with those of others in this small town, its grounding in this East Texas land that she began loving as a child and could not imagine leaving, the question returns. It comes not so much in the form of second-guessing my own decisions but, rather, from her point of view. How much did it matter, how much did it hurt her that the choices I made took me in such a different direction?

Just a few years ago, a thoughtless remark of mine provoked a rather definitive answer. Over the years I had tried to talk her into moving close to us in Chapel Hill by stressing the superior choices she would have when it came to shopping, entertainment, the arts, everything to support the good life she cultivated. The advantages were obvious, I said one night in her kitchen, while complaining that I couldn't even find fresh tortellini at the local grocery. "You've rejected my town, my state, my church, my whole way of life," she shot back.

"How can I not take it personally?" If I had wanted an answer to whether my permanent expatriation from Texas had hurt her, I'd practically drawn it in blood. (I later learned I'd been wrong about the tortellini.)

---

SATURDAY MORNING, 23 January. Here are some of the ways in which my life has embraced, and not rejected, my mother's. First and most enduringly, a love of literature and writing, passions of hers that led me to earn a Ph.D. in English. A love of classical music (also jazz), which found expression in a senior piano recital and a college organ recital. A love of cooking and fine food, engendered early as she took me to restaurants like Brennan's, in New Orleans, where to my astonishment I saw perfectly good food deliberately set on fire, and the fabled Old Warsaw in Dallas, my first real taste of Continental food: fresh sautéed spinach seasoned at table with cracked nutmeg—a revelation!

A couple of years ago while dining with my husband at City Grocery in Oxford, Mississippi, whose chef, John Currence, is a James Beard award winner, I remarked upon what an excellent cook my mother was. He looked at me in disbelief. Although I freely confess that wine was involved, his reaction moved me to tears. I surrendered to what I understand now to have been an overpowering wave of loneliness. It was true that he hardly knew this side of her. He had not tasted the venison chili she made out of roadkill, a warm carcass that she'd spotted and retrieved from the side of the highway. He had not been in my high school Latin Club when she was asked to serve the main course for the progressive dinner, where the challenge was to use only ingredients available in ancient Rome. (After careful research she came up with a delightful concoction of roast chicken with rosemary, olives, and grapes.) Nor was he among the college friends I impressed with her Caesar salad, a favorite from Helen Brown's *West Coast Cook Book*, the real deal, involving coddled eggs "cooked" with lemon juice and croutons made of day-old sourdough bread sautéed in garlic-infused olive oil.

When she visited me at college, we'd have lunch at a 1970s, hippie-style restaurant and cooking store. We drank Lancer's from little bottles, the kind you could turn into salt and pepper shakers. In the 1980s, newly divorced and in her fifties, she took up the nouvelle cuisine so excitingly reflected in the Silver Palate cookbooks and the like: she was a foodie *avant la lettre*. Packages of Alaska salmon smoked on alder wood displayed at my local fancy food store remind me of the cruise up the inside passage of Alaska we took together, where a side trip took us to a forest above Juneau for a dinner of alder-wood-smoked wild king salmon. As memories such as these flooded over me that night in Oxford,

I faced the realization, surely common to daughters of mothers everywhere, that these memories belong to no one but the two of us and that before long they will be only my own.

But there is tangible evidence of our relationship. In her closet she kept some two dozen shoeboxes of letters from me, from college until the 1990s, when a combination of my marriage, a baby, and the advent of e-mail spelled their demise. Of her letters I saved only four or five shoeboxes, and I'm surprised that it's even that. At some point I decided that the better course was to let them go, that looking back on them would only sadden me. But now I realize her instinct to save them—a record of two lively women holding forth across generations about the women's movement, the politics of the Reagan years, and the culture wars of the 1990s while one of them rebuilt her life as a solo business owner and the other made her way to law school, then graduate school, marriage, and her own footing in the world—was right.

No doubt my letters involved a good bit of self-performance. While there was much genuinely happy news to relate, especially as I embraced the life of a young professional (a yuppie) in the Washington of the 1980s, there would have been little mention of bad dates or heartaches, little of the looming anxieties of young adulthood. Prudent financial moves would have been emphasized over foolish mistakes. And yet our letters underwrote the time we did spend together with bonds of sympathy and mutual interests. I've even wondered if our relationship were not better, less complicated perhaps, for being negotiated across time and space than it might have been had we lived in close proximity.

It's a reasonable question. Her own mother, very much in proximity as business partner as well as mother, was a force of nature. Over more than forty years, Georgia Laschinger worked virtually every job involved in publishing the *Mirror*, except for operating the Linotype. A journalist, an ad manager, a civic leader, a local historian whose tireless efforts to gain historic markers for the county resulted in her appointment to the Texas Historical Commission, a politico whose work for LBJ landed her dinners at the White House, she enjoyed tremendous love and respect. For her funeral, all the shops on the courthouse square closed their doors.

In February 1970, nine months after her mother's death in a Houston hospital, my mother suffered a psychotic break. In her delusion, she was a great novelist coming into her powers. In letters she actually wrote to confidants (men of the Texas literary establishment), she explained that she "wanted to write something equal to Flannery O'Connor and Kathryn Ann Porter, something that would last," but worried that it might not be "worth the disruption in lives" of those she loved. Of the work she was writing (in manic sessions at the typewriter that confused and frightened me), she preserved only fragments. One outlines the novel's premise:

> This all started at a point outside of time in St. Luke's Hospital, Houston when my momma confronted me with her statement. It was her challenge to me to prove that I was as good a man as she was. She was saying if I met the challenge we would both have eternal life. The Easy Riders blew it, momma. We didn't. But we damn near busted a gut.

---

SUNDAY MORNING, 24 January. One of my clearest childhood recollections is sitting in the den, in the 1950s home that is not this home, vowing to memorize everything around me, knowing someday it would be only a memory. On this last morning in this house where I did not live, where my mother has hardly lived in years, it feels different. Again I want to sear every detail into memory. But it's not my memories that I want to fix in place, or not only that—it's my mother herself, and already she is slipping away.

The west wall of the living room is one built-in bookcase filled with inherited treasures, mementos from exotic trips (a Limoges ashtray I'd never noticed, from a Paris hotel where we had once stayed; how did she end up with that?), and books. Not her most valuable books, these are by writers she cherished. Updike, Bellow, and Cheever. Joan Didion and Annie Dillard. James Agee, Walker Percy, Wallace Stegner. Flannery O'Connor, Pearl S. Buck, W. B. Yeats. A photo I particularly treasure shows her whitewater rafting down the Nenana River, in Denali National Park, with fellow journalists on a post-convention trip. She's in her sixties, and she has never looked happier.

North-facing windows, including clerestory windows addressing the loft room, admit generous light. On this winter morning, soft sunrise colors outline bare branches in the hardwood bottom. The fireplace, on the north wall, is made of antique brick. On the mantel sit a tall rectangular antique clock, fat decorative candles suggesting the 1970s, and a miniature reproduction of one of the soldiers from the vast terra cotta army buried with China's first emperor, rediscovered in the twentieth century.

When we moved her last year from an assisted living institution to the home of a devoted friend, I took from the mantel a photograph made at this site and placed it in her room. It's of her standing beside a life-size reproduction of one of the soldiers. She asked me about it the other night. What is that? Where was this picture taken? I looked up the terra cotta army on my phone, and she took note, but recognition seemed just out of reach.

"Am I losing my memory?" she asks, as she has asked before and will ask again.

"I'm afraid you are, some."

"Oh, I hate that."

"But you're still you!" I said, and she smiled.

Is she, though? Who is she? I look into her wizened face and see behind it the image of a bright, generous, brave, and adventurous woman. Aided by photos, I see a young reporter for the *Dallas Morning News*, an eager sixteen-year-old beginning her studies at Stephens College, the valedictorian of her high school class, a girl who loved flying and a girl who loved horses. I see a woman who held fast to friendships from every chapter of her life. I see a native Texan who took tremendous pride in her state, who loved its geography, its food, its folkways, its literature, its history. I see a skilled journalist, never caught without pen and paper, ready to capture the next news item. I see her reading, always and indiscriminately reading.

The pleasures of reading are beyond her now.

"I am a part of all that I have met," says the Ulysses of Tennyson (a poet she learned to love early), which I take to include all those worlds that are met on the printed page. Though his physical strength is failing, this Ulysses remains existentially present, sound of mind and "strong in will." He can still beckon to his colleagues, "'Tis not too late to seek a newer world." For my mother, words on the page no longer translate into sustained thoughts or flashes of insight. There is no newer world, imagined or actual, although certainly there are moments of happiness.

Existentially, spiritually, who is the person, where is the person now, when her past is in pieces and her future inaccessible? Where did the rest of her go? The question is unsettling, unnerving, harrowing ("to harrow": to break up, crush, or pulverize [soil or land] with a harrow; to tear, lacerate, wound; to vex, pain, or distress greatly).

It's impossible to disentangle her condition of loss from my own. My mother is disappearing. Her mind is disintegrating. What part of me is disappearing in the process? Psychologists use the term "ambiguous loss" to describe this state: loss without understanding, loss without closure. Pauline Boss coined the term in the 1970s as she worked with the wives of fighter pilots who had gone missing over Vietnam, and she quickly realized its broader applications. Immigrants face the ambiguous loss of loved ones back home, whom they may or may not ever see again. An adopted child searching for her birth mother is attempting to resolve an ambiguous loss.

Naming it helps. But it turns out that recognizing one ambiguous loss leads to confronting another. "In order to heal from that last loss, you may have to revisit those that came before," writes Boss. "They are all part of your experience." Losing my mother to dementia is a kind of "goodbye without leaving," as Boss puts it. Its mirror image, "leaving without goodbye," is a type of loss I'm familiar with as well. I left my father without telling him goodbye.

Thanks to the papers she saved, I better understand the tortuous loss my mother suffered as addiction slowly turned the man she married into a cruel stranger. In letter after letter, even while laying out the reasons she must leave him, she reminds him in the most loving terms that he can still choose to reclaim his life. In one beautiful passage, she encourages him to open himself to spirituality, offering her own journey as a model:

> My spiritual awakening, since which I feel I am a much different person, came during the period from 1970 until 1975. At some point along there everything I had ever read on philosophy and religion, sifting, sifting, sort of clicked into place. And I knew that I could believe in some higher power, but that in my case it probably always would be manifested through other people. During that dark period in my life in the 1970s I thought about Albert Camus' idea that the only real philosophical question is why, on any given day, should a person not commit suicide. I thought about that a lot because I really wanted to be rid of my life. But I knew that there were people who loved me, and I owed them more than that. And I finally came to see that if I were stuck with this life, it was up to me to make the best of it.
>
> I got out a couple of books you acquired long ago, Liebman's Peace of Mind and Lin Yutang's The Importance of Living. I have another one that's along the same lines, The Will to Meaning, by Victor Frankl, a man who survived a Nazi camp. He tells about how people he knew in the death camps achieved a remarkable serenity, and others he had known with many worldly goods and power were miserable. All because of attitude, the only thing in the world that any of us can really control. (Our own, that is.)
>
> A wise old friend of mine once told me that the reason you need something, some belief, to hold on to outside of yourself is that when you depend on another person, sooner or later that prop will fall out from under you. I think it's true.
>
> One thing I learned from [my psychiatrist] a long time ago is that people set themselves up for a lot of pain when they build up expectations that are not necessarily going to come about. Try to separate out hope,

which you can always have, from definite expectations. As I've often told Sally and Russ, sometimes you just have to "go with the flow." Being in control, in other words, isn't everything.

The letters are photocopies. So she was not just writing to my father. She was working through her own grief and loss by reminding herself of the inner resources she would need to keep going. Did she ever reread them? Or was the act of writing and keeping them enough? Three decades later, they resurface unexpectedly as a gift. In her own words I find the thread of a way to live into the ambiguity that defines both of our lives. Frankl's "tragic optimism": hope in the face of unknowing.

---

NOON. IT'S TIME TO LEAVE. Where are the words, what is the ritual, what symbolic act is worthy of this moment? I remain unsure. But I'm perhaps more certain of my legacy. Bags loaded, I lock the side door. I look back through the window to the west wall of the living room, and I am still.

# The Good Fight

— JACQUELYN DOWD HALL —

MY MOTHER, Virginia Mae Branham Dowd (called "Jinx" by one and all), died in the summer of 2001. A few weeks later, I dreamed that she had called us together—me and my younger brother and three sisters, all children again. I left the room for a moment, and when I returned she was gone. I couldn't believe that she, of all people, would desert me. But then, I thought as I awoke, of course she would, with the same quiet, self-contained steadiness of purpose with which she had supported me all my life.

That calm stayed with me, flowing beneath the more expected storms of regret and sorrow as I took up the most ordinary and yet, for me at least, extraordinary of tasks: writing her obituary, a genre that offers special permissions and imposes peculiar restraints. Within the tiny frame the form allows, I had to work collaboratively, adhering scrupulously to the facts while telling a story on which all five of her children could agree. And not just a story but a well-made story, and one that carried within its strict confines a mutually satisfying moral and political point.

A few months earlier I had asked my mother what she remembered as the best years of her life, half expecting her answer to have something to do with us. She named the 1970s, when I was gone (pursuing graduate study at Columbia and starting to teach at UNC) and she went from being a secretary raising my two youngest sisters on her own to directing the Labor Action Coalition of New York. I had devoted my life to excavating the history of southern women, and when it fell to me to write about my mother, I took that conversation as a mandate to tell a story that would turn on one of that history's central tropes: the eruption, against the odds, of ordinary women into public life.

I spent the hours before her funeral in the Cornell University archives, searching the Labor Action Coalition papers for traces of my mother that would authorize that theme, knowing all the while that it left out as much as it told. It said nothing about the hidden continent of motherhood. It did not evoke the qualities that inspired our fierce devotion and made her so luminous in our eyes. To capture even a hint of the personal, which could not, in any case, be separated from the political, I had to leave the archives (with its comforting promise that the documents preserved there would, in some small way, keep the ripples my mother had made in the world alive) and plunge into the labyrinth of family memories, searching for the images, the emblematic moments, the conversations that signaled the grace, courage, and anguish of a life lived mainly in what the literary scholar Patricia Yaeger calls the "nonepic everyday."

I can imagine my mother watching with bemusement as I rushed home with my precious documents in hand, awkwardly "interviewed" my siblings, and then labored over the words that would appear fleetingly in the local paper after the morning news. I think she would have been surprised by all that clambered for inclusion—the many things I wanted to say but could not. I could not explain how she combined a stubborn desire to make her own rules with a transcendent, clear-eyed acceptance of things as they are. Or how she cultivated irony while taking such simple joy in the day-to-day, or how she hated self-dramatization while mirroring for others a dramatically heightened sense of themselves. "Really?" she had said on her deathbed, in response to a story about how, as children, we thought she was the most courageous mother in the world. "I didn't know you felt that way."

What she did know, and would have approved of, was the obituary's plot—the escape from a bad marriage and a small town; the poverty about which she never complained (never mind having a room of her own, she usually slept on a couch and often worried about making the rent); the loyalty of her children; the exhilaration of "fighting the good fight"—because that was a joint invention, told and retold by colleagues, friends, and family over the years. She might even have acknowledged that she had wordlessly designated me for this story-telling task, just as she had counted on us older children when she escaped Oklahoma and marriage to my father so many years ago. ("One for all and all for one," my teenage brother said in the mid-1960s, when we packed up the babies and the furniture and moved to Memphis, where I was in college.) But the urgency was my own. I was the one who could not rest until the inchoate experiences of a lifetime had been marshaled into chronological form. I was the one who put my faith in history, with its document-based rhetoric of persuasion, its promise that a woman might, if only by a daughter's proxy, "reach the conclusion of a life, and come into possession of [her] own story," as Carolyn Steedman put it.

My mother, on the other hand, had been preoccupied with dying, and she had done so in the same spirit in which she had lived. It was as if she had summoned us all to one last party and then retreated inward, keeping her own counsel as we filled the hospital room with our endless, self-involved, ricocheting talk. "I'm fine," she said at one point. "You all just keep talking." And later, just before she died: "I know what you're thinking. You think I'm afraid. But I'm not."

How did she do it? How did she manage those last words, in an atmosphere in which such benedictions almost never occur: the chaos and callousness of a modern hospital, which her children's vigilance and advocacy, demands and tears could not overcome? She had been determined to see that her almost hundred-year-old father had a good death. Now, in her own way, she was practicing what people used to call the "art of dying," taking comfort in our chattering presence, assuaging our guilt, drying our tears. But she was also reminding us, gently, that she was beyond us. We did not know what she was thinking. We could not know her mind.

Yes, as my brother said at her funeral, she was always a mystery to us. And in writing about her, not just for myself and my family but for unknown readers, I felt, in their most distilled and piercing forms, the impulses that drew me and many in my generation to women's history in the first place: first, the desire, always thwarted, to solve the mystery, to bring back that which is irretrievably lost; and second, the quest of the daughter/historian for the power to shape historical memory, to claim a place in the public record (whether in humble obituaries or in ambitious books) for the unacknowledged heroes of the past.

———

MY MOTHER AND I BOTH grew up in Oklahoma, a crossroad where the South meets the West. Her ancestors had inched their way up from Texas to sharecrop in "Little Dixie," the traditionally Democratic, cotton-growing, biracial southeast corner of the state. My father's parents came down from Republican, pro-union "bleeding Kansas" to open a dry goods store. I gravitated toward my mother's poorer, sprawling southern branch of the family. Her mother had gone to eighth grade; her father, a sharecropper-turned-barber, could barely read or write; her grandfather was stabbed in Seven Shooter, Oklahoma, leaving his wife—our delightful, snuff-dipping Granny Lou—to raise eight children by picking cotton and working as a cook.

No southern state had more homegrown socialists, more crosscutting mixtures of red, black, and white, a more violent heritage of appropriation, or a more multicultural, multiracial past. The history we learned in school, however, ignored all that. It turned instead on the land rush that opened Indian Territory to white homesteaders in 1889. I was amazed, years later, to see photographs of my hometown's founding citizens. They were not the lily-white settlers I had imagined; they included Indians and whites, slaves and free blacks. In the Old Cemetery, I discovered that outlaws and bankers, Confederate and Union soldiers lie buried side by side.

It was the social history of the 1960s and 1970s that changed how I saw this world, and, as with everything else at the time, I shared what I learned with my mother. It now seems to me that, while she might not have known the details, she had absorbed the cultural memories. The core values of rural radicalism seemed to run in her veins, guiding her sympathies unerringly toward the underdog. Children first: we were sacred, and there was never a time when she was not sheltering us and our wayward friends. Also African Americans, who lived virtually unseen by most whites—but not by her—across the railroad tracks, on the wrong side of our small Oklahoma town. Her best friends, two of whom were from the Choctaw/Cherokee families that had been pushed to the shadows by the time I was growing up. Vietnamese farmers, who lodged in her conscience before most people had registered the import of a looming, disastrous, undeclared war. Above all, the blue-collar activists with whom she felt such affinity and in whose company she spent those best years of her life.

As I changed—slowly, often painfully—from a student to a scholar, I remained my mother's daughter, carrying forward a project that links the rescue of others to self-invention, and spinning out, in my life and work, narratives that she and I both inherited and invented. At the time of her death, I was grappling with the limits of history's disciplinary conventions. In my own writings, I was trying to break the spell of the omniscient narrator and share with readers the travails of research and interpretation. My goal was not to rehearse the details of my own life, but I did long to show how the stories we tell grow from a process of forgetting and remembering our own encounters with the relics, fragments, and whispers of an always already recollected time.

In this effort, I felt called by my mother's spirit, which made her always the quiet center, the listener (whether at kitchen tables or union halls), the one who usually knew more about others than they knew about her. I knew that neither history nor obituary could bring the dead to life. But I could aspire to a more mortal form of writing: writing that admits its own limits, writing that respects the integrity of one's subjects rather than treating them as extensions of oneself, writing that—like memory, like my mother's last words—keeps the blessed conversation between the past and the present, the dead and the living, alive.

Looking back at the obituary I wrote, I'm struck by the degree to which I did at least push at the margins of the form—by stressing both motherhood and political passion and including my mother's last words, her decision to divorce my father, her poverty, her predilection for sleeping on the couch. But I'm also struck, again, by all I didn't say or sketched in but in a bare bones way. How I would love to write something that would really do her justice, but where would I begin?

I'd have to start at least with her mother, Dealva Mae Livingston, who married Roy Mack Branham when she was not yet seventeen and died too young and in too much pain. Here's how Jinx described her, writing to me in her beautiful cursive hand: "She made our modest little house in Wynnewood, Oklahoma, a wonderful home—beautiful flowers, fruit trees, garden, fish pond—even chickens and a cow. She was pretty, smart, generous—and worked too hard. But you know all of that—she was your grandmother and she absolutely adored you."

I did know, for I spent much of my childhood in "Deedle's" magical company. She made our clothes on an old treadle machine, hand cranked the laundry in a wringer washer on the back porch, wrung the heads off chickens in her backyard, and cooked memorably for us and for a sprawling extended family that always preferred gathering in her tiny house.

She passed on to my mother the generosity that guaranteed that anyone who was, as my mother put it, "displaced" ended up living at Deedle's house. Otherwise, she didn't bother to teach my mother her skills. Instead she let her live in books, become valedictorian of her high school class. But she and my grandfather had no money to send a daughter to college. It took everything they could do to scrape together enough to pay for one year of secretarial school.

On the eve of World War II, Jinx married my father, John George Dowd, a good dancer and a looker, a decision she immediately regretted. He joined the army while she was pregnant with me. When he returned, she followed him around the country as he worked his way up from shoe salesman to assistant manager in J. C. Penny stores. In 1953 he lost his job, sending us back to Pauls Valley, Oklahoma, a county seat town of fewer than five thousand souls where by now virtually all of our relatives on both sides lived. He went to work in his father's men's clothing store—a fateful decision: under "Papa John's" thumb, he bent himself to controlling her and us. She worked as a secretary, cleaned and scrubbed, took care of the kids, commiserated with us girls in the bathroom, the only private place in an aspirational ranch house that never felt like home. She was almost forty when she had her fifth child in 1961.

By that time, her marriage was beyond repair. Partly that was because she had changed. As for so many women, it started with the church. She taught a Sunday school class, learned the art of exegesis, became First Presbyterian's first female deacon. Soon she was joining one of those great democratizers of culture, a Great Books Club. She got a job as secretary to the superintendent of schools—the smartest man around, hated by the town fathers (including especially our Papa John) for integrating the schools. She would never have put it this way, but she was creating what she was hungry for: a life of the mind. My father wasn't his father, but he disliked her new friends, was discomfited by every sign of independence from him.

Meanwhile, we oldest children were becoming teenagers, and the 1960s were in the air. Her biggest grievance against my father had always been that if she bucked him, he'd take it out on us. Conflicts escalated as we became harder and harder to control. Soon after I left for Southwestern at Memphis (now Rhodes College) in 1961, she took my four siblings and moved out. When I graduated in 1965, my boyfriend and I rented a van and moved the family to Memphis, where she got a job as secretary to the dean of the college. The next year we all moved again, me to graduate school at Columbia, my mother and siblings to Ithaca, New York, where my sister was an undergraduate at Cornell.

One of my most precious artifacts is an Art Spiegelman–inspired graphic novel written by my niece a year after my mother's death. It memorializes one of the many family-myth-making stories we love to tell and retell: the epic move from Memphis to Ithaca, where Jinx and my two youngest sisters picketed the Mayflower moving company for leaving them stranded in an empty rented apartment for almost a month.

At that point, my mother was forty-four and embarking on a life she could not have imagined when she left Pauls Valley behind. It started when, working as secretary to the chair of the Cornell English department during the tumultuous years between 1964 and 1967, she befriended a cohort of radical graduate students and young professors. When they created Tomco Better Housing, Inc., she joined the staff, helping to build low-income housing and form a tenants' organization. In 1967 she met me in Washington for the March on the Pentagon, immortalized in Norman Mailer's Pulitzer Prize–winning *Armies of the Night* (1968). A few years later, with my two little sisters and eight other mothers and their children, she staged a Mother's Day sit-in at the Ithaca draft board, for which she was arrested and tried (the lawyer argued that by refusing to arrest the children the police had violated their constitutional rights). In 1969 she went to work for the Cornell Human Affairs Program, which was founded in response to the demand that Cornell offer students and faculty the opportunity to link intellectual work to activist concerns. In 1973 she met the man who would become the love of her life—the program's first full-time director, who elevated her from administrative secretary to assistant director almost as soon as he arrived. A year later, they and their allies created the

People's Power Coalition, a statewide, grassroots organization that sought to make public utilities responsible to the people they were meant to serve. When Cornell terminated the Human Affairs Program in 1975, the staff brought together delegates from nineteen international unions to found the Labor Action Coalition of New York.

Sustained by dues from local unions representing approximately eighteen thousand members, the Labor Action Coalition created ties between labor organizations and environmental groups at a time when they were usually pitted against one another and provided a voice for left-wing unionists who wanted to grapple with issues outside the workplace: protection against plant closings, robust health and safety standards, and especially municipal ownership of public utilities. First as the coalition's information director, then as its director, Jinx traveled the state by bus, wrapped in her signature brown wool cape (which, to my lasting shame, I later wore and lost), organizing conferences, lobbying the state legislature, testifying at rate hearings, and helping to produce a four-hundred-page "Organizer's Notebook on Public Utilities and Energy for New York State." She treasured the support of the charismatic reform president of the International Association of Machinists, William W. Winpisinger; the friendship of union stalwarts like Edward J. Bloch of the United Electrical, Radio, and Machine Workers of America; the thrill of Pete Seeger singing at a rally, the victory represented by the 1981 municipal takeover of the Niagara Mohawk facility in Massena, New York.

In the end, she was working out of a daughter's old bedroom, almost single-handedly keeping the organization alive. "Big Bill Haywood" (her parakeet), she wrote, "keeps me company and I have strategy sessions with him. When I start typing, he starts singing." In 1983 she finally "retired." Struggling to survive under the Reagan administration, unions were channeling all of their resources into strike funds and legal battles. Key Labor Action Coalition leaders were in failing health. Dues had slowed to a trickle.

All of this time—first in Pauls Valley, then in Ithaca—she had been taking care of us, as if whatever was going on in our lives was the most important thing in hers. She came to spend the summer with me when my first marriage broke up; she helped one of my younger sisters raise a daughter and restore a hundred-year-old farmhouse in rural New York. She was too intent on listening to whatever we needed to talk about to ever say much about herself.

Which returns me to the intensity with which I seized the opportunity to write about her after her death. I did it to keep from feeling what I was actually feeling: a loss, a vacuum that can never be filled. I'm so grateful to have had one more chance to keep her memory alive.

# The Persian Mom Mafia

## — MELODY MOEZZI —

PERSIAN MOMS don't work alone. They toil in teams, like professional athletes or ant colonies. Even in exile, even in the least likely places, even in Dayton, Ohio, they find one another, creating collaborative networks that would put habitual MVPs and ant supercolonies to shame.

I know this because I grew up in one such network, born of revolution, war, and exile. Iranian brains drained to all corners of the earth after the so-called Islamic Revolution, but one corner retained prominence: America. It wasn't as much a place as an idea, a hope, a dream.

And my parents' brains got us here. Both doctors, they were invited to practice in the nucleus of the American heartland. It wasn't New York or California, but it was *America*, and that's all they needed to know. So my sister was born in Hopkinsville, Kentucky; I was born in Chicago, Illinois, and our family settled in Dayton, Ohio.

There, the Persian moms found us and one another. In a land between lands, these ridiculously resilient women became both our refuge and our salvation: living testaments to the Prophet Muhammad's renowned assertion that heaven rests at the feet of the mothers. Time and time again, I've found paradise through the work of the women who raised me, nourished by the celestial bounties beneath their feet.

I call them the Persian Mom Mafia despite a notable absence of criminal elements in their activities, for they are the toughest and most protective humans I know, the people who would track me down to the ends of the earth were I ever abducted, and the women who would leave my kidnappers wishing they had been captured by real mafiosos instead of Persian mom-iosos. So, I call them my Persian Mom Mafia out of love and respect, because without them I'd be lost, and because if I *were* ever lost, *they* would be the ones to come find me and carry me home.

MY MOTHER'S NAME, Jazbi (short for Jazbieh), is derived from the word *jazab*, which means "attractive" in both Persian and Arabic. The name suits her, for beauty is her thing. She seeks it in her surroundings: her attire, her family, her friends, her face, her heart, her career, her everything. And she finds it. It's her magic. In her presence, even what seems gruesome becomes gorgeous.

A pathologist by trade, my mother has conducted hundreds of autopsies and tens of thousands of tissue diagnoses throughout her career, most of them during her twenty-year tenure at the Dayton VA Medical Center. For Jazbi, each autopsy, each brain cutting, each frozen section is a work of art as well as medicine. She revels in the challenge, the mystery, and the elegance of it all. She loves her work, and she made me love it too, from the moment I learned that she was the kind of doctor who investigated more than operated. Her devout fascination with the inner workings of the human form—how our cells multiply and rupture, how our organs atrophy and swell, how we live and die, and *why*—is contagious. Or at least it has been for me, if not genetic. Whatever the case, Jazbi has a preternatural knack for making the mundane exciting, the tedious intriguing, and the morbid life affirming.

I was still a kid when I saw my first autopsy, and somehow, my mother made it beautiful. I was visiting her at work and got bored waiting in her office, so I wandered into the morgue, where she was standing over a dead man, pulling out his heart to weigh it. I knew that cutting open dead people was part of my mom's job, but I'd never seen her in action. Standing in that deathly cold room, watching my mother holding this stranger's heart in her hands, I was in *awe*. I know now that plenty of people (children and adults alike) would no doubt experience fear, horror, nausea, or all of the above at a sight like that. But not me, not Jazbi's daughter. I felt only wonder and admiration. I knew what my mom did was important. I knew it helped get answers, heal hearts, kill cancers, and save lives. I *knew* she was beautiful.

"Every organ you must veigh," she tells me now. "Deh veight can be a clue. A heavy heart, *masalan* [for example], is a sign of heart failure. A light heart is a healty heart. You vant your heart to be tree-hundred gram, about."

While I don't know how much my mother's heart weighs, as thankfully, she is still with us, I do know the capacity of her heart, and it is vast. Though she is far more rational than emotional (the latter is my father's specialty), she loves fiercely and sensibly.

When I had trouble gaining height and weight as a kid, she took me to every doctor imaginable, for fear that I might be stunted for life. First and most often, she took me to Dr. Kardan, my pediatrician and primary care doctor until I was nearly twenty. Azar Kardan was also a member of the Persian Mom Mafia, and later our neighbor. Over and over again, Dr. Kardan patiently examined me and consistently came to the same conclusion: I had a fast metabolism, and I would be fine. In the end, she was right, but so was my mother, who persisted in dragging me to specialists galore, all to no avail. Jazbi was sure that there was a glitch in my digestion or absorption or *something*, and as it turned out, she was right too.

I grew to a respectable five feet six inches tall, and at around 130 pounds I was almost plump by Persian standards by the end of high school. But the day after my high school graduation, thanks to an excruciating stomachache that felt more like a heart attack, my parents took me to the emergency room, where doctors discovered a mass in my pancreas that nearly killed me.

My father, Ahmad, all but lost his mind, holding a seemingly endless array of kidney-shaped plastic containers for me to vomit into as my mother calmly held my hair back. He cursed himself for not bringing me to the hospital sooner; he cursed the nurses for chronically failing to land their needles inside my abnormally small and slippery veins, starting my IV himself at one point; and he constantly sought support and guidance from Amoo Nozar, a gastro-enterologist and my *amoo* (meaning paternal uncle, though we aren't actually related—our bond runs deeper than blood). Both Amoo Nozar and his wife, Auntie Mahboob to me (yet another member of the Persian Mom Mafia), showed up at my bedside. There was no way I could go through this alone, not even if I wanted to.

Unlike my dad, my mom wasn't freaking out. She was being reasonable; waiting for results; trying not to assume the worst; petting my back, my head, my hands, my feet, all in steady rotation—just as she had done nearly every day of my life for almost two decades, her way of waking me up for school, making those brutally early mornings practically tolerable.

The mass in my pancreas turned out to be a tumor that looked ominously malignant, so much so that the pathologist initially identified it as such. But thanks to my mother's photographic memory, resourcefulness, and relentless talent for tracking down the bright side, I was rescued from an effective death sentence. Having seen a tumor like mine at least once before, her bizarre ei-detic memory had filed it away, allowing her to recognize my peculiar pancre-atic mass as incredibly rare, impressively malignant looking, yet definitively benign nonetheless. She was accused of wishful thinking, but in the end she was right.

It turns out that sometimes wishful thinking is also smart thinking. My mother's life is a tribute to this fact. The second youngest of nine siblings, she lost her father when she was eight, and she describes her childhood in Tehran as idyllic, though it sounds chaotic at best based on the facts alone. She left Iran at the start of the revolution, carrying me in her womb and my sister on her lap, hoping for a better life in America. The irony: this America for which she and so many of my Iranian brethren longed was also the America that had fueled the nasty political conflagration engulfing the remnants of our ancient homeland. It was America's coup that paved the way for Iran's painfully un-Islamic "Islamic" revolution; America's weapons that fueled the eight-year Iran-Iraq War that killed an estimated half a million Iranians and Iraqis alike; America's greed for oil that nearly suffocated our souls.

But America remained the hope, the dream, the goal. She took a leap of faith that I can barely imagine: leaving everything she knew behind, moving to a faraway country, learning a new language, and raising children whose teachers warned her to avoid speaking her native tongue at home lest she hinder our education. And still, she had the wisdom and strength to ignore those teachers and all the other morons who treated her like an imbecile simply on account of an accent. My mother did all of this and more, and she did it smiling and laughing, with hope, love, and insatiable optimism, finding beauty in ugliness, and sharing it with abandon.

---

"PUT HIM IN THE FREEZER, and I be there soon," my mom said into the phone as she stirred her *khoresht-eh bademjoon* (eggplant stew). It's my sister's favorite, but she wouldn't be there to enjoy it. We had just dropped Romana off at college, and overnight I had effectively become an only child. My sole source of consolation: a brand new Duke sweatshirt and the prospect of something called "Lil Sibs Weekend" that no one would ever let me attend.

It was 1990, and I was eleven. My mom was on call and had just been directed to perform an autopsy, but she made the case that it could be put on ice until after dinner. One of the advantages of patients who are already dead is that they can generally wait a few hours. As my mother poured too much rice and *khoresht* onto my plate, part of the ongoing campaign to fatten me up, I asked my parents a question that had been nagging at me all week, ever since dropping Romana off in Durham: "What would happen if you both died? Romana is grown up now. She would be fine. But where would *I* go?"

Perhaps there are parents who would respond to their children by trying to comfort them, spreading lies like "We're not going to die, honey," and whatnot. But my parents have never called me honey, nor have they ever lied to me about death. Between their respective professions, it wasn't something they could get away with even if they had the will to do so, which they didn't.

A couple years prior, a woman had called the house screaming and crying. This wasn't entirely uncommon, as my father was still practicing obstetrics and cell phones were still the size of cinder blocks. What *was* uncommon, however, was the fact that the woman insisted that I stay on the phone with her, even after I explained that my father wasn't home. Long story short: she had a miscarriage in the toilet and was so panicked that she thought a nine-year-old might be able to walk her through it. I couldn't. But I did learn a lot about miscarriages after that. I also learned to tell patients to call 911 next time they tried to seek medical advice from a fourth grader.

In any case, being familiar with death wasn't the same as being prepared for it, and I wanted to be prepared—or at least to know that my parents were prepared, that they had a plan for me in the case of their untimely mutual demise.

To my relief, their response was matter-of-fact, immediate, and perfect: "You vould go vit Auntie Negar and Amoo Ali."

Like many in our tight-knit Dayton Iranian community, neither Auntie Negar nor Amoo Ali were direct blood relations, but again, our bonds ran deeper than blood. The Elmis (of said Auntie Negar and Amoo Ali) were my parents' closest friends, and the parents of *my* closest friend, Nobar. For a moment, before remembering the key premise behind the contingency plan, I grew almost giddy at the thought of living with the Elmis. The idea of a never-ending sleepover at Nobar's house sounded amazing. Because Romana is nearly seven years my senior, we never actually became friends until we were both adults. Growing up, our relationship was more master and servant, less big sister and little sister, but now that Romana was gone, I desperately wanted her back. The way I saw it, Nobar was the most alluring alternative: the sister I had left and, bonus, one who didn't order me around and came with two free brothers to boot. The idea of actually living in the same house together sounded like a dream come true—minus the dead parents part.

My father must've caught a hint of my initial excitement at the prospect of being sent to live with the Elmis, perhaps a smile or a glimmer in my eye, because he added, "Don't be too happy. If you kill us, you go to jail vit *baradar-hayeh* [brothers] Menéndez."

We all laughed as we cleared the table, and I assured my parents I wouldn't kill them. Then my mom headed to the VA to attend to the man in the freezer, and my father and I watched the evening news. I slept well that night, for the first time since Romana had been gone. It felt good to remember that my parents had backup, that *I* had backup, that I would *never* be an only child. Such is the comfort of a network like ours, for dead or alive, we all need backup.

Auntie Negar has always been my number one backup mom. And lucky for me, she's good at it. Family is her thing. Where my mother specializes in beauty, Auntie Negar specializes in babies. I'm pretty sure there isn't one Anne Geddes book or calendar she doesn't own, and I don't think she is capable of passing by a baby, any baby, without dropping an exuberant "elahi ghorboonet beram," literally "God let me sacrifice myself for you." It's a relatively common Persian expression of endearment, but she offers it to *all* babies irrespective of national origin, thankfully without translation. Honestly, on the off chance that a child's life ever actually depended on her following through, I don't doubt that Auntie Negar would do it.

For years I used to bite my nails, and in an effort to stop me she used to teasingly hold out her hands—elegant and pristinely manicured nails on full display—as an offering. "Here," she would say, "bite mine instead." I never took her up on it, but the sheer shame and absurdity of the whole scenario gnawed at me. While I knew her proposal was in jest, I genuinely believed—and continue to believe—that Auntie Negar would rather I mutilate *her* hands than my own. Knowing that she cared enough for my bloodied nail beds to offer her own immaculate talons as a sacrifice was ultimately the motivation I needed to quit, and I did. These were the exceptional lengths of Aunty Negar's powers—an imposing mix of empathy, humiliation, and persuasion.

She used to be the host of a children's television show back in Shiraz, and ever since, she has devoted her life to raising and protecting children: two sons, a daughter, three grandchildren, and God knows how many others, myself included. She has tended to my scrapes and bruises; she has tucked me in; she has wisely advised me on makeup and wardrobe; she has cheered me on at piano recitals, ballet performances, graduations, and more; she has treated me as though I were her own; she is my family, blood be damned.

When I finally had the surgery to remove my pancreatic tumor in 1999, Auntie Negar was there with flowers, tears, and kisses for my forehead and cheeks. And she wasn't alone. Nearly the entire Persian Mom Mafia showed up at my Chicago hospital room, and they brought the dads and kids with them. But now, like me, the kids were growing up. Auntie Shori's oldest son, Mehra, for example, was a surgeon at that same hospital. He just happened to be working with one of the best pancreatic surgeons in the world, so he hooked us up, scoring a coveted surgical time slot and making sure I got the best treatment America had to offer.

Such is the wonder and irony of networks in a diaspora: the farther we get from our original source, the stronger, tighter, and deeper our bonds grow. For distance expands perspective, and perspective revives memory. In the diaspora, we remember our oldest ancestors, the ones we *must* have shared, and we cling to them, knowing that we are all indeed related. Through joy and trauma alike, we find one another, and without fail, it is the mothers who make it happen.

And I say this as a woman who has actively chosen to forgo motherhood, for like my mother and unlike Auntie Negar, I am not exceptionally fond of babies. I don't go wild for the smell of their heads or the shape of their toes, and I've never wanted a child of my own. Personally, I feel the same way about children as I do about opiates: I've seen them ruin too many lives to want to pick them up for myself. Indeed, they are parasites from the very beginning, literally sucking life out of you. I know this because I have been and continue to be one such parasite. It's a trip, and I love my hosts dearly. I just wouldn't want to *be* them.

I'm not saying there's no joy in motherhood—of course there must be, or women wouldn't keep at it. What I *am* saying is that when you bear witness and run the numbers, there's a hell of a lot more joy for the child than for the mother, on average. For the devoted mother, there is an inevitable mountain of worry, torment, sorrow, sacrifice, and more sacrifice. Why else would heaven rest beneath her feet?

The only conceivable answer is that she worked like hell for it. Heaven isn't like a free gift at the Clinique counter. It's a big deal. It isn't bestowed upon just anyone who spends $35 on a qualifying purchase; it must be *earned*. And mothers earn it. They pay in sweat, tears, blood, skin, heart, bone, milk, and more.

I've done the calculations, and given the costs, I much prefer to lounge in or beside paradise than above it. In short, I'd rather enjoy heaven at the feet of the mothers than make the sacrifices required to earn it under my own. But let it be known that as I lie here—at the feet of Jazbi, Negar, Mahboob, Azar, Shori, Romana, Nobar, and all the other mothers, new and old, who have made me who I am—I lie prostrate, in worship, in awe, in gratitude.

# La Chingona

— STEPHANIE ELIZONDO GRIEST —

MOM SPARKED my writerly curiosity early.

*Where does she go?* In the mornings, I'd climb a counter stool and wait for Dad to stop fiddling with the Mr. Coffee machine and shake some Cap'n Crunch into my bowl. Mom would swoop into the kitchen in an aromatic whirl, wearing a pressed linen suit with a silk scarf knotted at her throat. After a gulp of Folger's, she'd kiss me on the cheek and Dad on the lips, and then dash out the door in high heels, not to return until almost nightfall.

*What does she do?* I asked this so often, Dad took me to her office once to try to explain. We drove out to the Corpus Christi Bay, where oil tankers bobbed in the blue distance, and then cruised the palm-tree-lined streets toward downtown. IBM occupied a wavy slab of concrete and featured row upon row of bulky computers manned by men in neckties. Mom stared into her screen as if in a trance, flicking a lipstick-ringed cigarette between her fingers as she rattled off numbers into a phone. Climbing into her lap, I joined her gaze at the hypnotic glow, willing it to reveal a secret. Yet the intrigue only compounded—until at home a few weeks later, when Mom called my big sister, Barbara, and me into the living room and plunked a hat atop her head. It was just like the one Captain Stubing wore on *The Love Boat*, only hers was full of crisp dollar bills. Hundreds fluttered across the carpet as she announced that IBM had rewarded her job performance with an all-expense-paid trip to Miami. My sister and I rolled in the money, squealing like people did on *The Price Is Right*. Barbara was stoked about the cash, but I was more excited about the clue. IBM must be a game show . . . and Mom, its star contestant!

*When does she eat?* I sometimes glimpsed Mom slip a Granny Smith apple inside her purse before waltzing off to work. At night, I occasionally watched her slice a block of H-E-B cheese and a tomato, sandwich them between Wonder Bread, and sprinkle pepper on top. But I rarely saw her eat. She informed Dad on their wedding night that she'd cook once a year. (Half a century later, we still relish the lasagna she bakes each Christmas.) For our remaining eleven hundred meals each year, Barbara and I turned to Dad for sustenance. A small-town Kansan, the man knew his way around a casserole. My favorite was when he blended a cup of instant rice with a can of tuna and another of cream of celery and popped it in the oven until the cheese started bubbling. Yet Mom disliked even the *smell* of food, preferring her kitchen to whiff of Pine-Sol. So Dad usually took us to Furr's Cafeteria or Andy's Country Kitchen instead.

*What is she saying?* Corpus Christi was a half-white, half-brown town about 150 miles from the Texas-Mexico border, so when the phone rang there was a decent chance the caller would be a Spanish speaker. I could tell if that was the case before Mom said even a word. English callers induced a certain rigidity in her: a stiffness of the spine, a curtness in the throat. When Spanish greeted her, however, she'd smile with her entire being. I would paw at the phone cord, trying to decipher the language inside it as she loosened her scarf and laughed and laughed. Dad used to complain that Spanish sounded "like a bunch of people arguing," but when Mom got on the phone, it seemed more like a comedy show—only I was never in on the jokes.

Dad I understood completely. I knew what he did each day because he always spent it with me, walking me to and from school and then whisking me off to the piers to feed the seagulls or to the ferry to watch the porpoises. His work was no mystery, either. I could actually *see* him teach students how to hold a pair of drumsticks and boom-get-a-rat-trap/big-ger-than-a-cat-trap against the practice pad. I could *hear* him smashing cymbals at concerts. He had only one brother, so when people called from Kansas, I knew exactly who they were and understood every word they said. Mom, meanwhile, had seven aunts, seven uncles, nine brothers, and four sisters, each with a spouse and several kids apiece. I couldn't keep their names straight. Barbara called all the ladies "Tía" and all the men "Tío," so that's what I did, too. They, in turn, called us "M'ija."

Once I (finally) started studying Spanish in seventh grade, however, I learned that "tía" and "tío" meant aunt and uncle. That made sense in most cases, but why did we use those terms for Grandma and Grandpa? Why not "Abuela" and "Abuelo"? More important, why did Mom call her parents "Tía" and "Tío," too?

It also occurred to me that, while I could rattle off dozens of stories about Dad's childhood—how he delivered the paper when it was five degrees below, how he walked to school in three feet of snow—I couldn't think of a single one about Mom. It's not that I never asked her questions. She just answered with as few words as possible. *What did you do today?* Worked. *What are you reading?* A book. *What's for dinner?* Ask your father. I'm full.

So I started sleuthing. Those first rummages through Mom's dresser drawers yielded little more than rosaries and pantyhose, but then a yellowing envelope appeared. Inside was a document soft from folding. The heading was ominous: DEATH CERTIFICATE. So was the name: Barbara Silva Elizondo. I recognized the former as my sister's name and the latter as Mom's maiden name, so I knew she must be important. A long lost tía, perhaps? I read on. From the dates (1925–49), I calculated that she had lived to be only twenty-five years old. Mom was born in 1946, so she barely would have known her. Why would she care about a stranger so many years later?

Then came the line that stole my breath: under cause of death, it said gunshot wound to the head.

———

WEEKS LATER, Mom's brother Valentín picked us up in his giant Ford truck, and we set off to see some tías. The cityscape gave way to cactus and oil wells as we headed south. Caracaras flew overhead. The sorghum glowed crimson. We passed cotton field after cotton field, knee high and miles wide, billowy in the wind.

"¡Híjole!" Valentín said, stroking his handlebar moustache. "Remember us out there? How many pounds did we pick?"

I shoved my head between their front seats. "Wait, what? You picked cotton?!"

My primary association with cotton had always been slavery—until Mom started laughing about how they used to team up with their brother Meme to drag their heavy bags over to the weighing station. "Every summer," she said.

Which meant in the hundred-degree heat, without a shade tree in sight.

"Nine cents a pound," Valentín added.

"But . . . why?" I asked.

Valentín peered up at me in the rearview mirror, eyebrows creased. "Because we were poor, m'ija! We had to help our tíos."

Poor. It was the first time I'd heard that word in relation to my mother, and it stung. But later that day, when we pulled into the neighborhood where they grew up, details that previously escaped my notice sharpened into focus. The houses were indeed humble, slumped over cinder blocks. A pit bull yanked on his chain wrapped around a tree. Teen moms pushed strollers down the street. We entered the home of the grandparents we called Tía and Tío and found her cooking in the kitchen while he cheered on the masked men wrestling on TV. I couldn't follow the Spanish conversation that ensued, but that let me observe other things. Like the couches wrapped in plastic. The crack in the glass of *The Last Supper*. The motion-picture waterfall clock that stopped ticking long ago.

When Tía ladled plates of beans and rice for us, Mom crinkled her nose and said she didn't want any. Maybe this is where she got her aversion to cooking. From age eight onward, she helped prepare dinner for her family of eight. Beans and rice was the staple, night after night after night after night.

Other insights followed. Struggling over my Spanish homework one evening, I griped at Mom for never teaching me. She explained that, when she was in school, Tejanos caught speaking Spanish in class had to hold out their hands and a teacher would smack them with a ruler. Either that, or a bar of soap got shoved inside their mouth. Discrimination was rife then; an accent, a liability. That's how generations of Tejanos lost their native tongue—mine included.

A difficult childhood explained other aspects of Mom's parenting as well, like extracurricular activities. Determined to give me opportunities she never had herself, she signed me up for everything the Texas Coastal Bend had to offer: ballet, jazz, and tap classes, piano lessons, gymnastics, cheerleading, catechism, a months-long course on how to be a model. A bookish child, I found each activity more harrowing than the last, until baton. To our surprise, I adored strutting around in a sparkly leotard, leading an imaginary marching band behind me. I even won a trophy. Then Mom glimpsed me twirling in the front yard one day and thought, *why is my daughter wasting her time, throwing a stick up in the air and trying to catch it?* Next thing I knew, I was catching fly balls with my face in Southside Little Miss Kickball.

When puberty came along, Mom honed her enthusiasm on my appearance. This was ironic, considering her own less-is-more approach. She might have accentuated her large brown eyes with mascara and reddened her lips, but that was it. She never went for blowouts, like her cousins, or manicures, like her sisters. When her thick, black curls started graying, she didn't try to disguise it (unlike Grandma/Tía, who remained a brunette well into her seventies). No matter. She invested in curling irons and hot rollers and Aqua Net and Clinique and coaxed me into using them. When my eyebrows started fusing, she took me to an electrologist, who yanked every hair from its follicle. When acne invaded, she took me to a succession of dermatologists before we finally crossed the Mexico border for the $5 tube of Retin-A that worked.

Mom also orchestrated my wardrobe. Grandma/Tía, a seamstress, had taught her how to sew her own dresses, so she had a keen sense of fashion. Thriftiness occasionally clouded her judgment, however. Like that time my freshman year in college, when my friend Shea correctly identified clips from ten music videos in a row and won a trip for two to the MTV Music Awards in Los Angeles. I called my parents screaming to announce I'd been invited along. Mom knew just what I should wear: my prom dress.

"Might as well get another use out of it," she reasoned.

That sounded logical, so I asked her to ship it. A week later, at Hotel Nikko, I slipped into the floor-length, sleeveless, backless, turquoise-sequined dress and sauntered into the MTV hospitality suite in my matching turquoise heels. Everybody there was clad entirely in black: black leather, black spandex, black suede, black velvet, black netting. Even Shea's mom had sent her a funereal cardigan. I darted into the nearest bathroom and called Mom from the phone hanging conspicuously by the toilet.

"I look ridiculous!" I wailed.

"That's not my fault. I told you to get the purple one."

She then assumed her role as disciplinary interrogator. She wanted to know *exactly* what we'd be doing that night, how and where and with whom, and most important, what time we'd be back in our hotel room, so she could check on me.

"If you're not in by midnight," she threatened from the living room couch in Corpus Christi, "*I will find out!*"

Mind you, that couch was fifteen hundred miles away. Instagram hadn't been invented yet. Caller ID hadn't made it to South Texas yet. I could have checked in myself from a payphone or another toilet phone or even Metallica's car phone. Mom wouldn't have known the difference. And even if she somehow discovered I got blitzed at the Roxbury at 4 A.M., what punishment wouldn't be worth the risk? Shea had just spotted Flavor Flav in the elevator. *Flavor Flav!* MTV VJs were our chaperons. *MTV!!* Nirvana was playing at the awards show that night. *Nirvana!!!*

Not even Kurt Cobain could drown out Mom's threat, however. As the night progressed, the thought of her hopping the next flight to California grew more and more conceivable. So after Shea and I had circled the after-party a couple (hundred) times, ogling at Axl Rose and Shannen Doherty, I convinced her to follow the other black-shrouded winners back aboard the MTV bus, just like we were supposed to. Around the time Mom should have made her midnight call, I was tucked in bed, ready to receive it.

Only, the call never came.

Mexicans have a term for a woman like this: *una chingona*. It's not very translatable, but "badass" comes close. Like all chingonas, Mom wielded her powers so confidently, so ferociously, she knew I wouldn't call her bluff. She didn't even have to check.

---

A CHALLENGE of having a chingona for a mother is they can be somewhat intimidating. Barbara formed a tight bond with Mom growing up, but I sought refuge in my happy-go-lucky dad. We did everything together, from Friday nights at Peter Piper Pizza to summer road trips to Kansas. The cashier at Furr's called me his "little shadow."

That parental dynamic shifted in eighth grade, however, when I started my period while taking a timed test in typing class. By the time Mrs. Robinson rang the bell and collected our papers, I had bled straight through my pants and onto the floor. Memory has kindly blocked how I made it to the nurse's office, but I remember my conversation with Mrs. Perez, the head nurse, distinctly.

"Go on to the restroom, m'ija," she said. "I'll call your mama."

"My dad's home. Call him."

She stared at me with horror. "You want me to call *your father,* m'ija?!"

And suddenly I didn't. Just like that.

Mom arrived surprisingly fast, wearing an IBM power suit with shoulder pads. I was so embarrassed I couldn't meet her gaze. We walked out to her Park Avenue Buick in silence. I don't know what Mrs. Perez told her over the phone, but it must have been drastic. As if channeling Grandma/Tía, she had wrapped the car's interior in plastic. Glad bags lined the passenger seat, the floorboards, even the armrest between us.

My stomach clenched like a fist when we turned down our street. I didn't want Dad to know about this. Not now, not ever. Before I could say so, Mom smoothly offered that he had gone to work. That was a lie. Dad had probably never "gone to work" at that hour in his life. But I accepted it with gratitude.

"And I guess you're going back to work, too?"

She glanced at me sideways and gave a soft smile. "Actually, I thought I'd stay home with you."

A new relationship didn't just seed that day. It flourished.

———————

SO NOW WE KNOW the proper title for a Tejana who lands a high-power job at IBM in 1976 while her gringo husband stays home with the kids. Chingona.

Ask Mom about her feminist achievement now, however, and she'll shrug and say, "He had patience. I didn't." There is no denying Dad was borderline Buddhistic then. He once drove Shea and me 240 miles to a U2 concert— "Achtung Baby" blasting through the speakers—waited in the parking lot for four and a half hours, and then drove us 240 miles home. But Mom's modesty discounts how she rose in the ranks of a multinational corporation armed with only an associate's degree from a community college at a time when few Tejanas could find work outside of a field or a factory. It also overlooks the uniqueness of their relationship.

My parents met at a jazz club in downtown Corpus Christi in 1966. Though curious about the world, Mom hadn't seen more than four hundred miles of it. She was twenty and radiant and looking for an adventure. Dad, meanwhile, had spent more than a decade with a U.S. Navy band, playing concerts around the globe. He was a twenty-nine-year-old searching for a home.

When Dad first took to the stage, Mom started crushing on the saxophonist. (That was her favorite instrument, plus she liked his curly hair.) My (slightly balding) father distinguished himself at intermission, however, by coming over to introduce himself and accidentally spilling a Coke all over her shoes. He led her backstage, cupped her feet with his hands, and gently wiped them clean. They got married three months later. Dad's next gig was Mardi Gras, and the only way Grandpa/Tío would let her accompany him was as his wife. So that's how they did it. After New Orleans, they packed up his red Mustang and headed northeast. Biracial couples were unusual there, but Mom's olive skin passed for a tan, plus she'd lost her accent years ago.

When they returned to South Texas seven years later, however, there was no doubting Dad was a gringo. The Tíos would clink their beers and sing along when conjunto music jangled over the speakers, while my blue-eyed, red-bearded dad would sip his Dr. Pepper and say, how about some Sinatra? His Spanish vocabulary consisted solely of menu items and ¡Vámonos! (Let's go!). Mom wished he'd made more of an effort to integrate into her culture but felt he more than compensated with his refreshing lack of machismo. Dad completely supported her career, no matter how many late nights or business trips it entailed. Plus, he brought her coffee every morning, right after she stepped out of the shower.

Growing up, it was clear who had the sweeter deal. Dad played tennis with his buddies all morning and then banged on the drums all afternoon. In the evenings, his bandmates came over for rehearsal. I could hear them out in the garage, living their dreams. Mom, meanwhile, was gone all day, and when she came home, the first thing she wanted to do was the crossword puzzle (New York Times, with a pen).

My writing compulsion initially seemed to have been inherited from Dad. He was the one who inspired me to never earn a paycheck for anything besides art, like he did. (It wasn't long before I realized this was a vow of poverty.) Dad was also the one who stoked my wanderlust by telling me bedtime stories about the places he had visited. Hong Kong. Corfu. Newfoundland. Japan. In college I studied the language of the farthest country I could fathom (Russia) and jetted off to Moscow with a pad and a pen. A yearlong stint in Beijing followed.

A theme soon emerged in the notes I took. Totalitarianism had dismantled a great deal in those nations: private property, intellectual life, community, idealism, trust. Even more painful, according to many people I encountered, was the government's attempt to vanquish heritage: the banning of religion, the outlawing of certain literatures, the silencing of native tongues. Yet time and again I heard heroic accounts of those who preserved it. Like the gentleman I met in Vilnius, Lithuania, who chose to be imprisoned and beaten rather than renounce Judaism. Or the Riga widow whose husband kept publishing Latvian poetry, though it ultimately meant perishing in the gulag. They had risked everything to honor their ancestral pasts. I, meanwhile, had ignored my own.

But how do you fight for something you barely know?

Mom flew out for a visit toward the end of my Beijing stay. On her second to last day, we packed a picnic and headed to Yuanming Yuan, an imperial palace that got obliterated by British troops a century and a half ago. Sitting among its ruins, I finally asked the questions that had haunted me since childhood.

*Who was your mother?* Her name was Barbara.

*How did she die?* She killed herself.

*Why?* She had five kids before she turned twenty-five. That's reason enough.

Mom explained that her mother grew up on the King Ranch, an 850,000-acre swath of South Texas that, in its heyday, was the biggest cattle empire in the world. Her family migrated there from Tamaulipas, Mexico, more than a hundred years earlier to work as its founding cowboys. They had been braving fires, floods, and rattlesnakes there ever since. Barbara was among the first to venture into the city. She had fallen in love with a handsome barber who owned his own shop on Agnes Street. They moved into a two-room bungalow and filled it fast with children. When the youngest was still an infant, she tucked them in for an afternoon nap in one room and locked herself in the other. A shot rang out soon after. The eldest, Maria, herded the little ones next door, where Tía/Grandma and Tío/Grandpa lived. Unable to have children of their own, they took in three: Mom, Valentín, and Meme. Another tío adopted Esteban. Just three years old at the time, Mom's lone memory of the experience was when they took Maria to live on the ranch. All the kids were huddled together in the back of Grandpa/Tío's truck when she got taken away from them. They cried and cried as the truck pulled away, their big sister running behind them.

*But . . . someone must have had a theory why she did it.* Oh, some thought Dad was cheating on her. Or she was cheating on him. Her own mom said someone must have come in and shot her.

*But . . . what about your dad? What did he do?* Remarried. Had seven more kids.

She reminded me that we used to visit him at Christmas. Cozy house, lots of people, a pot of tamales steaming on the stove. When I was little, he entertained me by removing his wooden leg. (He lost the real one in a motorcycle accident.) He succumbed to Alzheimer's long ago. I never understood who he was, until that moment in the fallen Chinese palace.

Beyond her death certificate, the only possessions Mom has of her mother's are two notebooks. One is brown and spiraled; the other is a Blue Horse tablet. Both are filled with song lyrics penned in tidy script. Love songs, mostly— old Spanish ballads. "Amor Chiquito" (Newborn Love). "Nunca, Nunca, y Nunca" (Never, Never, and Never). "Mariposa Pecadora" (Butterfly Sinner). She also has a few photographs, including a black-and-white portrait that is propped on our piano. Barbara is seated on a stool wearing a pinstriped dress, her arms by her side, maybe eighteen years old. Her lips are darkly painted, but she has no other adornments. Her face is long, like Tío Meme's, and her hair is thick and curly, like Mom's. Like my sister's. Like mine. She stares into the camera bereft of expression, neither happy nor sad, flirtatious nor mad. She left no note behind that day. Besides her young children, she said no goodbyes. None of Mom's elders ever spoke of the tragedy.

Looking around at the collapsed kingdom, I realized that my grandmother wasn't the only mystery that confounded me. So was the entire heritage that she represented. It was time to stop perpetuating that other form of death.

As soon as I returned home to Texas, I enrolled in an intensive Spanish class. My previous attempts had been fruitless, but now I felt conviction. After several months of study, I bought a ticket to Mexico and invited Mom to join me. Our first stop was Monterrey, where we visited cousins, whom to my delight I (somewhat) understood. Then we tracked down cultural artifacts. Diego Rivera's murals in Mexico City. Frida Kahlo's Casa Azul in Coyoacán. Mayan glyphs at the Museum of Anthropology. On New Year's Day we joined hundreds of pilgrims atop El Templo del Sol, the pyramid of the sun at Teotihuacan, and basked in the morning light. Mom and I descended from an extraordinary people. I hungered to learn more.

For twenty years now I have strived to do just that. Many of my essays and all of my books are an attempt to answer the questions Mom stirred within me long ago. *Where does she go? What does she do? What is she saying?* Dad may have motivated my artistic impulse, but Mom is my forever muse.

———

MOM HAD ME when she was twenty-eight years old. She had been married for seven years by that point. When I was that age, living in Brooklyn, I had yet to meet a man who would date me more than twice. She owned a three-bedroom house. For about the same price, I rented a room in a cramped apartment that had a futon, a dresser, and just enough room to stand between the two. She was forging a career path toward IBM; I was psyched to have a day job where I could sneak free photocopies now and then. She had successfully raised a child to the age of six. I couldn't keep a pot of basil alive. And around the time she birthed me into existence, I had sired but a single manuscript—and had yet to find an editor to publish it.

However erratic my journey must have seemed to her, Mom has never once questioned it. Not when I quit a perfectly good job with health insurance to write my first book—not even when it meant moving back home with her and Dad. Not when I left a surgeon who earned half a million dollars a year to attend grad school in Iowa. Rather than point out the inanity of such economics, she offers to edit everything I write. Much of my work is memoiristic, meaning she is a frequent character. Yet the only requests she ever makes for changes are when she fears that *I* look bad. She has even relinquished her hopes for getting any grandchildren out of me and takes pride in having books instead, scrapbooking their reviews and monitoring their sales on Amazon.

Lately, Mom has been mentoring me through the indignities of middle age: mammograms and gum grafting; graying hair and knee surgery. When my eyesight started faltering—despite my Coke-bottle glasses—we had lengthy discussions about the merits of progressive lenses. ("Just avoid the stairs," she said.) The night before my first colonoscopy, I called her amidst the agony of chugging one glass of salty liquid after another. "When will it start?" I asked moments before dropping the phone and darting into the bathroom, never to return.

Mom has aged with grace. Her curls might have whitened twenty years ago, but she has kept her muscle tone, sense of style, and slender figure. Sometimes, when she turns around, I see surprise in peoples' eyes. They weren't expecting such a glowing face. (Oil of Olay, she says.) Dad hasn't fared as well. After surviving prostate cancer, colon cancer, a triple bypass, two hernias, and a stent, he started mentally declining four years ago. Tennis was the first to go, followed by piano. Then he willingly handed over his car keys. He still drums, but only with his fingers. Any nearby surface will do. He rarely sits behind his Ludwig drum set anymore.

The patience that evaded Mom in our childhood has emerged in masses. Dad needs to be instructed on almost every task. Do I put my clothes on now? Or brush my teeth first? All right. Is this shirt okay? Okay. But maybe I'll just put on the same one from yesterday ... What's that, hon? Oh. Okay. So this shirt then? This one right here, and not the one in the hamper? Okay, now, where are my pills . . .

This is the aspect of life for which I am wholly unprepared. Hearing him mumbling in the background when I call on the phone, I wonder, *Where does he go? What does he do? When does he eat? What is he saying?* Mom tries to be reassuring.

Years ago, my parents bought a monument for the family burial plot in Dad's hometown in Kansas. My sister and I visited the cemetery with them during the last Griest family reunion. "I can't even find my own grave," Dad grumbled as we walked up and down the aisles, peering at the headstones. When we finally found it, right beside Grandma and Grandpa, I was shocked to see their names and birthdays already inscribed on the granite. I averted my gaze and shuddered. Just recently, however, Dad announced he wants to be buried at the Veterans Cemetery in Corpus instead. (He's a fan of their twenty-one-gun salutes.) Mom is pleased with this decision. Her entire family is buried in South Texas, plus she cannot stand the cold.

*But what about your plot in Kansas?*

They shrug. In fifty years, they'll just impress everybody with their longevity.

Dad has a few goals left. First, he wanted to make it to seventy-five. Now, he seems excited about turning eighty. Mom says, take me now, before it gets worse.

Barbara and I have tried to convince Mom to hire some help with Dad, but she refuses. That's another challenge of having a chingona for a mother: stubbornness. My sister and I have long passed the point in our relationship where *we* should be offering *her* assistance. Yet Mom can't shake her breadwinner's sense of responsibility. She still calculates our taxes. She flies out to help with every cross-country move. She tends to us after surgery. She remains the first person I call in times of need or joy. Our conversations always last the longest.

*How did she become such a valiant mom when she had no model herself?*

I have no answer to this, or to any other question these memories evoke.

*Will I ever love anyone as intensely as she loves us?*

*Could I ever love anyone more than her?*

*How will I endure without her?*

— PART V —

Legacies

# Scuppernongs and Beef Fat

## Some Things about the Women
## Who Raised Me

— RANDALL KENAN —

"You don't eat it because it's good for you.
You eat it because it's good."

I FORGET THE EXACT CAUSE for the occasion, but I remember it was a Saturday night in the 1970s. I remember we were at the Camp Lejeune marine base in Jacksonville, North Carolina, where she worked as a cook, "she" being Clementine Whitley, one of the women who raised me.

Saturday nights in those waning days of the Carter administration were marked by too much television viewing for me. TV of the mildest, most innocuous sort: *Hee Haw, The Lawrence Welk Show, The Love Boat, Fantasy Island.* Sundays were even more boring than Saturdays, which at least held a mythical promise of some type of weekend thrill—something *could* happen. These imaginary joys never materialized out in the deep woods and swamps of eastern North Carolina, despite my cousins' intense anticipation of such.

Imagine a "party" of sorts down on a military base, with lots of food, some dancing. (Perhaps it was Independence Day, perhaps it was some military promotion celebration, it could have even been a wedding reception—I do not now remember the reason for the gathering.)

Without a doubt I was the youngest person there. By most standards, then or now, this was a rather ordinary affair: the enlisted men with their dates; rhythm and blues and soul music playing; socializing of the loud and backslapping type, which—to the eyes and ears of a fourteen-year-old country boy—is as attractive as the prospect of oral surgery. And there was the food, which to me was the most special part of the special occasion. And though the fare was rather ordinary—fried chicken, potato salad, slaw, hushpuppies—I remember having recently been introduced to the grown-up and somewhat decadent charm of grilled beef. We are speaking specifically of sirloin and rib eye and the mischievous T-bone, something in which a boy can delight, in considering its direct and gruesome anatomy lesson as well as delectability. T-bone steaks were fun and still are fun to eat.

Those hearty and fun-loving Marines spared no expense when it came to the food and selected the most capable and gregarious cook they knew to helm the event, that being my aunt Clem. My being her sidekick in the kitchen that Saturday night meant I could eat my belly full. That is to say, steak galore!

I was not exactly a glutton. But the fact is, fourteen-year-old boys exist for very few things on this planet, and eating is very near the top of that brief list. Curiously, at the same time I had somehow come under the trance of "eating right." Probably by public service messages interjected in and around Saturday morning cartoons, or school nutritionists visiting classes. However it came to me, I had digested the notion that animal fat was BAD. While chomping down on a juicy steak cooked by Aunt Clem, I sliced off the fat and pushed it aside with some contemptuous comment about eating fat and how fat wasn't good for us, delivered with all the sagacity a self-righteous, greedy fourteen-year-old can muster. To which she replied by picking it up and popping it in her own mouth, saying, "You don't eat it because it's good for you. We eat it because it's good."

Family lore has it that I spent my first night in my ancestral home of Chinquapin, North Carolina, in Clementine Whitley's house located on a bend of the northeast Cape Fear River. Clem—Clementine—was one of my great-aunt Mary's best friends, and in truth my cousin.

Clem was descended from a very large family. Her mother, Viola, was at the time one of Chinquapin's oldest matriarchs. The family originated from and lived in what local people referred to as "The Quarters," for upon the land where her home sat was where the enslaved people of the long-gone Chinquapin Plantation lived. Miss Viola had many children, so Clem had a vast arena of brothers and nephews and nieces and cousins galore. This was exactly the web of family into which I was born. For, indeed, I was related to both Clementine (via her mother) and her husband, John, or Chicken (via his mother). Chicken drove a bus. Clem worked down on the marine base in Jacksonville. By the time of my birth, Clementine Whitley had grown small-town famous as an outstanding cook. Women who themselves were not slackers in the kitchen held her food in high esteem. My connection to her was a powerful thing.

It was into this world of taste and hardheaded common sense that I became conscious of the world.

## Mama. Clem. Nellie Mae.

Mama was my great-aunt, who took care of me directly. The night after I was brought down to Chinquapin by the twenty-year-old woman who bore me, a love child, I was taken to where I had been requested, my father's parents' home fourteen miles away. This had been the overarching plan: for this illegitimate but now-acknowledged boy-child to be raised by his grandparents in the railroad town of Wallace, North Carolina.

My paternal grandfather, at that time in the mid-1960s, ran a prosperous dry-cleaning establishment, and his wife, my grandmother, was a popular and busy seamstress. My father had led a somewhat privileged life compared to most of his black boy contemporaries. My future was so bright I should have worn shades.

I was recently reacquainted with the woman my grandfather hired in those days to be my governess. She told me I was a rambunctious baby who fought to get out of my crib. And that I actually succeeded on a few occasions.

Perhaps my grandfather's sister, Mary Fleming, recognized this spirit in me and liked it. She would spirit me away on weekends to the ancestral home in Chinquapin, the first village in which I'd slept. This weekend absconding continued and continued until, one sad day, her husband, Redding, died. My grandfather suggested my great-aunt keep me, to keep her company on the farm. This is how Aunt Mary became Mama to me.

Nellie Mae: she was a substantial woman of substantial proportions and the spirit of a mighty thing. Her hugs were crushing, enveloping, as genuine as heavy rain. She too worked down at Camp Lejeune as a domestic for a high-ranking marine officer. She spoke of that family as if she had been a true member, something for which Mama and Clem upbraided her, saying: "They don't care about you, woman."

And yet this was Nellie Mae's spirit, the purest example of agape I've come in touch with. Her laugh, her smile, her cooking, her generosity with time and things exuded a largeness of spirit, a positivity, a joy. Nellie Mae had a vast green Pontiac Bonneville, circa early 1970, when cars had more in common with whales than with the combustion engine. On Saturdays Mama, Clem, Nellie Mae, and I would take trips down to Wilmington, about a two-hour drive in those days before the interstate. The backseat of that sturdy automobile was my playground. We would stop en route at Paul's Place for one of their famous hot dogs. The first stop in Wilmington would always be Hudson Belk department store, where I would endure a couple hours of watching these women browse through dresses and shoes, my penance for a quantity of minutes downstairs in the toy department, ogling toys we could not afford. But I could afford a coloring book.

Coloring books! With my Crayola 64 box and my coloring book, I would be a child free in his own universe.

Back at Nellie Mae's house I would go down in front of the television, coloring. The women would be enjoying themselves, gossiping and cooking, and I would employ my burnt sienna crayon and sky blue and crimson to make a blank world real.

One story from that time I heard into my teenage years, I still remember vividly, though the retellings have probably polluted the event.

It was a humid spring day; the dogwoods had done blooming. I was hot and sweating down on the floor with my coloring book. The women were sitting about Nellie Mae's den around me. I became frustrated with the heat and declared loudly, "I'm having a hot flash," something I had heard my womenfolk exclaim quite a bit in those ten years, all being women of a certain age. All three roared with laughter, much to my confusion. It would be another decade before I understood their amusement.

At the risk of being self-aggrandizing or simply tedious, I include here a passage from my first book of fiction in which I wrote one of the most honest passages I've ever written about my great-aunt:

> He remembered his grandmother's hands to be small and firm, also callused from hard work, but still soft in a womanly way. People called her Retha. Aretha Davis Cross. A mother of the church. His mother. Hers were the hands that were his beginnings: In the beginning were hands, and hands were the beginning; all things that were made were made by hands, and without hands was not anything made that was made. In her hands was life; and the life was in her hands. Her hands reached through the darkness. Her hands lifted and supported. Undid and did up. Comforted. Scolded. Fed. Clothed. Bathed. Her hands did the teaching, the sending, the receiving, the mending, the strengthening. Her hands spoke and listened, smiled and encouraged. (*A Visitation of Spirits*, "1:15am")

## The Greatest Gift: Flopsy, Mopsy, and Peter Rabbit

Mama had been a professional cook, a domestic, a graduate of N.C. College (later N.C. Central University), and by and by a kindergarten teacher.

That she taught me to read at the age of four is not a curiosity. But sitting with her, looking at Beatrix Potter's bright watercolors, imagining Peter Rabbit and that sinister Farmer McGregor ("Why don't he leave that rabbit alone?"), introduced me to the keys to the world. I remember not only that book (ultimately written all over by this engaged child, who did not imagine the story could ever end) but also the pads with the blue lines, three in which to capture the print. The Rs and the Ts and the serpentine Ss. A life-long fascination with the word. "In the beginning was the word, and the word was God."

But more, for some peculiar reason, on the Christmas of my fifth year Mama gave me a children's adaptation of *Moby Dick*, full of lurid illustrations of the great whale and the doomed captain, and dramatic seas and thunderous skies. My mind was overstimulated, and happily so. In short, I was hooked. Soon would come *Treasure Island, Kidnapped, The Swiss Family Robinson*. (To this day I am slightly ashamed of my obsession with these blond kids marooned on a tropical island. Like Nellie Mae, my heart was just too damn large.) All this due to my great-aunt Mary Fleming, my Mama, her need to grow things, to give.

And so, as always, there are three things: a love of food, an instinct toward compassion, a love of words and story. To me these all work together, bind each other, make wonderful sense, make life *life*. How could a fellow not wax in gratitude recognizing the seeds of his life.

The three things these women gave me: love of food, love for my fellow human, love of reading.

---

MAMA'S GARDEN: We were, per course, cash poor and land rich. Mama's ingenuity and resolve and green thumb made us wealthy when it came to nourishment. In fact, she grew enough to share with many of the neighbors and church fellows.

We are talking a garden of over an acre. She grew sweet corn, sweet potatoes, tomatoes, green beans, butterbeans, carrots, radishes, beets, red potatoes, white potatoes, mustard greens, cabbage, collard greens, okra, okra, okra. She canned; she pickled; she blanched and froze. As a boy, I took all the work and time and energy to accomplish all this bounty for granted; now I look back in wonder.

But I write about childhood. Relations, connections, negotiations . . . adulthood brings different imperatives, different emotions. When one is a child one sees older folk, perforce, as fixed and unmoving in time. Experience helps us see our mothers on a continuum that gives us insight, inspires remorse, tenderness, and awe. Old age (Mama died at eighty-nine) engendered another type of sensitivity. Indeed, enough material for a roman-fleuve.

# One of My Most Precious Memories:
## Gathering Grapes in Fall

The scuppernong grape is one of the few grapes indigenous to North America, one of the muscadine family. They are plump spherical things, with a mighty thick hull, and a mucus-like sweet interior with obnoxiously large seeds clustered at its center. The hull is acidic and the pulp, when ripe, sweet like candy. Mr. Proust had his cookies; I have my grapes.

My dear friend Allan Gurganus once said to me regarding scuppernongs: "They are so *entertaining* to eat!" Which I have ever since recognized as the precise truth of the matter.

Come late September, just before the leaves commence to turn, the grape arbors grow heavy with ready grapes. In our county many arbors would invite folk in to pick their own grapes. My memories of those afternoons picking (and eating) grapes comfort me and keep me buoyed. The pop in the mouth, the sweetness, the early fall sunset, my Mama's laugh.

Mama would make wine from these mischievous berries, barreled in the fall when the grapes were plentiful, tended through the winter, and opened in early spring. I remember my first taste of this homemade wine. It was harsh, it was sweet, it was bracing. I remember the very character of it to this day, though no one seems to understand how to make it in this fashion today, despite my home county's boom in wineries and distilleries and grape growing. This method, this special witchcraft, left the earth with my Mama in 2007.

You don't drink life because it's good for you, you drink life because it is good.

# My Mother, My Muse

— CLYDE EDGERTON —

A COUSIN WAS CHASING ME, from his backyard next door over to my back-yard. In the middle of a brief fistfight I'd decided to hightail it for home. We were each five years old. I had decided he was about to beat me up.

I got to my backdoor screen, opened it, quickly slipped into our small back porch, latched the screen door, and just as he grabbed the outdoor handle, I turned around to walk into the house.

My mother blocked the way. She'd been watching from the kitchen window. She grabbed my shoulders, pushed me against the wall, and put her face to my face. I sensed her agitation, her frustration. "Don't you run from him," she said. "You get back out there and fight him. And don't you ever run from him again." She grabbed me by the arm, pulled me to the screen door, flipped the latch open, and pushed me into the backyard.

My cousin and I then fought it out—I can't remember who got the upper hand. I never ran from him again. We eventually learned, on our own, how to settle up without fighting.

I still choose to encounter situations I might otherwise run from because I sense my mother coming out onto the porch, grabbing me by the shoulders . . .

Going back outside, back through that screen door, ended up making me proud.

———

MOTHER, SUSAN TRUMA WARREN, was born in 1904 in rural Wake County, North Carolina, near the middle of what is now Umstead State Park. She was next to youngest of seven children in a family of sharecroppers for the Page family in rural Wake County—the same Pages that produced the writer, educator, and diplomat Walter Hines Page (*The Southerner*, published 1909). Mother's father, Israel Warren, died when she was seven, and soon she, three sisters, and her mother moved to town, to Durham, North Carolina. They took a cow with them.

At age twelve Mother quit school and went to work in a hosiery mill to help support her small family of women. She soon had to quit work due to the arrival of child labor laws. To my knowledge, she never considered her upbringing to be in any way adverse, but that upbringing left habits and traits like these:

> She'd never waste water. If she turned on a faucet for warm water, she'd collect the water that was getting warm and use it to water plants.
>
> She reused ice. She'd wash off ice from an empty glass of tea, put it back in the tray, and put the tray back into the freezer.
>
> She loved animals, vegetables, fruits—their raising, cooking, canning.
>
> She didn't like any overpraise of children, including her only child, me.
>
> She was a faithful friend to many elderly people—cooking for them and visiting.
>
> She enjoyed living alone.
>
> She was loyal to her family and had little interest in national politics until late in life, when she was won over by Rush Limbaugh. (Our conversations about Mr. Limbaugh's teachings were less calm than conversations regarding the teachings of Jesus.)
>
> She loved to read and study the Bible. She took the lessons therein seriously, though she was not a Goody Two-shoes.
>
> She loved to listen to and tell and laugh about family stories—often the same ones, over and over. Those stories were among my most special inheritances.

As a child and young adult, I spent much time with my mother and her two Durham, North Carolina, sisters, Oma and Lila. The three were together in some combination nearly every week. I heard them gossip, laugh, joke, and argue, and I heard them, in different combinations of two, complain about the third.

I'd like to introduce her to you through letters my mother wrote to her sister Lila (away at the beach for the summer), over a two-month period in the summer of 1980, starting two months after my father died, after their forty-six-year marriage. Mother had just turned seventy-six when these letters were written. Only when sorting through the letters did I begin to realize the connections between my mother's language and obsessions and the themes and peculiarities of my own fiction writing, particularly several of my novels.

I can hear her voice as I read—medium pitch, occasional light giggle, calm.

## THE SELLING OF AN OLD CAR
### that my father, Ernest, drove before he died.

Mr. Hackney sorta wants the old Buick for $50.00 Would you sell it for that?

Think I'll wait, maybe Fab [a cousin] will give $100.00 since Ernest was asking 200.00 before. Take care and write. It's 10 minutes to 11 o'clock.

Love, Truma

[A later letter:] I asked Fab if he was interested in buying the old Buick, right off the bat he said yes! how much you want for it. Just said how much will you give, and right off the bat again he said $150.00. So I made out I was thinking it over, but right off the bat *I* said I'll take that, because it's not doing me any good. Then before I left he came up and said I'll be up there soon and if anybody comes along and offered me a few dollars more, he'd go that too. I think he's sorta anxious for it, but he doesn't know I'm anxious for him to hurry and get it before he gets out of the notion. Somebody run into his old truck and sorta banged it up.

[A later letter:] Things about normal around here now, Mary was at the door, on her way to the garden real early. The gardens are looking real pretty now. Soon be getting squash and string beans, tomatoes good size too. Mary is going to call a man that she says might be interest in buying the Buick. Says she believes I can get more than $150.00. Maybe we'll stir up some competition anyway.

[Later:] This is one *tacky* writing tablet! Clyde brought it along with envelopes and a bottle of Jergens lotion when he came the morning of my birthday. I wish he had kept his money, far as this tablet is concerned. He didn't get any *chores* done, 'cept he did get my house numbers up. All the rest of the time was spent getting Fab off with the Buick. [—and later:] Haven't heard any more from Fab, cept Clyde said when he went by there to get the license tag, it had knocked off again and wouldn't start. I'm not sure if he got a bargain or not.

Love, Truma

This excerpt shows how sociable Truma was, and also how energetic. On a day when she did nothing much, she baked three coconut pies.

I sure do watch for the mailman. He's about my only outside contact. I wrote Bob and Berdena a long letter, started Tues. night and finished up Wed. A.M. I really haven't been doing anything much. I did make 3 cocoanut pies yesterday, late, one for the dinner Sunday, one for me and one for Craig (my neighbor) if he comes to fix my doorbell tomorrow like he said he would. . . . Haven't seen Oma since Monday but talk to her each day. She keeps on about the family reunion. Like: doesn't make any difference with me, I can go, or I just as soon not go etc. etc. Hortense said when she talked to her she said, "Well it doesn't make any difference with me whether they have it or not." . . . I don't know who *they* are that she *alludes* to so much. Well this is just something to write (or is it). I ought to be doing something else I guess.

[More on the reunion:] I had thought I would go to Sunday S. this morning, so I got up at 6:30, but, dogged, I barely did get ready by the time Oma & Gordon got here at 11:30. I did have everything ready to go by 11 o'clock, so I sat down & watched the church program from Raleigh 'till they got here. I had 2 cocoanut pies, (but I put one back in the ref. when Gordon told me he had a chess pie he had bought at *Byrds*) corn & butter beans, squash & onions, biscuits & ham, tea. Oma had a barbecued chicken (real good), potato salad, it was good too, she left me what she brought back. (I'm sitting on the side porch and can't see the lines) (or how to write either) a right good crowd there, mostly young people. The Haley children, Worth, A.C. etc., then their children, with wives and/or their families and so on. Even Faye, Hortense's daughter, had 2 grandchildren there. Fab, Oma, Jessie, Haley, me, Gordon, Hortense, and Mary were the oldest ones there. I think. 3 or 4 new babies. Clyde & Susan came. Eddie Haley brought 2 big pots of barb-q. We had plenty of food. We came back sorta early because Oma, Myrtle, & Edna were going to "Sylvester's" B.day party. (I'll go in the house maybe I will see better.) . . .

[After the reunion:] I got in and set all my pans and stuff on the counter I went and undressed came back took up my bag and opened it, my billfold was missing. So I began to look around, didn't see it anywhere, so I said to myself, I don't remember taking that out of my bag. So I began to look in earnest, couldn't find it anywhere. Looked in all the places I usually put it when I take it out of my bag. Couldn't find it. So I really did "go all to pieces," [private language] looked and looked. I had just $17.00 in it but I was thinking of my driving licenses. I remembered leaving it laying around on the table down there all the time 'till I got ready to come home, but I couldn't think anybody there would do such a thing. But I finally said well *somebody took it*, it's gone. So then I called Oma, she still hadn't left for the party. Then I called Clyde, then I called Hortense. Mary came in (they came back yesterday P.M.), I told her. Elizabeth called me to come-down there and eat some ice cream, so I told her. Then I went back in the bedroom, took my bag down again and looked, put it back up on the shelf and said: well it's gone and that's it. I happened to notice my white bag hanging there on a hook. I thought no use looking in there, but I did, and there was my billfold. I had used that bag last night when I went down to Hudie's and Lavoy's for a steak supper and homemade ice cream. He came and got me and brought me back home (sure was nice) and I hadn't even had my billfold in my bag all day. I felt like a nut. Then I had to call everybody and tell them.

The sun is shining so pretty this morning and everything so green and pretty, but how fast the summer is going.

Love, Truma

From *Walking across Egypt*, my second novel:

She walked into the kitchen, turned on the light and saw through the window that the eastern sky was dark red. It was her favorite time of the day. [And] she knew that for a minute before sunrise when the sky began to lighten, showing dark early clouds, there was often a pause when nothing moved, not even time, and she was always happy to be up and in that moment; . . . She hoped that when her time came, it would be close to morning, and she could wait for the still moment.

### SISTER OMA.

Not aiming to write much, just to report on our trip to Audrey's yesterday. To begin with, Oma was in a pretty good mood. She "acted up" a little when we first got there. I drove up pretty close to the steps, and she got out with her umbrella and says do you want to come on under my umbrella? I said, no, you go ahead and I'll come on. So I waited till she started up the steps, then I got out and started running up behind her, and she had stopped about halfway up to say a lot of *nothing* to Audrey who had appeared at the door and was holding it open. (It was raining, get the picture?) So I ran up right behind her and says: "go on go on" in a friendly tone, maybe a little loud, and she still took time to turn around and give me one of those silent scathing (spelling?) "stares." So I let her have it right back, by that time we were all in the little porch and Audrey was laughing and hugging us both, and that was the last of it, so the rest of the time, we got along just fine . . .

For supper Audrey cooked ham and biscuits, made a lot of red eye gravey, had a jar of honey with the comb in it somebody had brought her from the mountains, and coffee. We stuffed ourselves again. Gave us a biscuit with a *big* piece of ham to bring home for our breakfast. We left between 6:30 and 7 still raining some. I got along all right with my driving. . . . Oma just called to see if I "blowed up" last night. I told her no but sure did do a lot of *blowing off*.

Love, Truma

## THE CONTACT LENS

I got my "contac" Mon. when I went to the Dr. and it's doing great. They said I almost had 20–20 right then. I've worn it since without any trouble at all except yesterday morning I was washing my face over the lavatory in the bathroom with a rag and soap and then bent over to rinse it, and when I raised up I was seeing like I did before I got the contac. Clyde was here so I called him, and he looked real close and said he could see it had slipped over [we got it back in place]. Then last night I called Oma, and (thinking it was funny) I told her about it. Well right from the start she kept "butting in," such as: Well didn't you know better etc etc, and I'd try to explain, it was nothing just must have splashed too much water in it or some little something caused it. No harm done etc etc thinking she'd catch the funny part of it. (Not at all.) Next thing, she said why didn't you go back to the Dr.? I said Well I didn't need to, it was no trouble to slip back, Clyde could see good and it just slipped right back in place. By that time I was plumb *aggravated*, but I was controlling it. Trying to get her to see the funny side. Then she said maybe I'd be careful how I scrubbed it hereafter, I said Oma, I haven't been scrubbing it, I have been bathing it with warm water and cotton balls, but the Dr. told me when I asked him about my activities, he said do anything you want to. Then she said Well you didn't cut your eye did you? I said, No Oma, you know I *would* have gone to the dr. if I had. She said Well, I hope it doesn't happen again and right back I said "Well if it does I sure won't tell you!" (Ha ha) She said what? And I said it again and added: not if you're going to give me the 3rd degree, then she said well I didn't mean to make you mad, and I said Well I didn't mean to make you mad either. Then she said well let's hush. . . .

Any way we ended up O.K. and I'm carrying her some snap beans and cucumbers, so we're O.K. But honestly that took the cake.

Love, Truma

———————

IN *WALKING ACROSS EGYPT*, Mattie Rigsbee, seventy-eight and slowing down, has been discovered (by a dogcatcher, Lamar) solidly stuck down in a rocking chair without a bottom. They are in the living room. Mattie had started watching a soap opera after lunch—without cleaning the kitchen—when she absent-mindedly sat down in the bottomless chair. A dog is barking in Lamar's truck.

> "Listen [says Mattie to the dogcatcher], with all that noise I'm afraid Alora might—Alora's my neighbor—I'm afraid she might come over; I want to ask you if you'd do something for me. . . . Would you wash my dishes?"
>
> "Wash your dishes?"
>
> "It's just a few. If you don't mind. I'd pay you something. I'm just afraid that . . . Would you do it?"

That's my mother. I wish you could have known her in person as I did. I think of her almost every day. I know I find solace in natural things, simple things—like trees, flowers, and birds—because of her inspired example of embracing and finding pleasure in the simple free gifts the earth provides. And in these letters I see her word play, her love of language and narrative (to her it was simply "talk"). She never guessed that the son she hoped would be a concert pianist or a missionary would end up writing "talk" for a living. Of course we had disagreements, and she, like all of us, was a product of her family and culture. But that is for another essay.

She fell in the kitchen and broke her leg in 1998 when she was ninety-four, living alone, and she never quite recovered. She died soon after her ninety-seventh birthday. She was in my arms at her last breath, and I honor that final intimacy.

If I pass significant aspects of her spirit to my children, I hope it may be her stoic simplicity, her ability to live in the moment with simple objects and natural delights that are available to any of us, regardless of station in life.

I think she was perhaps a Baptist Buddhist but didn't know it. Which brings me to her corn bread recipe: fine white plain corn meal, water, salt. Mix and make thin patties, fry in a little oil in a cast iron pan. If you've never had it that simple, and you like it, thank my mother.

# Ties That Blind

— HAL CROWTHER —

DURING OUR ADOLESCENCE my brother and I must have heard, at least a hundred times, our poor mother's pitiful cry: "You boys are ruining/have ruined/will ruin my life!" The offenses that triggered this lament were various, but not what most modern parents would rank as ruinous. In those days—the 1950s, early 1960s—there were no drugs available to rural teens, and teachers' sons like us were rarely tempted by felonies, or any crimes more serious than vandalism or disturbing the peace. But there was beer, there were cars, there were draft cards that older boys shared generously with underage friends. Worst of all, in our mother's eyes, there were decent Episcopalian and Methodist girls who sometimes consorted with these reckless boys.

Not every respectable mother, to the best of my recall, was equally terrified by these predictable teenage activities. It's a strong thing for a fifteen-year-old to hear that he has ruined his mother's life. Our mother was a high school English teacher who taught drama, from Shakespeare to Eugene O'Neill, and when it came to drama she practiced what she preached. We had drama at the dinner table in our family—my father had a volcanic temper and an extended cocktail hour—but no matter what pyrotechnics the family dinner produced, my mother could upstage us all by dashing off to her bedroom in tears, locking the door, and weeping almost loud enough to be heard on the street. Besides the assertion that her life had been ruined, the worst thing we heard on these occasions was that she always wished she'd had daughters instead.

My little brother and I were no one's idea of truly bad boys. With my thick glasses, brush cut, and button-down shirts, no one except my mother ever mistook me for a desperado. But we were our father's sons, with a genetic disposition toward willful independence and a dogged resistance to the lofty morals of the Boy Scouts or the Methodist Youth Fellowship, both of which we had sampled without enthusiasm. Not everyone is cut out to be an Eagle Scout, or even a Methodist Youth. In a town as small as the Appalachian backwater where we lived, people kept close track of one another's children. The worst consequence of our worst infractions would be a ride home in the lone police car and a lecture from the lone policeman, Gene Wigent, who would deliver us to our parents with a gruff warning not to try it again. A benevolent small-town version of crime and punishment that never failed to reduce our mother to hysterics.

A traumatized childhood? Not exactly. But there were sacrifices. Prematurely tall, awkward with girls like many boys without sisters, at fifteen I was far from a polished lady-killer, and there was a whole lot of mileage left on my virginity. Yet I must have been the only boy in town whose mother had warned some of her friends to keep their daughters away from her son. That's hard to forgive, at an age when your hormones are working double shifts and overtime. And a lasting consequence of Mother's tragic scenes was my lifelong aversion to emotional extremes. There were several women I greatly admired and valued, later in my life, who never heard from me again after the first time I did something that made them shout or cry. I would just freeze up, close the books on that relationship, and withdraw.

Like most adolescents in their parents' homes, we had no idea that our domestic routines were abnormal. Other homes, we'd heard it rumored, could be much worse. Dad raged, Mom wept, and dramatic, hurtful things were sometimes said. But there was plenty to eat, no one beat us or even supervised us much, and we enjoyed our freedom. There were no "helicopter" parents in the 1950s. A submarine would have made a better metaphor. Our parents, both teaching full time, required nothing from us but decent grades and punctual appearance at the evening meal. The family narrative I constructed was all about me and my brother, of course—the burdens we had to bear, the stoic patience we had to learn. I never asked myself, until many years later, what might have made my mother treat minor violations of middle-class propriety like war crimes.

What wounded, what molded these adults, what had made them the way they were? These are questions none of us are equipped to answer during the years we're obliged to live with them. One of the admirable things about Richard Ford's memoir, *Between Them*, is his honest conclusion that there are many things about our parents we can never know. There are permanent mysteries, and our most educated guesses are often wide of the mark. Certainly these adults offered us very little of the personal history that might have enlightened us. I found this entry in one of my notebooks, under "Privacy":

"I tell my children and my closest friends everything about myself I want them to know—and if that's not enough for, say, my daughter, I assure her truthfully that it's twenty times more than my parents told me."

What did I know about my mother's life that wasn't common knowledge? She was born and raised in Boston, the oldest daughter of a sea captain's son from Nova Scotia. Her father—the most successful individual, financially, on either side of my family since the nineteenth century—was a regional sales manager for one of the big Pittsburgh steel companies. His wife, who had not finished high school, was the daughter of an immigrant craftsman, a decorative plasterer from Edinburgh. They were married before the First World War, and the marriage had produced two daughters and a son before the central, irreducible trauma of my mother's childhood, which occurred when her father left his wife for a younger woman, a private-duty nurse according to family tradition I can no longer fact-check (the last witness, Mother's younger sister, died at ninety-nine in 2017).

This Jazz Age crime against respectability produced some of the best but darkest comic material I ever harvested from my extended family. According to the gentleman's code that wayward husbands followed ninety years ago, my grandfather never divorced my grandmother or altered his financial responsibilities to her in any way. As far as I know, neither of them ever consulted a lawyer. He was just no longer present in the home, though rarely farther away than his office downtown. He attended to family duties according to his fashion. For years, when they were both in their seventies and eighties, he would drive my grandmother from her apartment to the family Christmas dinner he hosted at his club in the city. And all the way, a dozen miles or so, she would curse him vehemently in the subprofane language permitted to her generation of ladies, and repeat again and again, "Jack, you ruined my life." To which he would reply mildly, eyes on the road, "Yes, Catherine. Yes, Catherine." Once a year, every Christmas, this ritual shaming was repeated, even with grandchildren in the car.

It's only now, writing this, that I can see where my mother must have picked up the potent rhetoric about ruined lives that she recycled for her sons. But her father's great betrayal must have played a major role in the way she came to see the world. Here was a model American family in an affluent suburb, respected, perhaps envied. And then, overnight, the opposite: a family broken, the subject of malicious gossip, and worst of all, a family pitied. Pity is the emotional charity that isolates and even humiliates its recipients. Americans took these things more seriously back then, during the Coolidge administration. The Allens may not have been ostracized, but surely they were singled out and pitied. Added to the disruption and bitterness within her family, it must have been a lot for a twelve-year-old girl to deal with. My grandmother, to whom I was close in her old age, was also subject to fits of hysteria.

How do I think all this affected my mother? Her path, as the oldest child, was to grow up quickly and perform at the highest level, to become the kind of young woman no one could pity or reproach. She was the valedictorian of her high school class, she was Phi Beta Kappa and magna cum laude in college. She was the essential straight arrow—in fact, she was an archer, and in vintage photographs she looks the part of Diana the Virgin Huntress, tanned and long-legged with the ocean wind in her hair and a determined look on her serious square-jawed face that says "Don't underestimate *me*."

There are old boyfriends in many of these pictures, tanned, grinning, for-gotten suitors lying on beach towels or brandishing tennis rackets. She never spoke of them with any particular fondness or nostalgia, certainly never said to my father, even in her most dramatic moments, that she wished she had mar-ried Carl or Fred or one of the other boys in the photographs. My parents gave every indication that they loved each other, and often reminded their sons of this fact, occasionally in a way that made me, at least, feel less loved. In spite of the contrary evidence in my mother's own family, they seemed to subscribe to the maudlin Victorian myth that all marriages are made in heaven, between soulmates predestined to be together. It's a myth that would fit with my moth-er's need to rise above her family disgrace.

The unhealthy part of her search for wholesomeness and security was an excessive concern for the opinions of her neighbors and the community as a whole. This involves conjecture on my part, of course. But I sensed in her this hunger for propriety, for public approval, that the three males in her family never shared—certainly not my father. A man of considerable self-regard, he engaged the world with a kind of ironical condescension, almost contempt— an unwelcome hereditary tendency I've been fighting all my life, though it fights back tenaciously. My father never gave a damn what the neighbors thought; he seemed serenely confident that they admired him. He had not been a "good" boy himself, as his younger brother often reminded him, and his only objection to our trivial crimes was that they made our mother cry. But this was no casual objection. He was an autocrat who deeply resented anything that interrupted his reading or his monologues, and he could deal harshly with the hapless miscreants who provoked her tears.

He was a handful, my father, a man with a big ego and a big voice, a pres-ence like her own father only more so. By the time my brother and I reached puberty, I think my mother had had it "up to here," as she used to say, with the art of managing alpha males. She was wary, all her life, of unregulated testosterone. In the war between the sexes she assumed, not unreasonably but not always accurately, that the male was invariably and entirely to blame. She took my unsuccessful first marriage and subsequent divorce as a personal failure—if only her failure to give birth to respectable, reliable daughters. She was never the kind of mother with whom you could share your conjugal sorrows.

In the light of her family history, it's not surprising that she regarded adultery as a crime second only to genocide. The "soft" adultery I committed while my marriage was failing—the dating activity of a legally married man who is no longer living or welcome in his wife's home—was probably responsible for the coolest period in my sixty-seven-year relationship with my mother. Our low point occurred toward the end of this troubled period, when my girlfriend and I spent a getaway weekend at a rustic inn in western New York. When we came downstairs for breakfast, we found half the dining room occupied by a breakfast meeting of the Allegany County Retired Teachers Association—including my mother, who was the speaker, and half a dozen of my grade school teachers.

I can't honestly remember the look on my mother's face. We never talked about this disaster directly, but for the next couple of years she treated me as if I'd turned out just as she had always feared, back when I was a clueless kid drinking Twelve Horse Ale at Fox's Inn with Tom Baxter's draft card.

When you're nearly halfway through your thirties, with a decade in the Manhattan work force behind you and a daughter in the first grade, it's aggravating to be treated like a juvenile delinquent by your mother. It's more aggravating if you suspect that you might deserve it. But this tense phase of our journey together had a happy ending. My second marriage—to a successful writer and a teacher of English literature—convinced my mother that her civilizing influence and superior chromosomes had prevailed after all, in spite of everything. The more domesticated I appeared, as the years went by, the more she gloated. And doted—on my wife.

I've wronged my mother if this intimate history suggests that she didn't love me. I never doubted that she did. It's just that she came up short, like the rest of her family and much of her generation (and ethnic group), in the demonstrative part of loving: the hugs and kisses, the public declarations of her affection. She saved her demonstrations, unfortunately, for the mournful parts of her emotional register. And too much praise and approval, she seemed to believe, would only create another narcissistic male with the potential to make good women miserable. Withholding approval was probably the most toxic aspect of her parenting. In time she acquired enough self-knowledge to admit it.

HAL CROWTHER

"Perhaps I was too much the teacher," she once told my second wife, who shared her experience of raising two troublesome sons.

Perhaps you were, Mother, but as a teacher you were by no means a failure. Robbed of the daughters she deserved, my mother labored to protect her boys from the worst effects of that testosterone she so distrusted. She couldn't save us from sports, a local obsession and a family cult as well. But any accurate assessment of her sons as adults shows the depth of her influence. My brother and I took no interest in guns, cars, gadgets, or any sort of masculine hardware. We became Luddites who spent too much money on books and music, and we were competitive only in games. Thanks to my mother I developed an alarmingly feminine appreciation of flowers, sunsets, autumn leaves, landscape painting, and lyric poetry. I studied English poetry in college, though my grandfather was urging me to get an MBA while he still had the connections to launch me in the steel business. I disappointed him, even though he paid for most of my education. It occurs to me only now that this might have amounted to a bit of payback, with my mother clearly prevailing over the father, long forgiven and rehabilitated, who had once wounded her so gravely.

It's important, also, to note that her unnatural fear of scandalizing her neighbors did not extend to political conformity or timidity. My father was a liberal Republican, a nearly extinct animal—today he might be a centrist Democrat, liberal in everything but his economics. After he died, however, my mother rapidly rebranded as a liberal Democrat, a very rare animal in rural north Appalachia where she lived. Her causes included farm workers and Native American orphans, and her activism included a successful series of demonstrations against a hazardous waste dump. Her great commitment was to the peace movement. She had a father in uniform in World War I, a husband and a brother in World War II, and a son (not me) in Vietnam, a war she was the first in our family to denounce. She liked to remind us that she was born in August 1916 during the Battle of the Somme, when twenty-one thousand British soldiers were killed by German machine guns in a single day. War was the one masculine abomination, the one horrific manifestation of testosterone poisoning for which she would accept no excuses or rationalizations.

She was a good woman, a hard-working, clear-thinking woman fated to live her life with willful, verbally intimidating men. But she was armed with a formidable will of her own, and she was enough of a protofeminist to identify the patriarchy as her enemy and devise strategies to hold it in check. As her son, I could hardly endorse her strategy of dramatizing our mistakes and minimizing our successes, but I see now what she was up to. She had a vision of a better, more gender-balanced world that her parenting might help to realize, and over her very long life—unruined, I submit—she must have found many occasions to congratulate herself. We survived, her prodigal sons, to enjoy decades of her approval and support. She was there, at eighty-five, to share the day when the university closest to her home gave me one of its lifetime awards for journalism. When she died, at ninety-five, I cleaned out one of her closets and found a comprehensive archive of nearly everything I had ever published. I cried a little.

# Beatrice and Mamie

## — BELLE BOGGS —

MY DAUGHTER, WHO IS THREE, believes that she has always existed. "Where was I?" she asks when I tell stories about my own childhood: catching painted turtles in the pond with my brother, riding bikes with my cousins down a hill so steep my training wheels broke off, the time our cat hid her kittens inside our log cabin's walls. "And what was I doing?" she wants to know. "Did I hold you when you were a baby?"

Beatrice has had straight answers to most of the questions she's asked in her young life. She can name every one of her body parts, and she can tell you why Donald Trump is not a good president ("because he doesn't care about anyone but himself"), and also why you shouldn't mention him at the table ("because we're eating"). But I find the existential ones harder to puzzle through, in part because I don't quite understand them myself.

I spent more years—and probably more money—trying to conceive Beatrice than I have spent so far in raising her. In the worst of those years I avoided family gatherings and baby showers and couldn't get close to the children's section of a bookstore. If I had known that Beatrice was in my future, even distantly, the long wait for her would have been far less painful. But that isn't how infertility works—you can't know how you'll build your family, or when, or if. For a while I despaired; things seemed hopeless. I tried to reconcile myself to the idea of childlessness—I could nurture my students, be a good aunt, be someone to take my friends' children kayaking. I'd travel more, I told myself. I'd write more books.

Looking back, even in those lonely years it seems now that Beatrice was with me, in the things I valued about my own childhood and wanted to pass on to my children, things my own mother shared with me. I imagined that she'd one day be here to read my favorite books, to take meandering nature walks with me, to inherit and care for the cumbersome old baby doll she renamed "Mrs. Baby."

When she was born I was surprised that Beatrice was blonde, like my mother, instead of dark-haired like me and my husband. She is also, like my mother, tiny and hilarious and sensitive, the kind of person who remembers when anyone she loves is hurt, sick, or chigger bitten. She stands up to bullies, is constantly "rescuing" snails and caterpillars, knows all the words to "Diamonds Are a Girl's Best Friend." "She is my *soulmate*," my mother has said repeatedly, and a little fiercely, as if daring disagreement. My mother was her own grandmother's soulmate—she remembers taking daily driving tours of the Lutheran churches of Norfolk, Virginia, standing on the bench seat with one arm around her grandmother's neck as she steered.

This connection between generations—making my mother a grandmother as I became, like her, a mother—has been more gratifying than I even imagined. Bea wore the overalls my mother embroidered for me, mouthed the words to "Froggy Went a-Courtin'" long before she could talk, and sleeps under a butterfly mobile my mother made for her. She calls my mother Mamie, a name of her own invention.

---

THE SUMMER that Beatrice was two and my mother was sixty-five, I took them on a trip to Paris. My mother, an artist, had never been to Europe, and Bea had never been on a plane before. Transcontinental travel isn't the norm for me or my family, and as the date approached I wondered if buying the tickets had been a crazy (and expensive) mistake. Was a recently potty-trained toddler brought up in the woods of North Carolina a suitable companion for hushed art museums and endless city strolling? Would Bea whine about the six flights of stairs to the apartment we rented (would we)? Would she sleep?

No, Bea did not sleep well (at least, not at night), but I think it was the best trip any of us has ever taken. We walked ten miles a day, visited six museums and countless parks and playgrounds. We rode bikes to Monet's house in Giverny, ate *glaces* at every chance, and didn't tell Bea what escargots were. When the museum galleries were too crowded, Bea climbed into her travel stroller and fell asleep, and in this way we wheeled her through the Louvre, the Musée d'Orsay, and the Picasso Museum.

I felt a little bad, letting Bea snooze past the Rodins and van Goghs and Vermeers, but I was also relieved to take our time, aware that it was possible my mother wouldn't visit these museums again. The guards had looked suspiciously at Bea when she got too close to one of Monet's spellbinding water lily paintings, baby doll in arms, and I'd been afraid she might get her first spanking in front of the Winged Victory of Samothrace.

There was one exhibit where we stayed for hours, and no one slept or got in trouble. In the Louvre's design museum, an entire wing was devoted to the history of the Barbie Doll. My mother showed us the German doll that predated Barbie—her father brought her one home from a trip—and we took our time reading about the fabulously varied careers Barbie's makers had imagined for her (*president, snowboardeuse, docteur pour poneys*).

The exhibit was full of women—mothers, daughters, grandmothers, friends—all talking quietly, remembering their own dolls and childhoods. There was a small glass-enclosed room where you could sit on the floor, playing with the Barbies and their dream boats and dream cars and dream houses. I stood outside and watched while Bea and my mother, both dressed in black and white, pushed a Barbie coach across the hot pink carpet. It was unbelievable to me that we were there, that in a while we'd travel down the marble steps somewhere else, all three of us together in the most beautiful city I know.

This summer I left Beatrice for a weeklong conference in California. On the plane I read an article about a trip to Paris, and I scrolled, on my computer, through the photographs I'd taken on our trip. In so many pictures my mother and Bea are doing the same thing—staring up at a tree in the humid Jardin des Plantes greenhouse, resting their feet near a fountain, tossing bread crumbs to ducks on the Seine. I missed them.

On the last day of the conference, I watched as Amy Tan was interviewed on a panel about her new memoir. "Did your mother believe in ghosts?" the moderator asked. "Why don't you ask me if I believe in ghosts?" Tan suggested. The moderator hesitated, and Tan added, "My mother believed that I was the reincarnation of her mother."

The moderator didn't follow up—it was almost too profound and difficult an idea to talk about there, in a crowded room of tired writers looking for tips to record in their journals. What a burden to place on a child: to be the reincarnation of someone else, someone with a separate history and mind. But also, what a gift—to be aware of your own life's expansiveness.

*Yes*, I thought, as the panel moved on to other concerns. This is why my hard-won daughter feels so familiar to me, and perhaps why she sees her own existence as eternal, a mysterious nesting doll of ages, selves, experiences. I won't tell her, but I believe she held me when I was a baby.

— PART VI —

Secrets and
Lives

# Keeping Secrets

— SHARON K. SWANSON —

THE FIRST HOUSE I REMEMBER was a tarpaper shack, without plumbing, on our South Carolina farm. The window frames in the bedroom that I shared with my three siblings—we ranged in age like a stepladder, with me at the top, my youngest brother on the lowest rung, and two sisters placed evenly between, only five years separating the four of us—were filled with cardboard in the summer to keep out the mosquitoes, and covered with plastic in the winter. A single bulb that dangled by an electrical wire in the middle of the room provided the only light and created shadows on the dingy whitewashed walls, even on the brightest days. A patch of daffodils bloomed every spring next to a matching forsythia bush by the rough concrete block step at what passed for a front door. And during sweat-soaked summer nights, the unrelenting cacophony of cicadas and whippoorwills filled our dreams.

Our house, situated at the highest point of our two hundred acres, gave us a natural vantage point for watching approaching cars spinning up red clay typhoons as they passed on the dirt road but made us sitting ducks for frequent summer thunderstorms. Wind blew through the cracks in the joints of the walls, and dust swirled at our feet through holes in the floor where the linoleum was worn through, revealing the earth beneath the old wooden studs. One storm in particular raged with profound violence and fury and noise. As a child, it felt as if some mythical god was tossing thunderbolts, aimed directly at our tin roof. I could not think or breathe.

My father, a long-haul truck driver, was away overnight for work. But my mother quickly gathered us all in her arms, comforting each of us with the close softness of her hair and the smell of Ivory soap. Then holding each of us in turn, she sat with us by the open windows, encouraging us to enjoy the rush of refreshing cool air in our faces—a respite from the unrelenting humidity of our typical summer day. We could smell the cordite as the sky rumbled just above our heads in ever increasing waves. We startled with every rumble and crash. In a quiet, reassuring tone, Mama talked to us about her Southern Baptist God, who would always watch over us and keep us safe. I wasn't sure I could trust such an imposing and unknowable father figure, but I did trust her. In those moments, my mother reminded me of the only picture hung in our shared bedroom—a guardian angel watching over two frightened children crossing a bridge alone in the night.

As the storm receded and the lights went out, our mother lit candles and made shadow puppets on the wall, asking us to name the creatures we saw there. First a rabbit, then a dog . . . her repertoire was limited, but we were transfixed by the magic she created.

We thought we were safe. But that was before another storm.

---

I WAS NAMED after my mother, Katrina, who died more than thirty-five years ago. I thought I'd come to terms with her loss until the Hurricane Katrina headlines from the Gulf Coast in 2005 stirred up a new wave of sadness. Old grief reminds me of the pecan tree in the yard of our old farm: I didn't give its presence much thought until a storm exposed its roots.

My mother knew about storms. She was the daughter of hardscrabble to-bacco farmers on the North Carolina coast near Jacksonville, now home to the Marine base Camp Lejeune. She would not have been surprised to learn that the formidable Greek gods of the wind and sea carried the names of men. My mother also knew about legends. My grandmother, still a teenager when my mother was born, named her first child after a character from Washington Irving's *The Legend of Sleepy Hollow*. Perhaps she envisioned something better for her daughter than the crude patriarchal serfdom she herself was brought home to as a bride, during the early part of the Depression. Or maybe she just liked the name.

One day when I was ten, my father was home, although probably not completely sober, so the four of us were out playing under the shade of the pecan trees to stay out of his way. Mama was doing something in the kitchen. The images of that day are grainy but refuse to dim with time. I heard my mother cry out and looked up to see her sprawled on the big back porch, her right leg under her somehow or perhaps caught in a hole in the old wood. I was always afraid of what might hide under that porch—copperheads and spiders the size of my head. From where I stood, I couldn't see what was holding her down, and I wondered why she just didn't free herself and stand up. Then, as if in a delayed reaction, a sound crossed the yard to where we played. It was a

SHARON K. SWANSON

weeping so plaintive and despairing that her whole body looked paralyzed by her anguish. I had seen my mother cry before, but nothing like this.

My father, instead of going to her aid, commanded us not to go near her. His face a mask of anger, he yelled at us to get in the car. We obeyed like little robots, without protest, silent tears washing down our faces. Had my mother fallen in a "clumsy" moment, or was she being punished for some real or imagined offense?

My father determinedly put the car in gear and drove away from the farm. The four of us clung together in the back seat, my mother's place in the front passenger side inconceivably empty. We drove around the countryside for what seemed like hours, but probably was no more than twenty minutes, before returning to the house, where my mother was still slumped over on the porch, not moving.

My father, bidding us to stay in the car, approached her warily and called her name. She did not respond. With uncharacteristic tenderness, my tall, handsome father scooped up my petite mother and cradled her in his arms. Talking to her in gentle tones, he carried her to the car where we waited. Then my father placed her in the passenger seat and laid her head in his lap; I watched him stroke her soft hair as he drove. Mute in the backseat, we knew our mother must be dead if she could not acknowledge our silent pleas to open her eyes.

When we arrived at the tiny community hospital where my mother sometimes worked part-time as a nurse, my father carried her inside. As was expected, I took responsibility for my younger sisters and brother as we waited by ourselves in the car. Sometime later my father emerged without our mother, tersely letting us know she would be taken care of. Then he took us home where he made some attempt to give us a meal before sending us to bed.

Until that time, I could not remember being apart from my mother for even one night. For days, my father shuttled us back and forth to our mother's kind friends, who talked amongst themselves in hushed, sad voices. When I asked my father to be taken to see her, he told me, "Your mother can't see you now. She wouldn't know who you are."

*My mother not know who I am? How is that even possible?* I wanted to demand answers, but I had no voice.

"Your mother has had a nervous breakdown," my father pronounced, without elaboration, as he took off on one of his solitary hospital visits.

It would never have occurred to me to question my authoritarian father in the 1960s South outside a small Civil War town, home to peach orchards, an annual grape festival, cotton mills, Protestant churches on every downtown corner, and not-so-secret KKK rallies in the fields of local farmers. And everyone in our little community knew that the words he used to describe my mother's medical condition were the same ones used to encapsulate all kinds of crazy—from garden variety anxiety to full blown psychosis, like the time that a guy in town killed his mother on the lawn with an axe. We all knew that story.

About ten days later, my mother returned home, weak but gloriously happy to see us. Gradually, life returned to normal. Except to me. From that time on, I watched my mother for signs I might lose her again—and never get her back. More than before I helped look after my younger brother and sisters, redirecting them if I thought they were being too demanding of her energies.

A couple of years after her hospitalization, my mother, with the assistance of those same kind friends who looked after us during her illness, took us and fled the farm while my father was away overnight for work. I've wondered since how long my mother feared the loaded .22 pistol my father always carried in his pocket. There were no shelters for battered women in the 1960s; the sheriff's deputy who lived down the road from the farm was one of my father's drinking buddies.

I worried that the responsibility of being a divorced woman in a small, conservative town might prove to be too much for my mother. But with her nurse's training, she went back to work full time and seemed to blossom in every area of her life, taking on more and more responsibilities as a head nurse at the county hospital.

My siblings and I also flourished at the little house in town, with its one full pink-tiled bathroom and window frames with real glass instead of cardboard and plastic. Thunderstorms and other intimacies of nature seemed much farther away. Although I never completely gave up my guard, I did relax my vigilance, approaching something that felt like a normal teenage life and the corresponding testing of limits.

One night in the summer before I started college, I had just gotten in from a date and heard my mother's small, light steps approach my bedroom. Because she was up at 5:30 every morning for work, I had assumed she would be fast asleep. I quickly grabbed up a book, perhaps one of my favorite Jane Austens, and pretended to read although I couldn't follow a single line of the text.

"Have you heard from your sister?" she asked. "I am starting to get worried about her."

"No, but it's only a few minutes after midnight. I'm sure she'll be in soon," I told her, making a mental note to give my sister a piece of my mind for staying out past her curfew when Mom had to work the next day.

It was only after my mother left the room that I glanced down to realize my book was upside down. I hoped my sharp-eyed mother hadn't noticed the

SHARON K. SWANSON

words on the spine. I also hoped she hadn't noticed my glassy-eyed look. I sniffed the clothes I had dropped by the side of my bed for lingering traces of the pot my date and I had shared in his car.

My mother never said any more about it, so I figured the coast was clear. However, a few days later, I walked by her in the kitchen as she was making dinner after work. Handing me some salad makings, she nonchalantly mentioned that she was worried about my little brother.

"I think he is smoking marijuana cigarettes with his friends," my mother said.

I was shocked. My brother and I had always been close. I certainly hadn't seen any signs of this.

"Are you sure, Mom?" I asked. "He's only thirteen. I'm not even sure where they'd get it."

Busying myself with the salad, I avoided my mother's eyes. "I could talk to him about it if you want me to," I said. But my curiosity got the better of me.

"What would you do if it was true?" I asked.

My mother stirred the spaghetti noodles, and without missing a beat as she lowered the temperature on the pot, she replied, "Well, I know that marijuana is illegal, and I wouldn't have a choice. I'd have to report him to the police."

Really? Report a thirteen-year-old to the police? That didn't sound like my loving give-him-the-benefit-of the-doubt mother. Sure, my brother had been known to lob a few water balloons at me from the roof of the house as I exited with a date, but nothing more. And Mom had laughed that off as a prank, despite my profound embarrassment. Was my mother losing it? I needed to clean up my act.

Soon after, I realized that I didn't really enjoy those marijuana cigarettes. Smoking always made me feel as if there was a giant elephant sitting on my lungs. That feeling only grew after the conversation with my mother. And I never saw any indication that my brother was in danger of being ratted on to the police, or any reason for it.

I never talked to anyone about my fears about my mother's fragile mental state, especially her, for concern that even the mention of it would send her into a downward spiral. That knowledge became just a part of the scenery, the backdrop of my life. However, later as a young adult, I did have a conversation with her about the night of the thunderstorm. I thanked her for teaching me not to be afraid of storms, of the noise and the wind. I told her I remembered the shadow puppets. And although I grew up with a healthy respect for thunder and lightning, she made us feel that we would always be safe.

Her response surprised me.

"Honey, I am so glad that is what you remember because I was absolutely terrified of those storms. I still am."

We both laughed. In subsequent years, I couldn't help but think how vulnerable we all were in that shack of aged wood, perched precariously on river rocks, with no car and no place to seek shelter.

———————

MY FATHER LIVED another twenty years after my mother, at some point trading alcohol for a dependence on a fundamentalist religious faith and a church where he spoke in tongues. My relationship with him was tenuous at best, although he continued to be a part of our lives in various ways. After his death, I sat in the kitchen of my Aunt Arzell, my father's sister, as we reminisced about my parents. My aunt was never close to her brother for good reasons of her own, but she and my mother had remained close even after the divorce, as had the rest of my father's family.

Perhaps released from the secret of my mother I had held close for decades, I questioned my aunt about what she remembered about my mother's mysterious hospitalization, telling her what I knew.

My aunt had to think back before responding. When she did, her blue eyes were sharp with anger.

"I don't remember your mother ever having to go to the hospital for a breakdown," she said.

"That Katrina was probably the strongest woman I ever met," she said. "The only thing I can think of was when your daddy made her clean the floor of that broken down old shack with a mixture of bleach and ammonia. She inhaled the fumes and burnt up her lungs."

"If she wouldn't have known you, it was only because they had her on so much pain medication," she said. "I will believe until the day I die," my aunt went on, "that the damage to her lungs shortened her life."

My mother died during pulmonary surgery at the age of fifty-two.

Today, I can no longer recall the cadence or sound of my mother's voice. It is only the essence of her that remains—the soft hands caressing my face, the dimpled smile greeting my returns home. Although divorced for many years, neither of my parents ever remarried. After we all left the graveside at her funeral, one of my aunts witnessed my father kneeling alone in the rain in his best suit, his head resting on my mother's casket, sobbing inconsolably.

Dad later told us that a coworker had said to him, "If Katrina was the mother you say she was, she will have prepared her children to live without her." Although I still miss my mother—a calm center of a tempest in my early childhood and an unrecognized beacon of stability for the woman she knew I could become—he was more right than he knew.

After more than three decades, it is rare my mother is even mentioned at family reunions. There is no need to discuss legends. But recently, a younger cousin brought up her name in a phone conversation.

"When I was little," she said, "my family stayed at your house on vacation. My brothers and I were all on blankets on the living room floor when a big storm came up. We were all too scared to sleep."

"It was your mother," she said, "who came out to check on us."

# The Curse of Living in Interesting Times

## — SAMIA SERAGELDIN —

WHEN MY MOTHER didn't visit me right after she died, I thought I knew what she was waiting for.

It had to do with a promise I had made ten years earlier. I was visiting her in Cairo when, one day on a whim, I unearthed the big boxes that contained the albums of family photos, in the closet where she kept her wedding dress, the three-meter-long white satin train carelessly folded—I suppose, when you have lost as much in your life as my mother had, you either learn to be careful of possessions, or the opposite. Among the albums I came across three slim, leather-bound notebooks I had never seen before: journals that she had kept, sporadically, over a period of twenty years, filled with her distinctive backward-slanting handwriting in English, remarkably unchanged from her late teens.

I hadn't known she'd kept a diary. She took the journals out of my hands.

"I'm thinking of destroying these. They're private. I don't want them falling into anyone's hands and being read by the wrong person."

I promised her that if something ever happened to her, I would make sure they didn't fall into anyone's hands but mine, and that anything truly personal would stay private.

———

WHEN SHE PASSED AWAY, that promise was on my mind the entire long, bitter trip from North Carolina to Cairo. I was her only daughter, and although I took the first plane out when I heard she'd been hospitalized, I was too late to hold her hand. But I could at least keep my promise.

First, though, there was the memorial service to get through. The burial itself had taken place the same day my mother passed away, as is the custom, and the date of the service was coordinated to allow me just enough time to arrive in Cairo, so I had not had time to shop for mourning clothes and had packed what I found in my wardrobe. For the service, on that hot, late September day in Cairo, I dressed in a cap-sleeved black sheath and sling-back kitten heels, vaguely aware that my mother would not have approved of either, under the circumstances.

*That dress is too light as well as inappropriate*, I heard her saying. The odd thing, of course, was that it was my mother's voice from the time when she was still herself, her old critical voice that I remember from my teens onward, before she mellowed into benign vagueness in her last years. It was as if I knew that with death she had shed the debilitating mask of age and regained her old judgmental personality.

> *Have you put on weight? That skirt looks too tight.*
> *No, Mummy, actually I lost a kilo since school started.*
> *That's why your face looks pinched. It doesn't suit you, you shouldn't diet.*
> *But I thought you said the skirt looked tight?!*
> *It was riding up your legs when you sat down—horrible sight! It's too
>     short.*
> *All the girls in my class wear their skirts shorter.*
> *Yes, well, we're not everybody, we don't have to be slaves to fashion.*

My mother's memorial service was very well attended; I knew she would find that gratifying, and it assuaged my sense of guilt. In her later years she used to complain that, as her only daughter, I didn't pay visits of condolences or attend memorial services and that, as a result, no one would attend her own memorial service when the time came.

That night, I didn't dream of my mother. That didn't worry me too much, not yet. I had dreamed of my father three days after he died, and of my beloved maternal grandmother as soon, despite the fact that I was two continents away at the time. The dreams—I will call them that, although I experienced them as night visitations—had come as loving leave-taking, a welcome confirmation that their souls were at rest, a sense of closure. I craved a posthumous visit from my mother all the more, for the reassurance that she was at peace, not only with death but with me, for failing her at the end, for not being at her deathbed when she asked for me. Once I had found the journals, I believed, once I'd kept my promise, she would come.

The next day, fighting off fatigue and jet lag, I went back to my mother's home and engaged in the marathon of burrowing into her overcrammed closets until I found the boxes of albums and bags of letters and, among them, the three slim, leather-bound journals, her precious diaries. I got up off my knees, brushed off the dust, and expropriated the boxes and their entire contents to take with me and sort through at home, with the blessings of the rest of the family. After all, I am the keeper of memories in our family, the sentimentalist, the fabulist, the weaver of stories. There is one in every generation.

––––––––––

IN MY MOTHER'S JOURNALS I met a woman I never knew. She kept her diary for twenty years, from before I was born until a couple of years before I left home for London, but the entries are sporadic for the first few years. They start off with a happy young wife and mother, in love with her life, in love with her home, and in love with her husband. That last was a happy discovery for me. My parents' union, typical for their era and milieu, had been primarily conceived as an alliance between two compatible families. That it had blossomed into passion gladdened me. But with my mother, as with Carmen, "Si je t'aime, prends garde à toi." Reading between the lines of her diary, you glimpse a possessive, romantic young woman seizing the slightest pretext to test her new husband's devotion. I rather feel for my father, who was mature beyond his years and temperamentally averse to domestic drama. On the other hand, like many men with a deceptively long fuse, when he did lose his temper, the fireworks were to be reckoned with, and a few instances were recorded on those pages.

Another revelation from the journals was that my mother might be less secure about her appearance than she wished to project. As a young woman she was tall, with glossy black hair, strong eyebrows, and what her younger brothers called a Coca-Cola bottle figure: small waist and voluptuous hips. She understood, even as a nineteen-year-old bride, that her style had to be sophisticated rather than ingenue. In her wedding photos, taken at my father's family house, where the wedding took place one autumn evening, she wore a gown of pearl-embroidered white satin, with a strapless bustier and a three-meter-long heavy train. I can't imagine how she managed to move at all, let alone sweep down the high, curving marble staircase on the arm of her groom, as is the custom in Egyptian weddings. Later in the evening she went upstairs to change for the reception banquet, into a sophisticated yellow satin evening gown with a sash of jet-encrusted black satin. My mother was considerably taller than I, but I have tried these dresses on, in my late teens, and found the waist constricting, while the fabric around the hips and bust hung loose on me.

To look through photo albums of bejeweled women in glamorous gowns and men in white dinner jackets, you would assume that this early period in her married life must have been idyllic, but she had surprised me once with a comment. "You know, that life was empty, in a way. I had staff to look after the house and Madame Helene to look after you children. I woke up late, nibbled on a lettuce leaf for lunch and spent all afternoon in my boudoir getting ready to dress up and go out with your father in the evenings. I was no more use than a *poupée de salon*." We had one of these purely decorative, exquisitely delicate china dolls, with a white powdered wig and Madame de Pompadour silk dress, presiding on the gilded Aubusson sofa in the salon. I was never allowed to touch it as a child, until one day a cat somehow got in and ruined it. "Your father valued me more," my mother went on, "he needed me more, when the bad times started."

The bad times started in earnest in the early sixties. Although, a few years after her marriage, the entries in her journals take note of Nasser's coup d'état of 1952, the abolishment of the monarchy, and the agricultural land reform act that impacted large landowners like my father, these upheavals seem to have registered little on her overall satisfaction with her home life and, in due course, her pride in her young children.

The really bad times began in 1961. That was the year the so-called Socialist Decrees were implemented. Overnight, my father's family and other politically prominent families like them were targeted by the regime for the confiscation, not just of their cotton estates but also of every form of property, every financial or business asset, even personal possessions, like a second car or jewelry in a bank vault.

Even worse, the "dawn visitors," as they were known, could come at any time to arbitrarily take away one of the men in the family, for a period of days or months. It was a decade of dread, of frantic phone calls, of disappearances at dawn, of deprivation and social isolation. My mother's journal became her confidant, and she wrote nearly every day.

One incident she relates in scene-setting detail in her journal: how she rang for her breakfast one morning, but the *suffragi*, as menservants were called, did not bring her breakfast tray as he usually did, with the morning newspaper folded next to her café au lait, how she went down to the butler's pantry and found him sitting reading the paper, with her undelivered breakfast tray on the table. He pointed to the front page. "The Bey's name is on this list."

My mother took the paper from the *suffragi* but resisted looking at it until he had taken the tray to her room and she was alone. She scanned the long list of names, entire families, whose every penny of assets would be frozen and put under "sequestration" by the regime. My father's name was on that list. To make matters worse, as his wife, her own assets, inherited from her father, would be subject to the same confiscation. They would be allowed a monthly pittance.

The Curse of Living in Interesting Times

TWO THOUGHTS run through my mind when I read this entry. The first is that I had never grasped how desperate our situation really was, or the extent to which my mother worried, or how her pride suffered from her change of status, even vis-à-vis her own family. In her journal, she writes that she felt more at ease, after this reversal of fortune, socializing with my father's family, all of whom were targeted for the same persecution, rather than with her own family, who were not similarly affected and maintained their lifestyle.

My second thought is that it is from her that I inherit my storytelling inclination, although I always thought of my father as by far the more bookish of my parents. My mother subscribed to the *Ladies' Home Journal*, *Reader's Digest*, and Book of the Month Club, all regularly shipped to her from the United States, at a time when such things were still possible. Starting at age ten or so, I would surreptitiously pick a book at random off the bookcase, read it under the covers at night, and then replace it before anyone noticed. I remember especially Pearl S. Buck's *The Good Earth*, Frank Yerby's *The Saracen Blade*, a Restoration romance called *Forever Amber*, Somerset Maugham's *Of Human Bondage*. Any and all of these would have qualified as age inappropriate, and therefore verboten, by my mother.

Reading was my only escape from the pall that hung over our home. Immersed in her own misery and worry, my mother was understandably oblivious. In one entry, she writes that she doesn't understand why I have become so difficult and moody, and why my school grades are slipping. The new textbooks at my elementary school listed my father's family, by name, as among the most prominent "feudalist-capitalist enemies of the people." My brother was older than I and surely even more aware, although perhaps less sensitive. Two or three months later, my mother notes that I have made a complete turnaround, that I am suddenly cooperative and sweet and once more top of my class. There is no insight or, for that matter, curiosity as to the transformation. She needed to believe, for her sake more than for ours, that we were somehow oblivious to the disruption around us.

But she did try to protect her children from the harsher realities of their situation, even at the cost of putting herself in an unsympathetic light. The first summer after the draconian laws were imposed on my father and others like him, our parents announced that we would not be spending our usual three-month vacation in a villa by the sea in Alexandria as we usually did; we would be spending a week at a seaside hotel instead.

"It's no holiday for me, organizing the transportation of our entire household and setting up house for three months," my mother explained to my brother and me. "I'm looking forward to spending a carefree week at the hotel instead."

We resented this apparent selfishness at the time. I realize the real reason now, of course: we simply could no longer afford three-month seaside holidays.

One entry in her journals, written at the most stressful time, makes me smile. She writes: "Well, at least I've lost three kilos without even trying." How like her!

She kept a Mother's Day card I wrote her some years later, when I must have been fourteen or fifteen. I begin by telling her that I was taking the opportunity to write because, whenever I tried to express my feelings in person, we ended up arguing, and I wanted her to know that, although we had our differences, I appreciated everything she did to hold our family together. I must have had an inkling, even then, of the burden of worry she carried, given my father's repeated heart attacks and the risk of his lapsing into depression. Her relentless optimism must have cost her an effort, even if it was undergirded by her genuine faith in God's providence.

That card is a comfort to me today, when I remember how we argued during my teens, usually about my appearance. *Your hair's too long. It just drags your face down when it's so long and you blow-dry it flat like that. It doesn't suit you.*

If my father happened to overhear our exchanges, he would raise a wry eyebrow at me, wordlessly. *It's just your mother.* I would shrug. *I know.* And I did know, even at the time, that I should not take her criticism on its merits.

My father and I shared a moody temperament, chronic insomnia, and a sense of irony that escaped my mother. He was the one trusted by family and friends to safeguard their secrets, their reputations, their fortunes. They also knew he would rather lose a friend than collude in a white lie to help that friend cover up for an extramarital indiscretion. People like my father do not survive well in the real world; he died young. But while I had him as a father, he was a good listener and a reliable confidant, and we could discuss books, religion, or politics, late into the night. He had higher expectations of me than my mother did and encouraged me to dream about a career in diplomacy or journalism. To be fair to my mother, she never doubted my abilities, only she held a more traditional view of fulfillment for a woman, through marriage and motherhood, so nothing must be allowed to interfere with that priority.

When I married at twenty and left home to pursue graduate studies at London University—in the right order of priorities, as far as my mother was concerned—she wrote me twice weekly, ten-page letters that sustained me through the homesickness of those long, dreary English winters. We were closer then, I think, at a great distance, than we could be face to face.

When my father died, of the last of several heart attacks, I remember her crying out: "Not that! Anything but that!" As though she were bargaining, but with whom? It could only have been with God. It was cruel that her husband had died young, and crueler still that he had not lived to see the better days that were right around the corner for our family, and for Egypt.

She was still in her forties at the time she was widowed and often mistaken for her grandchild's mother. When I suggested, a year after my father's death, that if she thought of remarrying I would support her, she responded that if I were joking, it was in bad taste, and if I were serious, then it was in even worse taste. Why would she remarry? She didn't need a husband for either social status or economic security.

But remarrying excluded, as a widow she started a new life, using her new-found freedom to travel extensively abroad, in Europe, in the United States, even to Russia before glasnost, where she encapsulated the entire Soviet system in two words: "No choice. One kind of cheese, one kind of car, one kind of anything." She expanded her social circle with a new set of friends she made on these travel tours. Her calendar was full of ladies' lunches, and she entertained often at home as well, giving parties for me and my children when we came on our annual winter visits to Egypt, year after year.

She complained about my living abroad, but she was used to it; after all, I had left Egypt at the age of twenty. But she exhibited a deliberate lack of interest in my life in the States, my work, my friends, my social life, not even when I tried to tell her that, of all the places I had lived in Europe or America, only North Carolina had reminded me of home. The sense of family and community, the emphasis on courtesy and deference to elders, the way hostesses kept an eye on every neglected guest or empty serving platter while never letting a silence fall. Even deeper than that, the sense of faded glory and a contested history. I had lived in North Carolina by then for longer than I had lived anywhere else, including Egypt, but my mother simply didn't want to hear about a life led apart from her world.

Paradoxically, she never failed to mention that I lived in the States when she introduced me to someone, even to doctors I met when I accompanied her on her medical visits. Her pretext, when I protested, was that she needed to explain some oddity in my appearance or behavior, or why I had not been available to accompany her on previous occasions.

When I published my first novel, a semiautobiographical roman à clef, she refused so much as to look at the autographed copy I gave her. She thought it disgraceful that I would write about my family, and in fact I suspect she thought that she herself would come off badly in it. But as her friends read the book and

SAMIA SERAGELDIN

praised it, as she sensed that her standing in their eyes was enhanced rather than diminished by having a novelist daughter, I noticed that she placed the book prominently in her bookcase, although she still refused to read it, or at least to acknowledge having done so, if she had.

———————

WHEN HER DECLINE STARTED, it was gradual, difficult to pinpoint. She became more irritable and less sociable. She started to turn down invitations, and she stopped entertaining at home. When I urged her to take her friends to a restaurant if she didn't feel up to the effort of hosting at home, she agreed but only on condition that I went along. One of the few times I was in town and able to accompany her, she invited ten of her friends out to lunch at the newly opened Four Seasons Hotel on the Nile. She gave me her pocketbook and asked me to take care of the bill and the tip. I realize now that she was already having trouble adding up figures and counting out cash, which was why she needed me along. If only I had been less obtuse, or she had been more forthcoming!

A few years earlier, when she turned eighty—not coincidentally, the age at which her own mother died—my mother wrote her own obituary. She couldn't trust anyone to get it right, to remember every last relative and in-law, living or deceased, and their correct titles, those ancien régime titles of Pasha and Bey abolished by Nasser after the fall of the monarchy some sixty years earlier. But now she began to act as if her death were imminent. She complained that her children didn't spend enough time with her and that we would be sorry when she was no longer around. She reminded us of the Islamic injunction: "Heaven lies at the feet of mothers," implying that we would not be admitted into that select club without her benevolent intercession. At the time, though, the notion of her death seemed abstract, a whim of hers, a late-life ploy for attention that we affectionately but impatiently indulged.

But then one day, after a fall that resulted in a hairline forearm fracture, she took to her bed and refused to get up, seeming to sink into a lethargy of mute depression. Her mother had done the same, years before she passed away; I recognized the symptoms with alarm. I tried to jolt or cajole my mother out of her state, but she was impervious. I hired a retired army nurse to look after her and do physiotherapy. After observing the nurse at work that first day, I took her aside.

"You must never again address my mother in that condescending way. Never speak of her in the third person in her presence. My mother abhors indelicate language, so use euphemisms. Don't let her get away with lying in bed, make her get up and move around and walk, but cajole her. I hired you, but she's your employer, and if she takes a dislike to you, we can't keep you on."

It was a tall order, but the nurse stuck with it, and slowly, agonizingly slowly, my mother began inching up that slope that she had slipped down so rapidly. But every fresh blow—a sprained ankle, the sudden death of a beloved nephew—brought her tumbling down the slope again, back to the safety of her bed.

———————

THEN IT WAS THE ARAB SPRING and there were millions in Tahrir Square and around the country chanting and protesting, and army tanks were blocking city streets. One revolution is enough for anyone's lifetime. At my mother's age, and for someone who had gone through so much with that first revolution sixty years earlier, to relive the insecurity, the disruption, was too much. The Chinese curse "May you live in interesting times" had proved too true of my mother's life.

Increasingly, she seemed to be losing the will to live. Getting her to eat or to leave the house was a frustrating ordeal. She was so emaciated that her round-the-clock caregiver, a stout country woman, could pick her up easily. When we dressed her to go out, her skirts and slacks hung so loose that the waistline had to be tucked in with safety pins. There were moments when she seemed to regain sparks of energy or enthusiasm, but it never lasted. She lost her short-term memory and with it her sharp, argumentative personality—she couldn't hold on to her grudges.

But under the sweet passivity that replaced it, she was still my mother. I clung to the glimpses of her old self that I caught in the occasional acerbic comment or sharp look. When a nephew died, she was the only one who knew, or remembered, that he had a stepbrother by his father's second marriage, who would need to be informed. One time she was slumped in front of the television when she saw the Egyptian president bringing a bouquet of red roses to the bedside of a rape victim. She sat up and expostulated: "Red roses! How inappropriate! Someone should have advised him against it!" Then she lapsed into listlessness.

———————

"MUMMY, WHAT DID YOU have for lunch?" I would ask when I called her from the States, every day at the same time.

"Oh, let me see. Chicken cutlets, peas . . . and rice."

I could tell she was making up menus for my benefit because she couldn't remember what she'd eaten an hour before. Later she didn't even bother to do that much. I would put down the phone after one of these daily nonconversations, overcome with worry, with guilt for not being there.

She couldn't remember what she had for lunch, but she could remember every verse of the songs she sang to us as children. One summer night, at her beach house on the Mediterranean coast of Egypt, when I was visiting and we were sitting out on the veranda under the stars, I set her off with: "Mummy, do you remember how that song went: *Or would you rather swing on a star, carry moon beams home in a jar?*" She picked it up from there and sang song after song, with me feeding her just a first line as a cue: *Shoo Fly, Don't Bother Me, A Bicycle Built for Two,* and of course, her favorite:

> Row, row, row your boat,
> Gently down the stream
> Merrily, merrily,
> Life is but a dream.

---

THE FOLLOWING SUMMER, her last summer, she seemed to be in markedly better spirits, with slightly more energy. She spent happy days at her beloved beach house, surrounded by her favorite people, her grandchildren and great grandchildren.

"You're the only one who isn't here," she reproached me gently when I called from North Carolina.

"I know," I told her. "I'm waiting till summer is over and you go back to Cairo. That's when I'll come to make sure you don't get depressed. Right now you have everyone around you, you won't miss me."

"No one ever replaces anyone," she insisted.

And no one does. She was surrounded by three generations of family when she was hospitalized for the last time, but I wasn't there. And she asked for me. I booked the first flight out, when I heard she was taken ill, but it was too late.

At least I had not been too late to keep my promise; I had recuperated her journals. And yet, that night, I still didn't dream of my mother.

---

I RETURNED TO THE STATES, postponing for a few months my share of the job of unraveling her complicated estate. Back in North Carolina, I was immediately plunged into the stream of my life here, my obligations and preoccupations. A stream where my mother had never set foot, where the landscape evoked no memories of her passage, where no one knew her or commiserated with me or expected me to be wearing mourning. Although I thought of her several times a day, I began to lose hope of a nocturnal visitation.

And then it was November, the night of the presidential elections. I went to bed before the final results came in, confident of the outcome all the polls and the pundits predicted. That night, when I least expected it, I dreamed I was hurrying into my mother's bedroom, having rushed back from abroad because I'd heard she was ill, to find her sitting up in bed. "It's all right," my mother said as I hurried toward her, "it was just a cold."

Then I woke up. I puzzled what to make of the dream. What did she mean?

It was about three o'clock in the morning. Since I was awake, I thought I'd just check my cell phone for the election results. First there was disbelief, then shock, then dread: of an uncertain, ominous future, of what it might hold for those I love. The familiar sense of falling again under "the curse of living in interesting times."

And then I thought I understood why my mother had chosen that night of all nights to come to me. She had been through it all: revolutions, demagogues, and hard times, she'd seen them come and go and survived to see a better day. Perhaps, finally, that was her legacy to me. We were so different, my mother and I, in physical appearance, in temperament, in every way that counted, and my life had diverged from hers so radically and so early that I have sometimes made the mistake of believing I had not much to learn from her. But this she could teach me: how to live a life that is constantly buffeted by the crosswinds of history; how to survive in interesting times.

"This too will pass," she was reassuring me, "like a cold. You recover from a cold."

Or perhaps she was saying something even more difficult to remember and to accept. Life itself passes. Nothing you are going through, good or bad, lasts forever. So don't take it too much to heart. How did her favorite song go again?

> Row, row, row your boat
> Gently down the stream
> Merrily, merrily
> Life is but a dream.

# Drag Racing to the Promised Land

## — LYNDEN HARRIS —

CLAIMING THAT SOUTHERNERS have a sense of place is a nearly embarrassing cliché, except that I am standing in the cemetery where my mother's parents are buried. My mother's parents *and* her grandparents *and* her great-grandparents. So, if a sense of place means the bones that brought you here, well, these headstones are hard to argue with. Ours is a story of bones and dirt and the water that can wash away your sins. But I get ahead of myself.

There are many things a family may be known for; ours seems to be funerals.

My grandmother could never decide what to wear to hers. She was tall and effortlessly elegant and changed her mind about her funeral attire with an almost religious consistency. It wasn't just a question of seasonal suitability. She wanted to be buried in something she liked, preferably with appropriate accessories. When it's open casket, you don't want to startle your guests. So, Grandmama was forever telling her daughters she'd changed her mind again about her burial ensemble. Finally, one of my aunts insisted Grandmama pin a note to the current selection. Otherwise, we'd be forced to bury her in layers just to cover our bases, covering bases being a notion familiar to Grandmama. She was surely the Atlanta Braves' most stylish baseball fan, never missing a game and tolerating no criticism of her boys as she waited for the promised land of "next year."

A few years before Grandmama died, our extended family gathered for peach ice cream and eulogies. Grandmama wanted to hear hers while she was still able to make corrections. When she finally gave up the ghost at ninety-five, we stood together in the chapel as the pallbearers rolled her down the aisle to the slow and magnificent strains of "Take Me Out to the Ballgame."

She was my father's mother, but Mama called her "Mother" anyway. Mama said Grandmama was the only person she never heard say a single unkind word about anyone.

As my brother said at Grandmama's funeral, "Life is so short, the arc of it so long to learn."

My own mother abhorred funerals. And I'm pretty sure hers was at the bottom of the list. Mama refused to talk about it, other than to say she had written down the specifics, which, knowing Mama, probably meant she had *intended* to write them down. Or had written the words "Funeral Arrangements" on an envelope. An *empty* envelope. Do not ask my mother for directions or a recipe. You will end up with a sugarless pound cake somewhere in Kentucky. For all we knew, she had written the instructions in her head.

The last time we three children asked her about the details, she considered each of us in turn, and then pronounced, "I'd like a *Christian* burial." I fear we did not inspire confidence.

Mama did not always dislike funerals. When she was young, their garden stretched for acres. At the edge, a large square was outlined with rocks. When a kitten or chick or puppy died, my grandmother would give the children a box and the five siblings would pick flowers, assign roles, rehearse prayers, and then process toward the garden cemetery, minister leading, gravediggers in the rear, and everyone singing "On Jordan's Stormy Banks I Stand." A line of children bound for the Promised Land.

Sometimes when I had a column to write, I'd call Mama and ask about those days. Always, eventually, I'd get a story: about a Halloween when the boys hoisted the principal's car onto the roof of the school. Or the firecrackers Santa left in their stockings, because what kind of celebration didn't require explosives? When we were children, Mama gave us sparklers on rainy days and we'd light one after another, drawing fiery secret codes through the air. Or mason jars in the shimmery summer evenings to catch lightning bugs, nature's own hidden cipher.

––––––––

MORE THAN ONCE Mama related the story of a classmate who claimed girls couldn't drive worth squat. What choice did she have? Or so Mama explained to the policeman waiting at the end of their drag race down Highway 56. When the officer brought her home, my grandfather's only question was, "Did she win?"

Often the stories revolved around church. Church was dinner on the grounds or maybe drinking on the grounds if you considered the liquor-making facility at the creek down from the twin-towered chapel. When I asked how folks learned to make moonshine, Mama looked at me like I had lost my mind, even though we were talking on the phone. "*Everybody* knew how. It's just corn, water, malt, and time." She was right, which is amazing considering my mother's penchant for omitting ingredients. At the end of every story, Mama would add, "but you can't tell anyone that," and I'd reassure her, saying, "I'm not going to *tell* anybody. I'm just writing it for the paper."

Newspapers were serious business to Mama. Her parents read both the *Durham Sun* and the *Raleigh News and Observer* every day. More than radio, or later television, print was the medium of record. News was local and personal. If I were to wonder now what some family member wore to "a pleasant country dance followed by an oyster roast" a hundred years ago, those papers would tell me. The newspapers of record were a *record*.

This may explain why Mama called me one morning, indignant about an obituary she'd read.

"What didn't you like about it?" I asked.

"Well, anybody who knew that person knows it isn't true."

"What did it say?" I asked.

Mama snorted. "The first line was 'On Sunday, So-and-So went to meet Jesus face to face.'" There was a pointed pause. Then she continued. "In the *newspaper*, no less!"

"I don't think they fact-check obits, Mama," I noted. "Besides, that particular story would be a little hard to corroborate."

She sniffed. "And don't get me started on the loving children and doting husband. An obituary should say who died, when, who survives, and where the services are. That's all. And a designated charity so people don't spend good money on flowers."

I have met goldfish who were more sentimental than my mother.

She came from a generation for whom the words "I love you" were a foreign tongue. The language of love was what you eat, not something you speak. Cobblers, corn pudding, and fresh tomatoes. Eggplants and raspberries ripening out back. Love lives in the dirt where we're planted.

Though the dirt is meant to be metaphorical. It's that sense of place; you're supposed to sense it, not dig in it. Once when Mama was visiting and I was out dividing some dahlias, she sighed, saying, "You'd rather play in the dirt than do the first thing in the kitchen." I believe that may have been the moment she gave up hoping I'd turn into the daughter she intended to have.

A few years ago, when Mama saw on Facebook that I had broken my arm, she phoned for details and, when I complied, didn't even bother to muffle her snickers. Granted, such injuries usually involve backing into objects that move, such as the family dog, rather than ones that don't, such as paint cans and woodpiles. Mama hinted I might not want to keep the details to myself, given that it all sounded a bit, um, *redneck*. When I mentioned that the medical staff kept asking if I had been in any way light-headed or dizzy, she said, "I hope you told them that no, you were just clumsy."

But, back to the obituary. I suggested Mama might want to write her own, rather than leave it to our clumsy efforts. But she had no interest in participating in her death, much less her obit writing.

It started me wondering. What moments would my mother, for whom propriety was not a false idol because it was fully supported by church doctrine even if she couldn't pinpoint which one, what moments would Mama have found both pivotal and acceptable for print?

Surely, the early memory of her father returning from town, tossing a sheaf of papers on the table, and telling his family, "We've lost everything." The county bank had shut its doors and their accounts. Personal, business, investments: more than 190 banks failed in North Carolina during the early years of the Depression. "We've lost everything" must have been common as dirt.

However common, the hole went deep, though no one, least of all a child, understood its depth. How do you measure *everything*? All Mama knew was that on her fourth birthday, Grandmother had opened a bank account in her name. Now it was closed. Mama descended the front steps and wandered toward an enormous oak, stepping from one gnarled root to another, repeating with each planted foot: "I have no money anymore. I have no money anymore." Rolling the unfamiliar words around her mouth, she named them *loss*. Something that had been, was now gone forever. Telling this to me so many years later, her eyes reddened with tears.

But, of course, the family hadn't lost everything. Despite their shock, they retained the land, the farm, the houses, farmworker help, and a network of kin rooted in several counties. Like so many families, they made the transition through the Depression by pulling together rather than being pulled apart. Home, for them, would alter only in the amount of ease with which life there was accomplished. Home would not disappear.

I am certain these early years contributed to Mama's attitude of "drink (iced) tea and carry on." Part of functioning as a lady was the unspoken expectation that one simply keep going. And she always did. A tiny slip of a thing, with blonde hair and blue eyes, Mama was easily underestimated. Without a doubt, Mama was the most stubborn person I have ever known. Grandaddy called her his bantam rooster. She was, as they say, a pistol.

Yes, Mama was a straight shooter. There was right and there was wrong, and I was often in that second category. When I was four, I asked her why I wasn't Jesus. I don't think she ever recovered. When I reached my teens, Mama looked askance at many of my friends, reminding me often that we are known by the company we keep. I responded by bringing up Jesus again, whose example continues to be a thorn in parents' sides. Where would we be if Jesus had her attitude, I asked, Jesus being fairly notorious for hanging with the wrong crowd?

Ever practical, Mama replied, "You aren't Jesus. Besides, Jesus didn't have a choice. And just look what happened to him."

If you weren't sure what *right* was, Mama was happy to tell you. A few years ago, some family member spotted a news photo of me and others at a legislative breakfast. Moments later, my phone rang. "You're wearing your name tag on the wrong side," Mama said. And then, "You were raised better than that." Except, I'm sure she said "reared" not "raised," because children are reared; *plants* are raised. And don't get her started about the word "kids." Unless you're a goatherd.

But Mama had one fatal flaw against which propriety and even willpower was useless as buttons on a dishrag. Mama could be laid flat by any bit of slapstick. She may have inherited this weakness from her father, for whom April Fools' Day wasn't so much a holiday as a life strategy. When she was six and didn't want to climb out of bed one cold morning, he quietly left a baby screech owl at her feet. If you've ever heard a screech owl, you can imagine the explosion of sheets and running feet. Another time, he extended a hat full of freshly gathered eggs for her to take to the kitchen and then dropped the hat between them. Mama screamed but the egg gourds just bounced.

Once Mama started laughing, it was all over but the shouting. We took her to Tracy and Hepburn reruns not to watch the films but to watch her. Since she never learned to ride a bicycle, only horses, I decided one vacation to tote her around on a tandem bike. All went reasonably well until she forgot how to stop and we crashed into a police car. We were both laughing so hard at that point, it's a wonder we're not locked up still.

Mama was an *I Love Lucy* show all by herself. Restaurants were a fine setting for slapstick, as when she opened a paper creamer and expertly shot the man across the aisle's nose. Or when my young son accidentally squirted a table full of ladies with his water pistol and the women began searching the ceiling for a dripping air conditioner connection. I thought we might just have to bury Mama then and there. But what a way to go.

Mama and I shared an inability to control our giggles, but we didn't always share priorities. A couple summers ago she called, saying she had something for my bucket list. Intrigued, I asked, "What?" as I visualized Lisbon or Istanbul. "Organizing my cedar chest," she announced. I mentally reviewed my bucket list: um, not on there.

Mama's health was suddenly declining. She knew the situation was dire because she couldn't stand long enough to iron her pillowcases. When I was a child, our housekeepers ironed entire sheets, but Mama didn't want to ask her current housekeepers to iron even the pillowcases. When I asked why, she said, "Because they speak Portuguese."

Then, that September, Mama awoke one morning unable to put two words together. We thought she'd had a stroke, but soon the doctors discovered a "benign" brain tumor. Within days, Mama was nonresponsive. The palliative care doctor hinted at three weeks and suggested we call hospice.

A few days later, out of nowhere, Mama suddenly opened her eyes and said, "My interim minister visited and even though he doesn't always follow the liturgical calendar, I do like him." A major breakthrough, and I don't mean just her speaking. We called hospice back. Never mind. Mama may have lost the familiar neural pathways, but she was clearly finding her way around. She always loved a good puzzle.

Mama graduated high school at sixteen and enrolled at North Carolina State. There were so few women, they were escorted across campus to the dining hall, not because it wasn't safe but because a woman walking alone simply wasn't proper. To make things worse, Army scouts came to State and administered qualifying tests for a secret mission in Washington. Mama was the only girl who tested into the Signal Intelligence Service. Her extended family was horrified. Washington, D.C.? It was bad enough that she was away at college, but the capital? Unchaperoned?

———————

THERE WAS NO CHANGING Mama's mind. (Trust me on that.) The more you tried to convince her of a thing, the more she stuck to her guns. For forty years, Mama refused to talk about her work at Arlington Hall as a code breaker because "loose lips sink ships." So, family opinion be darned, Adelaide Wilder Jones was going to Washington. The only person who flat out approved, and so bore the brunt of the family's disapproval, was her own mother. I am sure she wished she could go along.

Some of Mama's facility with puzzles was surely due to an inherited love of games. In our family, card playing was how you learned to count. Rook and pit, Michigan rummy and Chinese checkers. When the speech therapist arrived at Mama's rehab facility with word games for the group of elderly ladies, Mama objected to the other ladies' including Pluto in their list of planets, on account of Pluto not following the new rules for planets. When the therapist called for a drink that began with M, Mama did not quickly lock down *milk* but instead hollered MARGARITA! She won the final round decisively: Things one finds in a closet.

*Skeletons.*

Because who doesn't have skeletons in their closet?

One rainless summer when I was little, my brother explained the reason the soil was cracking was that the ground was made of dinosaurs. I assumed the fissured dirt was actual skeletal plates and walked carefully, alert for any bones that might poke through. Maybe Mama felt the same, coming of age at a time when roles were both so proscribed and, at the same time, starting to crack open. Women were breaking ground. Opportunities were flickering on the horizon. Had Mama been born a decade or two later, well, it hardly bears thinking about. She went from the heady work in Washington to being an executive secretary in Florida to marrying my father and having three children, which didn't require her zippy typing skills but at least required countless trips to the library. This wasn't really the end of her story, because she loved children. Or, at least, babies. She might have been happy to farm us out for a few years later on.

But once she married, her talents would require workarounds. As my brother noted, these were early *Mad Men* days, a time when a wife working outside the home implied something about the husband's inadequacy. Mama's love of numbers, puzzles, and codes went underground, only to resurface as thrice-weekly bridge games, jigsaws, sudoku, not to mention the Women's Club and the Garden Club and, really, too many clubs to remember—lions and tigers and bears, oh my! I remember trying to convince her that the Garden Club directory, which listed the women by their husband's name, Mrs. John Smith, and then in parenthesis their own (Jane), should be revised. It's not like there was a single husband anywhere in the vicinity of the orchids. How about Jane Smith and (Mrs. John)? But the women knew their place. Not that they thought men were in charge, Mama clarified. It's just that they needed to *think* they were.

By the end of the sixties, rolling waves of change had smacked against the shores of this country, flinging Mama and Daddy's marriage asunder. It was a time of protests and promise, ruptured gender roles and revolutionary possibilities that left both my parents unmoored but for very different reasons. What do you cling to when the pilings have been washed to sea? Daddy dove into those waves and lived to pay the price; Mama put on sunscreen and stayed on shore, and then, when that was not sufficient, retired inside.

Sometime during those rocky years, I found a scrapbook tucked away in a bookcase. In it Mama mused, in her perfect Palmer Method penmanship, about a date with my father. "He thinks we should get more serious. So do I."

The flowers he'd given her were now pressed past any possible hope. It broke my heart. But Mama was one of those never-look-back Southerners, and soon after, she asked me to help her examine his bank records and canceled checks. It was not the only time I was instructed, "Don't tell the boys." There were some things only a daughter should know. We stood before the closet, confronted by a paper trail neither of us wished to walk, knowing that once we opened that door, nothing would ever be the same again.

Sure enough, the names on those canceled checks were reason enough to send Daddy packing. But he always asked to come home, and she always let him. This part of Mama's story does not have a happy ending, at least not in the time frame of a human life. She struggled mightily with our father's complicated life, moving through disappointment, despair, and devastation as she tried to reconcile her dreams and expectations with what was, in those days, an unspeakable reality.

Since they loved each other, my parents finally divorced.

The night my father died of AIDS, my mother brought a single white rose, the flower of his beloved fraternity, and laid it on his chest.

He left her everything in his will.

At his funeral, she requested the song "Somewhere" from *West Side Story*: "There's a place for us. Somewhere a place for us." I thought the stones of that small chapel might crack from sorrow. "Somehow. Someday. Somewhere."

What had happened to her promised land?

But as Mama often admonished me, "You don't need to know every little thing." Plenty, in her opinion, should remain in whatever closet was closest. And in the end, what does it matter? Life is a code that no one, not even Mama, could break.

Before she died, Mama spent some time at a facility named Hidden Lake. According to her, the reason the lake was hidden was because it was actually a pond. Hidden Lake was only a lake if you thought your birdbath was a pond. When I mentioned I was writing about her, Mama said, "Well, don't write something frivial." Apparently, the brain tumor had opened new pathways, allowing Mama to coin words at need. Frivial: frivolous and trivial, both.

Both my parents took sudden, unexpected, near-death dives, with doctors offering prognoses of mere days, and then, as if some unseen force had slapped them upside the head, just as suddenly woke back up for another year and a half. It allowed us the chance to say all the things we maybe meant to but never found the right time. I told Mama how grateful I was to have had her as my mother. I even wrote it down. Mama smiled quietly, tucking my letter into her Bible, which meant into her heart.

The day I turned eighteen, Daddy forgot and missed the party. Late that night, he left me a note in his tiny script saying he was sorry for not having been a better father. A single line, but it cracked me open. Ten years passed and he was dying and I was typing my own letter, a kind of eulogy to our relationship, deeply personal and private. I wanted him to know I forgave him, if such a thing is even ours to give. I wanted my father to remember what we shared, rather than what he had missed. The following week, one of my uncles patted me on the shoulder. "That was the *sweetest* letter you wrote your Daddy." Yes, my father was so proud of that deeply personal and private letter, he had photo-copied and distributed it to every member of his extended family.

At Hidden Lake, Mama's windowsill danced with letters and cards. Her favorite was of a long-stemmed rose under an elegantly scripted "Thinking of You." If you looked closely, you saw it was handmade from colored construction paper and recycled glitter.

"Say a prayer, my friend. The Creator is always listening."

"By letting go of all that is heavy, you become free to fill with all that is light. Holding you in that light."

"My heart goes out to you in this difficult time. Keep faith that all is well even when it seems it is not."

Mama said the words were the truest she'd ever read. I told her she was likely the only person in her facility with cards from men living on death row. My hanging out with the wrong crowd had not abated. Mama was perpetually baffled as to why I worked with people who lived behind bars, no matter how many times I reminded her about you-know-who: "I was in prison and you came to visit me." Mama would just sigh, "I suppose you have a calling," as if it were some unfortunate inheritance like different colored eyes or alcoholism, and probably from Daddy's side. But she treasured those letters. At one point, she got really tickled about receiving so many envelopes stamped *Mailed from a state correctional facility.* "I wonder if the rehab staff thinks I used to be in there." And then she added, "I hope so."

The men's kindness tore a wider hole in the screen of her heart because who doesn't have skeletons in their closet? Mama's acceptance of these men was a reminder that the real paths on our bucket list may be ones we fail to see we're walking. By this point in her life, she was fairly drag racing to the Promised Land. The night Mama died, my daughter sang her "Ave Maria," Mama's favorite song. Blessed mother, virgin of the sky. A few minutes after Mama passed that July evening, fireworks started exploding in the night sky.

"Peace and quiet and open air, wait for us somewhere." The song played a final time at Mama's funeral. That afternoon, our mother and father came together again under the enormous oaks and rolling green hills of the cemetery—not quite the fair and happy land she imagined as a child. But they were finally side by side as they had requested, and perhaps proximity is its own kind of peace.

For those of us fortunate enough to have been born into a family whose guide star, or lodestone, is love, the promised land is not where we're bound but where we live. The place for us is where we stand. Life is so short, the arc of it so long to learn. This is the truth of what is "frivial" and profound. Holes are dug and filled, but the ground remains.

# This Is Your Mom

## —ELAINE NEIL ORR—

THE DOG LOOKED LARGER than most bush dogs, perhaps because he loped with a sideways tilt. How far away was he when we first noticed him? A hundred yards? The length of a football field? Perhaps he stepped out from shade. Then he was in the street, a two-lane paved road in southwestern Nigeria. Surely he would cross to the other side. The entire episode took only a few seconds, though in memory the time is elongated. Because he did not cross but loped toward us, coming straight for the car. A brown bush dog with a squarish head. Until he ran straight into our oncoming vehicle, my capable mother driving.

---

WHEN I WAS VERY YOUNG, growing up in Nigeria, my parents, elder sister, and I took long trips in our Chevrolet station wagon, long trips on winding roads. Without air conditioning, my legs stuck to the plastic-covered seats, and I seemed always to need to go to the bathroom. To distract me and though none of us had a singing voice, Mother suggested a hymn, and we sang every stanza. We played I spy. Sometimes my mother and older sister gossiped, which I found immensely boring. I remember napping and waking with my hair stuck to my cheek, and asking over and over: "How many more miles?"

When we finally arrived at our destination, I still felt the motion of the car, so interminable were these travels. And yet I remember the journeys as beautiful cloistered hours of family togetherness: my father at the steering wheel, my mother to his right, often in curlers, which she took out at the last minute before we arrived at our destination. My sister and I shared the back seat, windows down, the huge green of the African rain forest ten feet from the car, our father braking to a dead stop for a herd of long-horned cattle moving in the other direction. Mother packed lunches of pimento cheese sandwiches and homemade cookies and a thermos of hot coffee, as well as Kool-Aid for us girls. Right this moment I can see my mother as we stopped for lunch. She stands by the car in a crisp cotton dress, belted at the waist, feet sandaled, her head tilted slightly, a near smile as she begins to remark on something to my father. My mother kept her cool even on those hot roads. For a woman driven from the age of eight to save the world, she composed herself like a queen, and not just any queen, the queen of England. I knew about Queen Elizabeth and how she looked. After all, we were her subjects in Nigeria. She never had anything on my mother.

———————

ONCE WHEN WE were living in the town of Osogbo and I was thirteen—this would have been in 1968—my mother and I loaded into our Peugeot sedan and took off for Ogbomoso, my birth city, thirty-five miles away. I don't recall the occasion, whether we were going for a day visit or an overnight. It would have been unusual for us to leave my father even for a weekend. By this time, my sister had left Nigeria to continue her education in the United States. We drove on the left side of the road in those days. The Peugeot was a stick shift and still smelled new. To either side of the road, grasses and low vegetation sprang up. We had not been traveling ten minutes, windows down, warm wind whipping through, a smell of dry grass filling our nostrils, when a bush dog appeared ahead of us. It began to run straight for the car, straight for the front fender. Like most bush dogs, he was a medium-sized, short-haired, sleek-looking canine. What I most remember is the sideways gait. My mother swerved, but there was no avoiding the hit. A shudder ran through the car. "Rabies," she said, and I understood: the dog was mad. We were quiet in the aftermath, my mother and I in our cotton dresses. The sun blazed. I remember nothing else about the trip but that dog and "rabies" and the silence that followed. The dog coming for the car. There was no avoiding the hit.

What am I close to here? There was no avoiding the hit? At the time, I found no parable in the experience of that morning. I only remember taking off from Osogbo with my mother, happy in her smart, reasonable presence, her blue-gray eyes behind glasses, her large, capable hands—which taught me piano—on the wheel. And then the dog we couldn't avoid.

That is something.

Bush dogs appear to roam free in Nigeria, though they are generally owned and trot alongside their masters. Yet they aren't leashed. From the time of earliest memory, I feared crossing their paths. They look something like an Italian greyhound, though they likely descend from the Basenji. Every bush dog I ever saw had a white tip on its tail. A dog with an owner is given a name. A name such as Tanmyinola? "Who knows the future?"

FOR THE MOST PART, I have imagined we could have avoided the hits. Who do I mean by "we"? To begin, I mean my parents and me. We might have avoided my being sent to the United States alone when I was sixteen. I could have attended boarding school in Jos, in northern Nigeria, where most of my friends were headed. The pattern had been trending in that direction among most missionary families for years. Rather than sending teenagers to the United States for two years to finish high school before college, families were keeping their children in Nigeria through high school graduation. I surmise that my parents thought I should follow my sister's footsteps. A recently discovered letter from my mother to a friend, written in 1970, reports that she did not believe the school in Jos was the best choice for me.

But was it suitable to put an ocean between us? To repeat the pain of separation my sister had experienced? *We can't avoid the hit.* Is that what she believed? That separation was inevitable? Age sixteen or age eighteen. A career as lifetime missionaries required partition. What difference two years? And then again, my mother's own father had died when she was fourteen. She left home at seventeen for college, and then she left for nursing school in New Orleans during World War II—attending many a death in early morning hours. And left again for seminary in Louisville because if she wasn't destined for marriage, she was still going to be a missionary. She did come home one summer and work for the town doctor in Fairfax, South Carolina, living with her mother and younger sisters in the house where she was born. Only after she died did I learn that she slipped home at lunch, changed quickly into a bathing suit, and laid out in the yard to sun. My mother? Never was she so frivolous in my experience. She sewed lovely rickrack onto my dresses and made a special birthday cake every year and planned my Christmas presents years in advance—after all, they had to come from the United States. But playful, hardly ever.

But to return to the question at hand: what difference would it have made to keep me in Nigeria, schooling in Jos?

Two years is the difference it made. Exactly that. Seven hundred thirty days. Seventeen thousand, five hundred twenty hours more I might have had my mother in my home country. Though perhaps my parents reckoned that in sending me to Jos they would not in fact have those hours. I would rarely see them. The trip was two days by car. I would be home at Christmas and Easter. So how many hours really would we have gained? How many times would I have driven with my mother to the Ogbomoso market or to Ibadan to shop at Kingsway department store and see friends or to Ede to visit missionary aunts in their lovely home on a hill overlooking the reservoir?

I would have been on the same continent, among friends, rather than living in Arkansas, a state I had never visited, with people I had never met, because my sister was in Arkansas attending college.

*We could not avoid the hit.*

Or could we?

I loved my mother. I coveted her hand. When I was eight, nine, eleven, even twelve, I woke in the night fearful, crazed by the abysses in my dreams. I'd dreamed of the abyss since age two. Was America the abyss? Or Nigeria, moving into civil war? She held me when I woke from those dreams—until I was no longer with her.

---

WE TOOK ONE FAMILY TRIP to Jos in my seventh year, 1961. Traveling up up up the Jos Plateau, red dunes to either side of the car. Did I imagine that? No subsequent research suggests Jos was then a place of red dunes. Rather, it was—until recent conflict and warring turned it into a combat zone—a green zone, the jewel of Nigeria, luxurious destination of ex-pats, including Southern Baptist missionaries. We traveled there once, and other than the red dunes, what I remember most is buying a glass animal, a translucent brown rabbit, at Kingsway. That, and I remember wearing a sweater as we sat outside—perhaps at a café—for breakfast or lunch. And then we were back in the car, heading down hill, away from Hausa land, back back back to Yoruba land: the rising heat, savannah grasses, and then high crowning palms, enormous palms, forested land. Always my father driving, the back of his head the very image of faithfulness. My mother in profile. Our family never had an accident on a Nigerian road. I don't even remember a flat tire. And yet, we could not avoid the hit, the bush dog.

After that trip to Jos, my parents and I moved a far distance from the town where my sister was in boarding school. For the first time in my life, I saw my mother despondent. Until "our" house was ready (missionaries never owned homes; we occupied them—I did not comprehend this reality at the time), we lived in a dark bungalow without our "things," and my mother wrote long letters to my sister, appearing blind to the blond daughter at her shoulder. I took off on my bicycle and rode like mad. Of all the famous sacrifices missionaries make, the one that took down my mother was separation from my sister. And yet, after a few months she recovered her composure. Years later, my sister and I (separately, for she was older and went first) were sent away again—across an ocean. And so we lost sisterhood as well as our mother, again and at intervals.

Our mother's sacrifice was ours. It was the very same. Coming directly at us.

IN THE 1950S there was no bridge as yet across the brown god, River Niger. By the time we arrived at the ferry, from whatever town we had departed, I was already exhausted from the heat and winding roads and fumes pouring from the lorry in front of us. We parked. I stumbled out. We stood beside the car and my parents enjoyed a cup of coffee while my sister and I sipped Kool-Aid. Just about the time my head was clearing and I was sturdy on my legs, it was time to board. Who knows how long it actually took to cross to Onitsha, the famous market town on the other shore, or to unload. There was no bathroom. We never used "public" bathrooms in Nigeria in those days. They didn't exist. Finally we were headed out of town. Grasses and trees and bush reappeared. My father found a place to pull over. Mother and my sister and I headed out to find a suitable spot. Squatting, the release was salvation: warm, yellow urine, its vinegary spoiled egg smell, the splatter of it hitting my legs. On and on it went, a steady stream. I was so grateful then and loved my parents so much because we had survived one more time. All was forgiveness and sweet light as we took off down the road.

Though they always observed rest time after lunch when we were home, my parents in their shades did not require rest in Nigeria when we traveled. Eight hours. Nine hours. We never tried a road trip of more than nine hours in Nigeria. We didn't travel at night, and evening came on in a rush. We left in the morning and arrived by dinnertime. Dinner was always prepared at another missionary family's home. My mother took the pins and rollers out of her hair. I sat up straighter, thinking of the girl my age who would not have been in a car all day and thus would not look like a crumpled mess in shorts and sweaty top. She would have had a bath and put a bow in her hair. My parents, even after all we had been through, could emerge from the car looking lovely and alert while I seemed to slide out, a little drunk, a bit cross, wishing I could retreat into their mutual shadow.

What made my mother so strong? Her father's death? His requirement that she make something of herself? Her love of God? God the Father. Once she told me I reminded her of her father. *Because you are so demanding*, I thought she meant. And it angered me. "No, *you* are like your father," I said.

I DIDN'T MAKE IT in America, where I was sent at age sixteen. I flamed out after a year and a half. My parents came "home" to be with me—and with my sister too, though it was I, not she, who asked them to come. I asked for that sacrifice, and carried the guilt for asking them to leave their mission. Though they had always said, in unison, as they said everything: "You girls are the most important thing to us." But how could I be as important as refugee children in the former Biafra to whom my mother was ministering? I study the pictures now: she squatted in her well-fitting dress before a child, her pocketbook at her side, her eyes on the infant's face, her hand grasping his. Who am I to speak of taking hits?

I admired my mother. Everyone did. On the mission, she was sought out for leadership positions. She preached in the 1950s in Ogbomoso, Nigeria, from the pulpit. In her eighties, she was finally ordained. When she and my father came home to the United States to be with me and stayed five years, she became an academic adviser at a Baptist college in Kentucky. She pursued and received another degree. The valedictorian of her high school class, my mother held degrees in music, nursing, theology, and counseling. I pursued a Ph.D. to best her at last.

---

IN MY LATE FORTIES I published a memoir about my Nigerian girlhood, written during a period of poor health: kidney failure, dialysis, and finally, transplantation. My life with my mother became a subject of study. During the writing and publication I was so enthralled by the journey home that I didn't dwell on the hits. In my mind I dwelt among rivers and my mother's zinnia beds and our beautifully appointed rooms, decorated to look like a picture out of *Southern Living*. I road my bicycle again and forgave her forgetfulness of me or her mantle of aloofness or the thousands of miles between us. But later, in my early fifties, came a time when I felt the full blow of all those shuddering hits. As if I, having lost her so early, going solo in the United States at age sixteen, had delayed my adolescent rebellion.

Why did it take so long? Here I was past fifty and my mother past eighty—how could we possible make it up? Was that what caused me to hit back? The news of mortality, my own and hers? I needled her. "How could you not have known? How could you not have seen, that summer before you sent me back to the U.S. and I lost forty pounds, that I was anorexic?" "But you wrote letters to us from 'Happy USA.'" And I guffawed. "Wasn't that a little over the top?" "You seemed to make friends. We never heard you were unhappy." Or of a later period, I would complain, "Why didn't you come live closer when you retired? I was working on my Ph.D. and had a baby and was working. I needed you." "You think we should have done that?" *Yes, yes yes! But how could you not see—you're a smart woman, a nurse, practiced counselor and adviser— your own daughter.* And I thought—you were so smart about everyone else.

And begrudged her enormously for having had servants as a missionary. And a cook and a gardener and a nursemaid and a housekeeper. It's not all sacrifice. I wanted to hit her.

---

FINALLY, AFTER SEVERAL YEARS of this struggle, this back and forth, she cried. I was cruel. There is no justification. Perhaps understanding. I had never in all my years seen her cry over me, though she must have. But she was guarded.

Mercifully, we had several more years together. We drove to Crabtree Valley Mall in Raleigh, where we shopped to our mutual satisfaction, she picking colorful prints while I selected solid pastels. She was my best friend when it came to shopping, a pattern that had begun long ago in Nigeria, after my sister went to boarding school. We drove to the beach and sat together looking out across the water that once divided, holding our coffee cups. Finally our driving was limited primarily to my picking her up and bringing her to my house, where my husband and I fixed dinner and we sat around the table, the three of us, because my father had died. She spent beautiful Christmases with us, and it felt like home. She napped on our couch. As the Yoruba say, those times were a sweetness in my belly. Sweet as her hand on my back.

These things about my mother:

She loved blue.
When she called me, she always began, "This is your mom."
She was a walker.
When I was young, she homeschooled me for two sweet years,
    the music of rubber tree pods popping across the fence.
She waited for my father to bring her coffee.
She read books.
Others found her charismatic.
She had a following.
I was envious of her power.

My mother died of congestive heart failure. She died of old age. She suffered dementia. That last was a hit we hadn't expected any more than the bush dog—the dementia. My smart mother. How it pained her. Because she knew, even as she pretended not to know, that she could not remember, that when she reported on a story she had read, it was likely something she had overheard and she didn't have her facts straight. Surely she could read her daughters' faces, tell that pieces were missing. She was like a beautiful woman disfigured, looking in the mirror. Her loss of self, devastating. Not just to her but to me. She was gone before she was gone.

In the last year before her death, trips were difficult. On our last journey, six months before she died, she became increasingly confused. "We just passed that store," she said, though we had never passed that store, never been on that stretch of highway. "We were just at this intersection," she might say five minutes later. I stopped correcting her. At night in the motel, she kept asking where we were. "Just remind me why we are here," she said over and over. Out of her natural rhythm, out of her apartment, she was more disoriented than usual. Even with her walker, moving about was difficult. She tired easily.

––––––––––

THE EVENING of the last night she spent in her studio apartment in a retirement home, she had soiled herself. Because she was too weak to stand alone, I entered the shower with her and held her up as I bathed her: her breasts, her back, between her legs. Her skin shone like the petals of the magnolia blossom. I helped her to bed, dried her, and slipped a gown over her head.

Driving to see her one night in the hospital, I saw the crescent moon, hanging low in the sky. I found her sitting upright in bed, waiting as if for an angel. "The most beautiful moon," I said, "in the sky tonight." "You're all the moon I need," she said, reaching for me.

––––––––––

WHEN THE DOG HIT the car my mother didn't lose control. Though it was shattering to watch him, in the heat of the day, heading toward us, anticipating and then feeling the hit through the body of the car, the horrible thud.

Later I would believe my mother's sturdiness was part of the problem between us. She was too strong. Only in the final six years did she lean in, needing me.

I had thought I would outshine my mother. I won't. I no longer wish to.

"How is your writing?" she said in our last visit, all the moon I need.

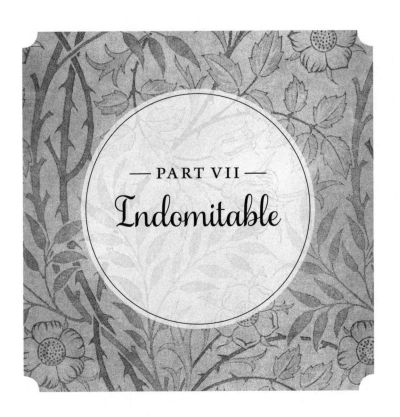

— PART VII —

Indomitable

# One Hundred Years of Letters

— MARGARET W. RICH —

AT THIS WRITING Mama has been dead not quite a year. Until she took her Ultimate Voyage without me, two months shy of her 102nd year, we had traveled many miles together: up and down the South Carolina highways of my childhood, from Caesars Head in the Blue Ridge Mountains to Pawleys Island, and over the dirt roads of my early marriage and across the Atlantic Ocean three times. She stuck by me when my high school grades were so bad I couldn't get into her alma mater with a crowbar—the first domino to fall away from the straight and sure path she had chosen for herself and the path she had hoped I would follow. She hung tough with encouragement ("tough" being the operative word) through that ill-considered young marriage, consequent divorce, single parenthood, and my going back to college in California ten years late. Those were the years I was trying to get away from Mama. Throughout, there are the letters we exchanged—a few fireballs when I didn't hold up my end.

---

AS ADULT CHILDREN DO, I gained an appreciation of that tenacity of devotion Mama was famous for, not just for her family but for her community of friends, too. She never wanted anyone she cared about to feel forgotten. She didn't want to be forgotten either.

In one of our timeworn duets on her porch in Greenville, the rattling of ice cubes the only sound that interrupted the silence that would fall when the subject of eventualities came and went with increasing urgency and decreasing actionable results, she said, "I just can't imagine *not* being here." We laughed at that out-of-the-clear-blue and uncharacteristic existential moment. I guess that's why we laughed. Anyway, it was an effective segue away from my line of thought and back to short-attention-span theater, hopping from one story to the next about people in our past and present, well away from what I thought was urgent: what to do about all the stuff in her house and what was her plan for the future. "Darling, just leave all that alone. You can tend to it when I'm gone. You'll find a lot to laugh about."

She got out of her chair, the spring-steel bouncer, and walked over to the cabinet under the bookcase to get the album she had painstakingly put together in 1980 when she retired from her career as a social worker. At that time, one of her goals had been "to get in a dying condition." I thought that meant she was going to clean out the attic, but that didn't get touched. Instead, she hooked up with a merry bunch who owned a Winnebago and a history professor who led another bunch on tours to Europe. She hit the road. If Daddy didn't like to travel, she did!

However, here in this leather-bound book was evidence that she had tried to sit still and apply her organizational skill to make it possible for somebody else to find the ancestors; in this case, the pictures of all the ancestors from her side of the family. I needed her tutorial because of Great-great-great grandfather, Charles T. Gibson, the Forty-Niner of Gold Rush fame, and all his namesakes down to my brother, named Charles. There was Great-Uncle Charlie, too, from another branch, and his three wives. According to Mama, "Uncle Charlie was a real charmer," *or a lady-killer, maybe.* It was important to her that I know something about the chain of people who had loved her and whom she had loved. My Grandmother Cooper was the only one I had known, and I thought she loved me better than Mama did. The old comedian Sam Levinson explained it this way: "The reason grandparents and grandchildren get along so well is that they have a common enemy."

───────────

WHEN I THOUGHT I knew everything there was to know about Grandma Cooper I found a box under my bed at home filled with Victorian baby clothes and doll clothes for my china dolls from a hundred years of beautiful sewing. I showed Mama three pair of little black kid, high-button shoes in the bottom of the box. She said, "Those must have belonged to Mother's brother and sisters who died." Three out of four children in one family had died of whooping cough or worse before the age of two. No wonder the fierceness of love for the only living child who married a young doctor and moved away from Baltimore to rear her family in the scrub pines of South Carolina. That gave new meaning to all the pictures of Mama as a child, duplicates mailed to Baltimore, and the zero pictures of daddy from his childhood. Hardly anybody in Daddy's family ever moved out of South Carolina or even Pickens County.

At times when mama and I spoke of Grandma Cooper, who died my last year in high school (two months before Kennedy was shot, as it happened), she said, as she also wrote to my friends whose mothers had died: "Your Mother will never leave you"—a comforting thought to me then, because who else could I call at any hour and hear: "I was just thinking about you"?

---

MAMA'S HUNDREDTH birthday party was a sort of last hurrah. On 29 November the Poinsett Club was already decked out for Christmas, and she was ready to celebrate, looking her usual radiant self in a teal blue silk dress, a becoming color with her soft snow-white hair twisted up with silver combs. The final touch was the brown-tipped feather boa she looped around her shoulders with just the right pizzazz. I used exactly the same props this time as for her ninetieth. At ninety who could know there would even *be* a next birthday? And who the hell would remember the decorations? Besides, I was out of ideas.

---

I HAULED IN the door-sized laser reproduction of a sepia photograph of Grandmother Cooper, a Gibson Girl in a long white dress, holding a baby Uncle Charles in her lap and my eighteen-month-old mother standing at her knee. That reproduction leaned up on the mantle. For place cards at five tables for eight I updated her 1936 bathing beauty picture from the Lido, in Venice, a favorite memory of her trip to Europe with her best friends from Agnes Scott College: "I was at Margaret's 100th!" Those leaned on "MCW's Survival Kit," the rerun party favor, a miniature white shopping bag filled with a small gold box of dark chocolate nonpareils and a minibottle of Jack Daniels. Everybody had a good time toasting her and roasting her. "Good Sport" was her middle name. She loved it. After we cut the cake the cast for the Café and Then Some, a satirical theater group led by a former caseworker under Mama's supervision at the Department of Social Services, burst in looking all messed up, ostensibly to petition Mrs. Williams to get their children back from foster care. To heighten the fuss (to the tune of the Tube Rose Snuff jingle, by Arthur Smith's Cracker Jacks) they sang:

I'm a twiddly twat from Agnes Scott and I go with a boy from Tech.
He took me to the Varsity and taught me how to neck.
He filled me up with whiskey. He filled me up with beer.
And now I am the mother of a ten pound engineer.

I lit a fire under the bartender to keep an eye on Mama's Bloody Mary because the last time I had to run my legs off to keep her glass topped up.

IT WAS DOWNHILL FROM THERE.

Efforts to make it possible for her to stay in her own home were thwarted by the real danger of her falling up or down the ten brick steps to her front door, or she could go out in a flaming wreck driving on Augusta Road. Also a problem were the mysterious disappearances of some of her favorite things, February ice storms, and her habit of firing the round-the-clock help after the latest fall. I couldn't keep driving 250 miles to Greenville and 250 miles back to Chapel Hill, every two weeks. None of the above was a problem for her. She had a gunslinger's determination to play her hand the way she saw fit and was going to gamble that she would just drop dead and only have to leave her house once, feet first. Her doctor told me it was time for me to assume the parental role. Who would tell Mama about this role reversal?

IT IS PAINFUL TO ADMIT I thought about her "never leaving" differently in the last year and a half of this part of our journey, when she reluctantly came to live with my husband, James, and me in Chapel Hill. She was finally persuaded, after a fall, that this would be her best option, at least until her "transportation"—her walking—improved. For safekeeping I packed up the family silver, her jewelry, and the boxes of family information to bring with us and promised to leave everything else exactly as it was at her house.

In a month or two she recovered from her fall and got a trainer, twice a week, at the Meadowmont gym. She was highly motivated to maintain her ability to walk so she could travel back to Greenville often to visit her friends and her house.

CONSIDERING THAT MAMA wouldn't be caught dead in gym clothes or take off her orange leather sandals, it was interesting to watch her with my husband's trainer, a highly credentialed physical therapist with short, spiked purple hair and tattoos up one side and down the other and who specialized in difficult cases. Mama shows up at the gym pushing her red walker with hot pink, leopard-spotted pockets; wearing gold and beaded bracelets up to her elbows, earrings, Revlon's "Cherries in the Snow" red lipstick, perfume (who pays any attention to fragrance-free zones), and ironed, colorful, pastel linen blouses and slacks, along with her Hillary pin, maybe a scarf and/or a sweater draped around her shoulders. I'm beside her carrying her sizable Italian leather pocketbook that must go with her from workout station to workout station. Neither one of them blinked. It would not be long before Mary Hale-McDonald had unfrozen Mama's shoulder and talked her out of the sandals. After years of my trying to get Mama to wear more supportive shoes, Mary ordered some neon-pink Nikes, to match her walker, which suited Mama just fine. On our next visit to Greenville a lawyer at her lunch place said: "When you're finished with those shoes, I want 'em."

---

MAMA REMAINED in complete charge of her mental and physical self, her finances, her correspondence, and me. If she had slowed down, she hadn't abbreviated anything. Her ablutions took forever, but she "made the effort," everyday, to put herself together in bandbox order to come to the table for meals and to be ready to receive visitors or go somewhere. The smart money was on the likelihood that Mama would live to be 110. I wondered if she would outlive me. So did my friends.

---

HER ROOM AT MY HOUSE was familiar to her and the most cheerful room in the house. From the start we called the downstairs bedroom "Mama's room" because she would be its most frequent guest. The red and white wallpaper is an old pattern of rose and foliage tracery (there is enough white background in the wallpaper so it's not as frightening as I thought it was going to be when that first roll went up). To amplify the sunlight, a large mirror is hung over the bureau across from a double window with lace curtains. Scattered on the bureau are pictures of three generations of us wearing the wedding veil Mama bought in Venice for her Hope Chest, before she even met my father: Mama wore it; I wore it; my daughter, Mary, wore it. Her engagement picture is on the wall across from her bed, a 1940s vintage photograph of her in a white organza evening dress with a wide band of black lace at the waist. She looks very sophisticated and dead serious.

Another picture on the wall is of Mama in the May Court at Agnes Scott the year she graduated, 1936. Naomi, her cousin and roommate all four years, was the May Queen in all white, of course, and a dozen attendants flanked Naomi at a reflecting pool to double the effect. The picture is in sepia tones, but Mama told me of the brilliant colors of their full-length chiffon costumes, with a simple long rectangle of chiffon, in a darker color, tied at the corners around their shoulders. The combination of colors were chartreuse and purple, yellow and orange, rose pink and blue . . . she couldn't remember the rest, but all different. Another photograph hung with that one is of Mama as a bridesmaid in Mackey

Crisler's wedding. When I was a little girl looking at that picture in Mama's room, I thought I would have a wedding like that. I liked the bouquets of Rubrum lilies that cascaded down to the bridesmaids' toes and Mackey's bouquet of lily of the valley. Mackey was another Agnes Scott friend on that European trip. Likely the one who snapped the picture we used at the birthday party. It's good to have pictures like that around, not just to make Mama feel at home but for new friends and the people who helped take care of Mama. Through the pictures they can meet her in the context of her whole life.

Mama settled into a routine here in the midst of a swirl of helpers in and out with mixed reviews. My friends whom she had come to know over the years dropped in to see her. Her friends wrote often. The postman was impressed with the increased volume of letters to and from Rosemary Street, and if he saw a straggling letter in the mail slot after his first pass to pick up her mail he picked it up on his way back by the house. Everybody coming from Greenville to Durham for a Duke basketball game or to Chapel Hill or Raleigh for any reason came by to see her. The Ham House, where her lunch crowd gathers in Greenville—her laughing place—sent a cooler with some of her favorite food by someone coming this way.

I realized, though, that no matter how acceptable I thought her accommodations were here, and how well she seemed to be adjusting at my house, she might feel isolated. I let my friend Bill Ferris know that I had a hundred-year-old woman over here if he had a student that might want to take an oral history. He immediately sent over one of his top graduate students from the Center for the Study of the American South. Mama wasn't thrilled because it was an effort to meet a stranger, but she went along with it that one time. When the student left, Mama said, "Can you believe it? That girl had never heard of May Day."

---

OUR ROLES NEVER REVERSED. My role expanded from personal shopper to secretary, cook, chauffeur, and laundress. I have my limitations in the day-to-dayness of the domestic sphere, but I have always loved making up beds and ironing the pretty old linens I got to use every day for Mama's place at the table. And I loved fixing Mama's flowers. I never went to her house without seeing the flower arrangements she made for the secretary in the living room and the dining room table. My whole life she put a flower in my old room when I came home. One of her trademarks she will be remembered for are the fresh camellias she wore to church. "Just because," I kept Mama covered up with flowers in her room and at her place in the kitchen. She liked the catbird's seat at the end of the kitchen island, the clerk's chair, a tall chair, padded for comfort, with a footrest. Sometimes a dozen single flowers in mixed up bud vases were right there at her place for her to enjoy in detail. Camellias were in bloom in midwinter when she arrived, followed by peonies, lilies of the valley, hydrangeas, magnolias, and gardenias. To fill in the blanks from my garden there are always beautiful oriental lilies from Whole Foods, just around the corner. She liked a pink poinsettia at Christmas.

She kept up her maternal duties at my house by reminding me of things she thought I ought to know. By now. "Darling, be careful not to wash that cutglass vase in hot water. It can easily shatter. . . . The dresser scarf would look prettier if you ironed it on the wrong side. It pops out the embroidery." She was right. "Those strawberries might taste better with a little more sugar. . . . You better put the date on that picture . . . and be sure to write in that book the name of the person who gave it to you." As she checked out the obits she kept up with in her subscriptions to the *State Paper*, from Columbia, and the *Greenville News*, she continued the short course for me about the fine points of writing a good sympathy note: "You can't really say 'I know how you feel,' if you haven't experienced it. Keep it short. Do it now." She had acquired some opinions in a hundred years. She was sort of amused by the well-meaning sentiment: "I'm sorry you lost so-and-so." To her: "People die. They don't get lost. I know where all my people are."

———————

I GUESS I KNOW where Mama thought she was going. If Mama knew for sure, where would Faith be? She had that Faith, and roughly, she thought she was going "to join that innumerable caravan . . . beyond sunset and evening star." In her condolence notes she often cobbled together those lines from both Tennyson and William Cullen Bryant. Mama had lived so long she also thought her friends who were waiting for her out there might be "thinking she went the other way." At her funeral at Westminster Presbyterian Church, her minister of some thirty years said he was sure "there would be a happy hour in heaven when those friends and she were reunited." In life everybody was glad to see Mama. Usually it involved a glass of Early Times and Coke. "Not much Coke."

———————

I WOULD HAVE TO return to those stacks of letters on her desk, squeezed into drawers and empty shoe boxes—many stuck around, singly, inside books and folders marked with one thing that *was* in the folder and fifty unrelated things that had nothing to do with the label. Mama had muscle memory of where things were, but the power center of her retrieval system was no help now. The conventional wisdom of some who had been through the breaking up of a household was to get a dumpster and start throwing all that paper in the trash. I couldn't do it.

Overwhelmed at the enormity of the task at hand, I was at the same time comforted and at times amused, as Mama said I would be, by the thousands of artifacts of her life that I must tend to and keep, lest she come back to haunt me. One note floated to the surface in Grandma Cooper's handwriting: "Broken switch. Might be good in an emergency." The switch in our gene pool was stuck on "keep it." I am a marked woman.

Furniture is the least of what there is, a good cherry secretary from Grandmother Cooper's home in Baltimore, the one piece of furniture Grandma had hoped would stay in the family. Forever. There are two handsome double beds (standard sheets are impossible to find anymore), several dainty chairs and small tables with pressed glass knobs—the big things like that have been meticulously listed and divided between my brother and me. I was going around in circles scratching the surface and finding things I had forgotten or had never known were there—some untouched, like the box of baby clothes under my bed, since they came to Greenville from Grandma's house in Columbia; seven 4-½ cent stamps, a handful of silver dollars, Daddy's waffle iron with the fat black-and-white speckled cloth cord, the front page of the *Baltimore Sun* about the Great Fire of 1904 (Grandma was twenty-two at the time), which makes sense of the way she almost insisted that the smokers in the family sit by a wet bucket of sand; and pictures of four Kendrick ancestors who fought in the Battle of Kings Mountain.

I had to have a system to organize all Mama's belongings. A song from "Sesame Street" came to mind: "One of these things is not like the other..." Categories! I needed to put things in categories.

The first thing was to get my brother, Charles, to come and take the things Mama wanted him to have. Without the dining room table, the place where Mama spread out her resources, there was operating room in the house on card tables and the floor. Unloading the art deco desk in her bedroom was a revelation of letters piled three feet high on top, crammed into its recesses, and bundled neatly with rubber bands about to break: letters to and from Daddy before they were married, some from a few also-rans, every check register and pay stub from her first job in Pickens, and every letter I had written to her since I went away to camp. As tempting as it was, I could not stop to read a one of these letters or I would fall into a black hole.

I packed my car to screaming-at-the-gills with the Letters category to sort through in Chapel Hill and turned my attention to the garage, attached to the basement. It would be good to get the most dreaded job out of the way before the venerable black snake that lived in there woke up from hibernation. Besides, I had the offer of a friend who would come with his pickup truck to take the port-a-crib and whatever else away. *Mama, why on Earth did you keep all those glass jars, bundles of newspaper, and old rugs?* She had her reasons. I was not laughing while three men and I hauled all that into the driveway.

The last thing I came to was a rectangular cube Mama had wrapped in plastic. After a concerted effort to undo what she had put her mind to *doing*, I could see that she had saved the blue cardboard trunk with all my letters and papers from the seventies. I thought these papers were lost somewhere, perhaps in the morass of my attic. Now these details of my life in California might help me finish the hardest part of the book I had put on hold. "Thank you Mama!" For the past five years I had blamed Mama for the necessity to put my work in the drawer, when it was just as likely that I was afraid I couldn't finish the book and I used taking care of Mama as my excuse.

At the sight of that carefully wrapped job of all I needed, I remembered a moment when the gloves came off between us. We were driving back from lunch at the Ham House through Cleveland Park, touching on the ongoing and going nowhere discussion about her plans. I wanted to help her stay in her house for as long as possible by coming home often, but the what-ifs of all the things that could happen to her, any minute, were gaining in my imagination, a real list of possibilities, none too good. She didn't really want to come live with me, but she would not fill out the paperwork to save a place at the Presbyterian Home—the only place like that she would consider. I mentioned that I really wanted to be able to work on my book and that I needed the peace of mind about her well-being and stretches of uninterrupted time. "Well," she said, "if you can't finish your book, don't blame me." Did she say that? I couldn't believe she said that. But the moment she said it I knew she was right. For a writer anything can become a shiny object of distraction, and Mama was the shiniest. It seemed to me, now, that what I may have lost had been given back to me.

---

IN THE MONTHS BETWEEN trips back to Greenville I have got the letters from everybody in chronological order, each page and envelope in its own plastic sleeve, the sleeves in three-inch binders. I'm up to twelve binders now.

I am grateful that Mama had some method to her collecting and keeping. The letters were in decent and even thematic order. Cards and letters she received when I was born were in a box marked "MODERN-MOTHER, Nursing Brassiere"; the letters she exchanged on her trip to Europe in 1936 were in a cookie tin with a ship's life preserver embossed on the top: "CONFECTION-ERY IZUMIYA," maybe a gift from Otska, her Japanese friend, whom she corresponded with for decades.

Over these months, as I got the bulk of the letters in binders, I began to feel the reward of all my tedious work. I had had to read a few letters in the process because, when the stamps fell off the envelopes, there went the postmark—the contents would be the only clue to their place in the unfolding story. I eased up on the lid I had put on my curiosity. Now, I could easily find out the sequence of events and confirmation, perhaps, of what I already knew. Certainly, I would not find anything that would raise eyebrows because Mama would "never put anything in a letter that she would mind seeing on the front page of the newspaper." However, in the process of merely handling the letters it was hard to miss the many instances of "Braxton dearest" and "My Darling Margaret" between Mama and Daddy—I never heard any of that when I was around. They could always make each other laugh, but the atmosphere at home could get adversarial in spells. I wanted my parents to make love, not war. Now I could go back and find what had to have been there in the beginning.

If Daddy had a past with other women, I didn't hear about it, except once, when Bob Ariail's mother told me Daddy was a great dancer. *Daddy could dance?* However, it's on record in these letters, if anyone would ever have doubted it, that Mama could keep a few balls in the air.

Daddy was fun, though, and I think he, in particular, caught Mama's eye from the minute she hit town in Pickens for her first job. Pickens was Daddy's stomping grounds, having grown up on a cotton farm in Pickens County. Immediately, the new girl in town had been adopted into the popular crowd, and as the story goes, she and Daddy soon met at a party at Sue McFall's house. The next day Daddy called on her at Mrs. Craig's house, where she had a room:

Mrs. Craig: "Margaret, Braxton Williams is here to see you,
   downstairs."
Mama: "Braxton? Where's Sue?"
Daddy: "Well, Sue's not here."

Although they were not dating seriously for a while, Daddy liked her well enough to write from Atlanta, where he had a good job, and well enough to let her charm him into using his considerable drafting skill to make posters for the county fair, advertising the services of her position at the Department of Public Welfare. In Mama's letter to thank him for his efforts, while he was slaving over his drawing board and taking engineering courses at Georgia Tech, she also told him of all the fun she was having at this poker party (how much she won), at that dance at Clemson, and that house party in Highlands. And with whom she was having it.

> Braxton, I'm just delighted that you found your job was still waiting when you arrived in Atlanta! I know you were quite surprised to find that you still had one—do you still have it? I'm just kidding—and, if there is any doubt about your capabilities as an architect, you know that you have a talent in another line and you could easily get a job making posters for "The Government"!! I personally will recommend you.

In October of 1938 Mama was off to the University of Chicago, courtesy of FDR. She took a leave of absence from her job in Pickens to do graduate work at the School of Social Work. She arrived by train in Chicago at the Windermere Hotel, and her first order of business was to get a room off campus because student housing was not available. Two days later, on 3 October, she sent Daddy a postcard—a little hand-colored print of the Holy Name Cathedral with one tiny red Ford Model A parked beside it—addressed to his new digs on Peachtree Street.

> Already so homesick I don't know what to do.... Have to be here 'til Christmas.... The Univ. is so huge I'm 'fraid I'll never find my way around.... Please write me c/o Mrs. Newton Davis, 5716 Kenwood Ave., Chicago.

Now, all the way off in Chicago, I think she was a little bit worried about Daddy, a young architect "with his newly acquired tails, and all those debutantes floating around Atlanta." (The only action those tails got in Atlanta, that I know of, is that they went to the premier of *Gone with the Wind*, 15 December 1939, on a friend of his, alongside a group of Confederate veterans who were guests of honor.)

By the end of October she wrote again, to the strains of "Home Sweet Home" by Abe Lyman's Orchestra signing off the radio:

> I have become quite a hiker ... having difficulty keeping north, south, east, and west in their proper places. Haven't gotten lost yet. In Pickens, you know, one goes by stores, mail boxes, creeks, etc!

She had found a "fellow sufferer" from Kentucky, Laura Berry, who didn't like it there either.

> The rude way streetcar conductors pulled you on and pushed you off ... she was the only person I've found so far who takes things the way I

do—you know, trying to see the funny side. But, instead, here all the students just *search* for the serious and intellectual! I guess I really should be inspired but I'm not in the least—no ambition, I know is the reason.

The letter to Daddy continues to tell him how her day went as she and Laura

hiked together through a sort of second class neighborhood to have supper . . . just so we could get in a few sours—so good. . . . The Windy City has so much to offer in the way of entertainment but, so far, my recreation has been very, very limited—in fact, almost entirely to a few good shows, taken in on Sundays, and visits to some of the bars—don't misunderstand me—I'm not a regular barfly but the whiskey sours, such an innocent looking drink, are mighty fine and especially so after a hard day.

Mama always did have a hollow leg. And she could hold it.

By November 1939, Mama would be back to her old life in South Carolina, thesis in hand. Daddy would be moving home from Atlanta to work with Mr. McPherson at J. E. Sirrine's, an architectural and engineering firm in Greenville, about thirty miles from Pickens.

Pearl Harbor, 7 December 1941, got everybody's attention. It clarified Mama and Daddy's thinking about whether to get married or not. They did: 13 April 1942.

Daddy sold his car to buy Mama's ring and had the good sense to let her pick it out, if she was going to wear it for the rest of her life. Their engagement was announced in February. In March Mama joined the Red Cross and was addressing letters to 2nd Lt. Braxton H. Williams, 4th Regiment, 14th Battalion, Camp Wheeler, Georgia. Not only was everything about the "job" of planning a wedding complicated by gasoline shortages, tire shortages, and logistics of friends being stationed in different places with limited and uncertain leave, but ten days before the wedding Daddy was in the infirmary with a fever, near pneumonia, and bleeding from his sinuses. His bad sinuses and chronic bronchitis had been a problem since childhood and would be a problem for the rest of his life. "You can count on me," was Mama's response. Before he got sick and "on the funny side," after one of his leaves to visit Mama in Columbia, Mama wrote to Daddy:

I am returning your gold bars I found in my car. The catch must be broken. I can't think of any other reason this could happen. Can you?

---

MARGARET RICH

AS IT TURNED OUT everybody could depend on Mama for all our lives. Even Hillary. A lifelong Democrat, Mama had her absentee ballot ready to go—in North Carolina, too, where it might have done some good. When Mama died in September, I had a serious moral dilemma about not sending it in anyway. God, I wanted to. Imagine thinking of that in the midst of planning a funeral.

Looking over some of the e-mails I sent while I was taking care of Mama, I found one to Sara Foster, who was also caring for her mother, who had come to the Cedars Retirement Home to be near her. We were both always looking for some good helpers for our darling, sparkling mothers.

> This time of life with our mothers is such a soup with every possible emotional ingredient—love, of course, admiration, anger (in my case)—I get so frustrated with how it is she can make seemingly EVERYTHING 10X harder than it has to be. I'm sure I'll be able to add guilt to the recipe before it's over. The thought I am having now is: "She might outlive me."

In all these letters of Mama's I see the seasons of life played out in the spates of gifts you buy and the letters you write. If you live long enough these seasons of community and connectivity start over and over. It is helpful to have that template of experience with a parent—you get to see what's reasonable to expect, or *what* to expect and something of what kind of attitude you will need to cope with the ravages of time. Mama wasn't a saint. I'm not a saint. But who loves a saint? I think it is safe to say that it is good if you can endure to the end of a long life, but it is better if you can do it with a little style. It costs nothing, and it is so appreciated.

# A Mother and Son Reunion

## — STEVEN PETROW —

CONFESSION: I've always hated Mother's Day, with its saccharine cards and marked up flower arrangements that oversimplify a complicated relationship. My antipathy toward this most contrived of celebrations only deepened when I joined Facebook in the spring of 2009. Within a few weeks came the mother of all holidays, and by Saturday night, before the day had even arrived, my Facebook news feed had been hijacked by public displays of affection.

Oh, the boundless devotion my friends put on display: "Mom, I love you so much!" (Really? Your mother's not even on Facebook and you're making a spectacle out of your emotions.) Their public memes: "Did you ever realize that Mom spelled upside down is Wow?" (No, in fact, I hadn't, but I did know that "dog" is "god" spelled backward. Good enough?) I quickly found myself hating my friends and their mothers—so much so that I copied and saved much of what they posted to make sure I never forgot.

Okay, so maybe I didn't exactly hate them. Perhaps envy is closer to the truth.

For starters, I didn't have any kind of classic TV mom: Not June Cleaver. Not Carol Brady. Not even Marge Simpson. My mom, then in her seventies, was a bundle of contradictions, coming of age in the netherworld between Mamie Eisenhower and Betty Friedan. For years Friedan's *Feminine Mystique* lay on Mom's bedside table, a silent warning to our father and her three kids: don't tread on me. I can still recall one passage she had marked: "Each suburban wife struggles with it alone. As she made the beds, shopped for groceries, matched slipcover material, ate peanut butter sandwiches with her children, chauffeured Cub Scouts and Brownies, lay beside her husband at night—she was afraid to ask even of herself the silent question—'Is this all?'"

Did this description apply to my mom? Let me just answer it this way: I was a Cub Scout.

My mother's feminism was both culinary and political, with the two often intertwined. Other moms in our predominantly Jewish neighborhood cooked from scratch; we subsisted on a diet that included Rice-A-Roni ("the San Francisco treat") and Pillsbury cinnamon rolls (the kind that came ready to bake, in a cardboard canister). Mom's nom de cuisine was Shake 'n Bake because she—and we—loved Kraft's wildly popular "bread-crumb-style coating for chicken." My sister, brother, and I sang along to the ad jingle ("Why fry? Shake 'n bake!"), as did our friends, who I'm sure secretly envied my mother's "modern" cuisine. Given the choice, what kid wouldn't choose Shake 'n Bake chicken, tater tots, and Le Sueur ("premium canned") peas over brisket and kasha?

Her name itself was the perfect emblem of how she navigated the changing conventions. She was "Mrs. Margot Petrow"—neither "Ms." nor "Mrs. Richard Petrow." After she died, I found piles of her old Crane's stationery with that moniker. I had a matching set emblazoned with my precollege name, "Steve Petrow." Not Steven. Two Le Sueur peas in a pod.

Channeling her inner Friedan, Mom went back to school when I was about thirteen—and she just under forty—to earn a master's in social work and then hung out her own psychotherapy shingle. After Nixon's reelection she declared herself "Another Mother for Peace," and in January 1973 she took me to the anti-Vietnam counter-inaugural in Washington, D.C. "Isn't this exciting?" she commented as we exited the bus and got lost in a crowd of a hundred thousand protestors. The "brisket and kasha" moms all stayed home.

By the mid-1970s, Mom had updated her stationery: it now proudly read, "Margot S. Petrow, MSW," with the acronym standing for her master's in social work. Replacing "Mrs." with "MSW" wasn't so much a repudiation of her marriage as an embrace of her new identity.

If anything about Mom was conventional, however, it was the smoking. Like many of her generation—she was born during the Depression—Mom smoked insistently and persistently. She took her first puffs as a young teen and kept up the habit for seventy years. As a kid I was sure she was trying to either asphyxiate us or give us cancer when she lit up cigarette after cigarette in our family's hermetically sealed Ford Country Squire (with its requisite woody panels). All of us kids hated it, and we tried over and over to get her to quit. "Mom!" we protested. "We can't breathe." "You're going to give us cancer." She made numerous attempts: patches, acupuncture, and gum, even hypnosis by a Russian. She did manage to quit a few times, but soon after each "success" I would smell the tar back on her breath or see the burnt-out butts in a poorly obscured ashtray.

Our entreaties went on for decades, and Mom was no more receptive to them as she got older. I remember when she was in her late seventies I begged her, yet again, to stop, and she replied rat-a-tat-tat: "I very much appreciate your concern—but f*ck off."

So it was ironic, to say the least, that I was the one diagnosed with cancer at age twenty-six. My mom was nearly as devastated as I was, but her pain was mixed with self-recrimination. It wasn't about her Kool habit, but about DES. Like other moms in the sixties, she'd taken it to reduce the risk of miscarriage (which was news to me). DES had already been shown to cause a rare form of vaginal and cervical cancer in daughters of women who'd taken it; cancer of the testes in their sons was then suspected. (Subsequent research has not shown a definitive link.)

After the orchiectomy, a procedure to remove the malignant testicle, my California surgeon told me I was "free and clear" and then explained to my mother: "I've never lost a patient." I was overjoyed, but to my mother he might as well have said he was a serial killer because she raised her voice, hitting back at him hard: "How can you be a cancer doctor and have never had a patient die? That's not possible!"

She insisted I get a second opinion, even though I was happy to accept the first doctor's good news without question. I finally caved to her endless haranguing and flew twenty-five hundred miles to Memorial Sloan Kettering Cancer Center in New York. Mom was there by my side when that surgeon explained—taking us completely by surprise—that I had metastatic cancer and needed additional surgery and chemotherapy. Chalk one up for my authority-questioning, rule-breaking mama bear. I asked the Memorial surgeon what would happen if the first doctor was right, and if I went with his easy-to-swallow conclusion over the second opinion? With no hesitation, he replied: "If you follow the other doctor's advice and he's wrong, you'll be dead. If you follow mine and I'm wrong, you'll have had an unnecessary surgery."

I had the eight-hour operation. A dozen malignant lymph nodes were removed. Mom took no pleasure in this outcome, but we all knew that if it hadn't been for her persistence I probably would have died.

Fast forward three decades. Now eighty, Mom had wound up in the ER with her carotid artery 90 percent blocked. She needed surgery, stat. A routine pre-op chest X-ray revealed a mass that turned out to be lung cancer. "Did my smoking have anything to do with this?" she asked the handsome lung surgeon, almost flirtatiously. "Yes," he replied without sarcasm. "Then I'll quit," she told him. And that, finally, made her stop.

The diagnosis was completely predictable in light of her two-pack-a-day habit. Still, I was angry with her—for being so sick and for having brought it on herself. It also scared me that Mom had to face cancer—especially lung cancer, with its rocky road and lousy outcomes.

A few weeks later "Dr. Handsome" took out part of her left lung at the same cancer hospital where I'd had my surgery decades earlier. Anticipating PTSD-like flashbacks, I had taken all the necessary precautions. I went to the hospital supported by several preparatory shrink visits, a new Xanax prescription, and the "4–7–8 breathing technique" to take the wind out of panic attacks. I knew it would be tough to be back on the cancer ward, even if I weren't the patient this time.

I was right about that.

But during Mom's hospitalization something unexpected, magical, and indeed life changing happened to both of us. We exchanged our lifelong roles: I became her caregiver and advocate, and she became my charge.

The lobectomy had left Mom weak and in pain, barely able to speak. I became her voice. When the aides were busy elsewhere, I was the one who made sure her bedpan got changed. When she needed more meds, I made sure the nurses contacted the surgeon. Just as important—maybe even more important—I made sure Mom's daily milkshake was chocolate, not vanilla.

My own stays in a hospital had taught me a few things about how to get the most from the hospital staff, and I was glad to be able to use that experience to help her when she needed it most. One afternoon the nurses couldn't get an IV inserted, pricking her time after time, and it pained me to hear her cry out and to see her grimace as they repeatedly stabbed her. I'd been through this nightmare, since like Mom I have delicate veins—veins that aren't easy for phlebotomists to reach. I explained how they must do it: Palpate the area. Warm it with a wet cloth to get the vein to pop. Insert needle. Then draw.

I had firsthand knowledge of what it meant to suddenly become a cancer patient, temporarily dependent on the kindness of strangers and family alike. "The way I finally accepted help," I told her, "was to realize that it would allow me to get better, faster." That made sense to Mom, who began to let go.

I also knew what it was like to face the possibility that your book of life may be coming to an end sooner than later. We talked about all that together. And we drew nearer and dearer. I realized I'd become her travel guide in this new country of illness.

Some days I just held her hand, her Jungle Red manicure always perfect, and let her talk. About my father. Her parents. And herself. Other times she'd ask me questions: "Was it like this for you, too?" "Were you afraid?" Increasingly, she asked me about my illness, making me into more of a hero than I'd ever been. "I can't believe you went through all this," she said time and again. Of course, there was no real comparison: she was now eighty, and I'd been twenty-six. Her prognosis: terminal. Mine: good odds for a long, if not happy, life.

Mom recovered from the surgery only to step directly into another twilight zone I knew too well: the "after" cancer stage, during which you struggle to believe it's over, all the while dreading its return.

During that interregnum, I continued to share with her what I'd learned along the way: Wait to worry, which translates to, don't freak out with every ache and pain. Do your research—or let me do it—and hold onto it. Ask for the support you need. Make up your own mind. Oh, and don't schedule appointments—especially for a blood draw, scan, or other diagnostic procedure—late in the week or before a holiday, when results take longer to get. Why draw out the anxiety of the unknown any longer than necessary?

But most important: live your life. "What's most important to you now, Mom?" I queried. Her reflexive and honest answer: spending time with her kids and grandkids, eating lots of chocolate ice cream and coffee cake, and watching political coverage on MSNBC in the run-up to the 2016 election. She'd never lost the fire in her belly when it came to politics, and what she had to say about Donald Trump can't be repeated here.

When I learned that Mom's semiannual CT had been set for Christmas week, I moved it to mid-January, following my own scheduling rule. I was especially glad I'd done that when the scan showed a new mass. My brother, sister, and I broke the news to her, assuring her we'd be there to help with the important decisions soon upon her. The very first one we faced: to have radiation or not. Dr. Handsome, the surgeon, didn't advocate for it, saying he didn't think it would increase the time she had left.

With our roles fully reversed, I now insisted Mom get a second opinion. After all, I reasoned, there's longevity and then there's quality of life. We met with a radiation oncologist, who agreed that the fifteen-day radiation regimen wouldn't give her more time, but it would erode the new tumor that would soon be pushing against Mom's trachea. Left untreated, the tumor could soon make it difficult for her to breathe. We did not want her gasping for air.

Mom wanted me to tell her what to do, which is precisely what she had done when she had stepped into the role as my advocate. I told her everything I knew but then—in a twist—explained this was her life, her decision. "Would it hurt?" she asked the radiation oncologist in one of her few direct queries. His reply, "No," but that her skin might feel like it was burning. I looked him in the eye much as Mom had with my first surgeon and said: "In other words, you mean 'yes.'" He nodded in agreement.

She completed twelve days of radiation before succumbing to fatigue, the constant burning sensation, and, I think, a sense that her fate had arrived.

One afternoon during the second week of treatment, I was taking Mom home in an Uber when I felt her grasp my hand tightly, telling me in no uncertain terms how glad she was that I was with her. I said that I felt the same way. She squeezed my hand again, her manicure perfect even though the rest of her wasn't, and I squeezed back. At that moment, Mom realized the Uber driver had taken the wrong exit off FDR Drive and she let him have it, full force. "Why are you getting off here?" She demanded, thinking he was trying to boost the fare, which only happens in taxis not Ubers.

That's when I realized that I did have a classic TV mother after all. Her liberal politics, the refusal to take flak from anyone, the habit of calling it as she sees it, no matter what—it's all there. She wasn't Laura Petrie, or even Carmela Soprano. She was more like "that old compromisin', enterprisin', anything but tranquilizin'" giant of 1970s sitcoms, Maude.

At Mom's memorial service a few months ago, my father and my siblings and I had the opportunity to talk about her, how first my cancer and then hers had changed our lives, and how complicated it all can be. It's not something that condenses easily into a Facebook meme, any more than it once did into a greeting card. I'm starting to get over my hatred of Mother's Day, and this year I even posted a photo of her nine months pregnant with me. She's exuberant—and as big as a house. I can almost hear her throaty laughter. A few weeks ago I found some old episodes of *Maude* on YouTube, and they made me laugh out loud as I recognized the brash, no-holds-barred style that was my mother's hallmark.

Her last coherent words before she became unresponsive: "Donations to Planned Parenthood, please!"

Right on, Mom!

# The Last Word

## — BLAND SIMPSON —

WE WERE RETURNING to Kitty Hawk from Ocracoke Island in our ivory Chevrolet station wagon one dark summer evening in the early 1960s—my kerchiefed mother driving, my younger sisters (eight and nine) in the back, and I (fourteen) in the passenger seat. A long day trip: ninety miles of the rippling coastal highway N.C. 12 and two ferry rides across ocean inlets each way.

Somewhere along about Frisco, between Hatteras village and the great Cape itself, without much warning she pulled into the parking lot of a small gift shop, and then we tired children traipsed inside with her to look at whelks and sand dollars and scented soaps. We bought nothing and did not linger, but on the way out the door, my mother said something offhand to the woman whose shop it was, how nice it smelled in there.

"Why, thank you!" the shop mistress said with enthusiasm, adding: "Here, I'll get you something really smells good!" And she followed us outside, quickly picking a half a dozen gardenia blossoms and giving one to my mother, one to me, a couple to each of my sisters.

"Thank *you!*" Mama said. "They smell *so good!*"

The Chevy filled immediately with the sensuous, even cloyingly sweet scent of the gardenias, and away up N.C. 12 we went. Just as soon as we rounded the first bend and were out of sight of the gift shop, my mother fairly shouted:

"Throw those damn flowers out of this car, now, *now!*"

"But you said they smelled good," one of the girls started in.

"Roll down your windows and *throw 'em out!*"

"But she was so nice!" said the other. "She *gave* them to us."

"Do you want me to *stop this car? NOW!*"

There was no negotiation. Our mother had spoken, and there was an end to it. Gift or not, the flowers had to go, so we desultorily, dutifully rolled down our windows and pitched them out against the breeze, for half a moment channeling, way out on this celebrated sandbar in the Atlantic, a little bit Steinbeck's

*Chrysanthemums.* Our mother always liked to have the last word, some pronouncement that lay beyond questioning or *any* sort of further comment, like something she might have heard Bette Davis say in an old black-and-white film just before turning on her heel and disappearing from a room. After a few more seconds, here it came:

"I hate gardenias," she said triumphantly. "They remind me of *funerals!*"

---

THOUGH DIFFERENCES between us in coming years would take on far more substantial subjects than those flowers that night, far more intractable and bitter, among them race, the war, and choice of career, the moments my mind turns to most often in this first decade since my mother's death at ninety tend to be ones of bemusement and odd comedy, as if one beneficent function of grief in memory is to steer the heart away from the grim and toward the light.

This clearly does not mean the heaviest of moments did not occur, simply that there may be a form of mortal danger in dwelling upon them. As Sir Walter Raleigh himself observed, obsessing on sorrows does not pull the dead back toward the living but, rather, pulls the living toward the dead.

---

IN THE FALL OF 1997, I gave my mother a copy of my wife Ann's and my first book about eastern North Carolina, and early that evening she called, as I expected her to do once she had leafed through it and seen, I trusted, that it was dedicated to our parents.

When I answered the telephone, she said briskly: "I'm not speaking to you."

"Well, you just did," I said. "And why not?"

"I'm not speaking to you because anything I say, you might put it in a book."

"That's right," I said. "I just might."

"I can't believe you made up that story about Daddy and put it right in the middle of your book. I'm not speaking to you."

"There are quite a few stories about Granddaddy in there, Mama—which one are you talking about?"

"Oh, you know very well which one," she said.

"Could you help me out a little bit?"

"You know: where he rode a horse to a river and . . . all that mess!"

So now it came to light. My mother had just happened to open the brand-new book to the precise page where lay the naughtiest (if one could really even call it that) tale my grandfather, a terrific storyteller, had ever told me. He had been a master builder, had directed during the 1920s and early 1930s the construction of many of the University of North Carolina's grand edifices, Kenan Stadium, the Bell Tower, and Wilson Library among them. Well before that, though, during the nineteen-aughts, he had been a journeyman builder, in charge of renovating and fireproofing old eastern Carolina courthouses, building small jails in such places as Manteo and Columbia.

When he arrived in a small county seat for his next project, he would quickly get to know the town fathers and mothers, as they were the most interested parties in the new construction, the ones who had willed it so. As a regular happenstance, he would dine with them in his hotel's dining room, and after one such occasion one Sunday after church, somewhere in the Big Empty, the sparsely populated, swampy southeastern part of the state, as he was bidding Mister and Mrs. So-and-So good day, the lady of the pair said, "I hope we'll be seeing more of you, Mister Page," to which he replied, "I hope I'll be seeing more of you, too."

Not long thereafter, he received a note in his hotel mailbox from her. She and her husband were inviting him to a dinner down by the river with several dozen others on a Sunday afternoon or two hence, and he accepted.

On the appointed day, Granddaddy, still wearing what he always called his "Sunday-go-to-meeting" clothes, walked over to the stable after church, rented a horse, and rode to the gathering several miles outside of town. When he got to the right place and rode up amongst the buggies and the tethered horses and looked around, he was not surprised that he recognized and, by now, knew most everyone there.

He was more than a mite surprised, though, that every last one of them was stark naked.

And now here, striding up to him (he still on his rented horse), came Mrs. So-and-So, the inviter, in all her glory, calling jovially, "Mr. Page, we're all so glad you could join us!"

Granddaddy maintained his composure and said evenly, "You know, when I told you the other week that I hoped I'd be seeing more of you, I had no idea I'd be seeing so *much* more of you!"

And there the tale stopped, my grandfather being a proper man, leaving me always to wonder to what extent he really did—or did not—join these small-town naturists. This was the family anecdote my mother had hit smartly upon when she first opened our book, and now she was skirmishing over it.

"I can't believe you made up that mess and put it in a book," she said.

"I didn't make it up, Mama—Granddaddy told me that story at least a dozen times."

"I don't believe it."

"Well, he did."

"Even if he did, and I don't believe it," she said, "you didn't have to put it in a book."

"Sure I did," I said. "It's a great story."

"He never told *me*."

"I can't help that," I said.

"I never heard it in my life."

"Well, *I* did." We were at a standoff, always the precise moment for her last word:

"Good night. And I'm not speaking to you anymore."

---

MY FATHER FINISHED law school with Carolina's vaunted class of 1948, along with such grand university and state leaders as William Friday, William Dees, and John Jordan. He graduated in June 1948, passed the state bar exams that summer, and that fall made ready to move back to his hometown of Elizabeth City with my mother and me.

Once I was born and fattened up a bit, that is.

My parents at that time lived in a small, gray-shingled house on Glendale Lane just off East Franklin Street in Chapel Hill. Because there was then no hospital in Chapel Hill, my parents elected to have me first see the light of day at Duke Hospital in Durham, under the watchful eyes and experienced baby-catching hands of Herbert "Daddy" Ross, who helped me into this world at 11:18 P.M. on a mid-October Saturday night.

We spent a couple of days at Duke before being sent back to Chapel Hill, and I do know my mother was mighty indignant about the nurse who looked into the hospital room one of those evenings and, after a few seconds of watching my mother hold me, declared noisily:

"My, what an *ugly* baby!"

Many years later, when being interviewed about a show or some other project, I would usually be asked where was I born. This was a matter of fact and was no secret, yet whenever the results of such an interview appeared, the phone would soon ring, and, answering, I would hear this from my mother:

"Is this the 'Durham songwriter'?"

Or this:

"I'd like to speak with my son, the 'Durham native.' Why do you tell them *such things?*"

"Because—"

"Why don't you just tell them you were born in Chapel Hill?"

"I *would* if I had been, but my mother taught me to tell the truth."

This standoff went on for thirty years or more, till finally her exasperation one evening reached a severe, fevered stage. I had just answered her why-do-you-tell-them-you-were-born-in-Durham question with my standard reply—because I *was*—and then she fairly shouted this last word:

"All right, then, all right—you were born in Durham," she said, surprising me now with near-ferocity, then adding: "You were *born* in Durham. You were born in *Durham*. But you were *conceived* in *Chapel Hill!*"

---

MY MOTHER AND I drove to Lexington, Virginia, to attend the funeral of her sister-in-law's sister. We arrived in that lovely old mountain-bound Rockbridge County town early in the evening before the funeral, just in time to join kin for supper. A note greeting us at the home of the kinswoman with whom we would be staying advised us that they had gone ahead to Harrison's and we could meet them there.

Harrison's back in Chapel Hill was a popular spinach-salad spot, the sort of place that was just beginning to be referred to as a "fern bar," and I was not at all surprised that Lexington, a college town, had an affiliate. Toward good food and good beer, off went we.

The address given was not downtown, as I had expected, but rather out on the edge, on the road back toward Buena Vista, and we somehow overshot the mark, because we found ourselves barreling down the narrow road through the dark woods along the riverside in no time flat.

"Think we missed it, Mama," I said, and I found a picnic table pull-off spot and turn around.

"I didn't see anything," she said.

"Neither did I, but there's nothing out here. We'll find it."

Several minutes later, we were back at Lexington's edge, and she said, "Let's look down there," whereupon I slowed and remarked, "That's just a neighborhood, Mama."

"Well, let's see."

Just a handful of houses, large lots, up on a wooded hillside overlooking a creek—I found a dark lane and again turned around to resume the search for Harrison's.

"Wait—let's stop here and think a minute."

"Think about *what*, Mama?"

"I mean, let's just pull over here and have a little drink."

We were clearly going to be late to the table at Harrison's bistro, and my mother feared it would be unladylike or somehow impolitic to order a beverage (particularly a whiskey—she did not like wine) when everyone else was halfway through dinner, or more. So while we were stopped here in the dark, sparse suburb, from the trunk she produced a small leather case containing a small glass flask with a small amount of bourbon and a pair of metal thimbles, each about one-quarter-ounce capacity.

It would indeed be "a little drink." In keeping with her very steady habits, she allowed herself a wee dram, only a thimbleful.

One of us wondered aloud what our kinfolks, or even the strangers who lived here, would think of an older mother and her grown son all dressed up and just sitting here in a dark car (she *had* used the interior light just long enough to make the pours) in a neighborhood we had never been in before, and never would be again, and having this miniature cocktail party.

This was laughable, and we *did* laugh—so much so that, had we been observed by the authorities during that one minute or so, we would have been certified.

We quickly regained our composure, though, returned the minuscule bar to the trunk, and got back to tracking down Harrison's. Once back on the main road heading into town, we saw it immediately, perched well up on a hill beyond a vast lawn, with a large, white, tastefully low-to-the-ground, all-lit-up sign we had just plain missed earlier:

*Harrison's Funeral Home.*

We had drawn quite the wrong conclusion from the note. Our kin had not gone to dinner this evening—this was the visitation.

"I wasn't quite ready to come to the funeral home," my mother said.

"Nor I, and yet here we are."

"I'm glad we . . . stopped."

"Me too, Mama. Thank you."

I parked the car, got her out of it, and took her arm, and we walked into Harrison's as if we could have hardly waited to get there. My aunt (my mother's sister closest to her in age) spotted us in a trice and cut quickly through the lobby crowd to invite us to go into the viewing room, where the hushed, sibilant voices would try to speak *Don't she look natural?* both quietly *and* authoritatively.

I gave my aunt a quick kiss of greeting and demurred, saying I was going downtown for a little while and would see them back at the house, and just as I was turning for the door, I heard the last word (this one disguised as an *opening,* though no less definitive for that), not from my mother's lips but from those of her competitive sibling, with an accent of judgment virtually identical to the one I knew so well:

"Dorothy! You've been *drinking!*"

———————

NOT TOO MANY YEARS AGO I took on a challenging administrative post at the university, and about a month into it I realized that the work was necessarily going to cut into my ability to perform one of my most important extracurricular jobs: driving my mother to and from her weekly Friday afternoon hair appointment at an in-home beauty shop in Carrboro.

I set out to explain this to her one Thursday, intent on suggesting a taxi service as the best and most appropriate solution, after enumerating and explaining the duties that were going to keep me from continuing to serve in that capacity myself both the next day and on many Fridays to come. My comments would have landed better on the ears of the Mount Rushmore presidents, because what I got for my carefully detailed efforts was this simple, sympathetic-sounding, nullifying remark:

"Oh, son, I know you're so busy. What time will you be by tomorrow to pick me up?"

———————

LATER ON, well into the period where I was doing light grocery shopping for my mother, occasionally I had to ask one of our children to do this. Once, after our son Hunter had gone to the store for her, I received a call.

"Your son can't do any more shopping for me," she said.

"Oh—why not?"

"He just doesn't know *how.*"

"Of course he does. What's the matter?"

"He doesn't know how to shop for lemons."

"Lemons? What on earth?"

"He bought me *organic* lemons."

"What's wrong with that?"

"They're a lot more expensive than real lemons."

"All right," I said. "Next time he goes to the store, I'll remind him: nonorganic lemons only."

"And these organic lemons don't taste a *bit* different."

"I'd be surprised if they did, Mama."

"I paid a lot more for them, and you can't tell any difference."

"They're *organic*, Mama—they're not *flavored*."

"This just didn't work out very well," she said. "Your son can't do any more shopping for me. Good night."

———————

THE ONE REMARK I should have been quite prepared for, but was not, came in mid-January of 2009.

My mother and I were visiting in her assisted living apartment in Chapel Hill, on the edge of the Glen Lennox apartment complex, where we had first moved in June of 1959, and where she had lived until April of 2007, keeping the apartment well after moving into assisted living.

At our previous visit, several days before, I had ventured the possibility of my wife, my sister, and I moving her goods and furniture *out* of the Glen Lennox apartment and putting things into storage. She shook her head vigorously.

"I'm not ready for that," she said.

"Well, when might you be?" I asked.

"I don't know, I don't know, not yet."

Then I advised her that we had already blocked out six successive weekends, late January through February, during which to tackle and complete the task, methodically so.

"No—I'm just not ready."

Against this intransigence, and on the way out, I said in true, flat-out frustration: "The way our calendars are, Mama, if we don't get this done in January and February, we won't be able to do it until May."

When I returned with the dozen grocery items I brought her each week (Lipton's Tea, lemons [nonorganic], five bananas [two ripe, three partially green], five Roma tomatoes, potato rolls, etc.), we sat down and she immediately straightened up and said:

"I have made a decision."

"Yes?"

"About the apartment."

"And?"

"I'd like for us to do it in May."

"*May!?*"

"Yes, you said either February or May. May will be fine."

"Mama," I said firmly. "When I said if we couldn't get your things moved out between now and the end of February that it couldn't happen till May, I didn't mean that to be a *choice!*"

"Nevertheless," she said, "I choose May."

"Mama," I said, "we are all set up to do this—we won't have six straight weekends in May and June. We need to go ahead."

"May," she said again, and then she leaned a bit toward me, eyeing me fiercely, and forthrightly added her intended last word:

"It's my *dying wish*."

Which old film had I wandered into? I recall looking away from her and over at the portrait of my proud and lovely then six-year-old grandmother that hung above my mother's bed, as if I were seeking advice and counsel from her (*Grandmama, how do I deal with your future daughter when she's eighty-eight?*), and thinking, *Now I have heard everything*. And then I turned back and, as calmly as I could, I said,

"Well, that's just fine, Mama. Except that you're *not* dying."

She clenched her jaw and shifted a quarter turn to her right, yet I could still plainly see what was happening—she was attempting to appear dead-level serious to me, while at the same time trying very hard not to laugh. She shifted a mite more, and then sat stock still—we both did—without speaking for a couple of minutes, posed as if for a sculptor working on a vexing piece to be entitled *The Debate* or *The Pregnant Moment* or, perhaps, *The Locked Horns*.

"I've got to get back to campus," I finally said, and she stood and followed me down the short hall to the door, which, once I was outside, she closed as she always did to an eight-inch gap and then, before she shut it fully, again said swiftly, seriously, Bette Davis style, "It *is* my dying wish."

Maybe it was, but I failed to believe it, even though it still resounded in my mind the rest of the afternoon. Such a pronouncement, coming from one's *madre* and delivered so gravely, and twice at that, could not easily be dismissed, even by one attuned and even inured to maternal melodrama.

What did it in, though, was my learning from our three children, early the same evening, that my mother during the afternoon had called each one of them and reenacted our conversation for them all, pretty faithfully I must say, and, according to their quick reports to me, she was chuckling and laughing her way through these recountings—as if she were letting them in on a juicy amusement she had designed just to see if she could get a better deal out of me than the one I had originally announced, the one we ultimately executed, without any further Sturm und Drang.

Despite our not insignificant differences over the years, these blither moments of contest, with their comedic underpinnings sooner or later revealed, are where my mind drifts to as I look back. Better that way, and sweeter too. Sometimes they had come less as moments of contest than of conundrum, like the task she—who had grown up as a girl in Chapel Hill collecting small spatters of gold leaf when it fell during application from the column capitals down onto the floor of Wilson Library's rotunda and putting them into a matchbox for safekeeping, her future riches, and also playing with her Pittsboro Street friends in the vast stadium woods that once rolled over and blanketed the valley and the hilltop south of that library—over many boyhood years often set me to when bidding me goodnight.

"In our dreams," she would say, "if *you* get to that big oak tree in the clearing first, make a mark."

"I will."

"And if *I* get there first," she would go on, "I'll rub it out."

While I understood the gardenias and the not speaking to you and the side-street nip and all the rest, even the dying wish, I am not so sure that I ever came fully to appreciate and understand the depth of this one.

Yet there will come a time when I do.

And that, my friends, really is the last word.

# Contributors

**Belle Boggs** is the author of *The Art of Waiting: On Fertility, Medicine, and Motherhood* and *Mattaponi Queen*. *The Art of Waiting* was a finalist for the PEN Diamonstein/Spielvogel Award for the Art of the Essay, and *Mattaponi Queen* won the Bakeless Prize and the Library of Virginia Literary Award. She teaches in the M.F.A. program at N.C. State University.

**Marshall Chapman** (www.tallgirl.com) is an American singer-songwriter, author, and actress. To date, the Nashville-based artist has released thirteen critically acclaimed albums, and her songs have been recorded by everybody from Emmylou Harris and Joe Cocker to Irma Thomas and Jimmy Buffett. Chapman is the author of two books—*Goodbye, Little Rock and Roller* and *They Came to Nashville*. Most recently, she's landed roles in movies that include *Country Strong*, *Mississippi Grind*, and *Novitiate*. Chapman is a longtime contributing editor to *Garden & Gun*. She's also written for the *Oxford American*, *Southern Living*, *W*, *Performing Songwriter*, and the nationally syndicated *Bob Edwards Show*. "But music," she says, "is my first and last love."

**Hal Crowther** is a critic and essayist, author of five books of essays, including *Freedom Fighters and Hellraisers: A Gallery of Memorable Southerners* (2018) and *An Infuriating American: The Incendiary Arts of H. L. Mencken* (2014). His collection *Gather at the River* was a finalist for the National Book Critics Circle prize for criticism in 2007, and *Cathedrals of Kudzu* (2001) won the Lillian Smith Book Award and the Fellowship of Southern Writers' Fellowship Prize for Nonfiction. He is a former screenwriter, a newsmagazine editor for both *Time* and *Newsweek*, and a syndicated columnist whose columns won the *Baltimore Sun*'s H. L. Mencken Writing Award in 1992. He lives in Hillsborough, N.C., with his wife, novelist Lee Smith.

**Clyde Edgerton**, born in Durham, N.C., is the author of two works of nonfiction and ten novels, including the acclaimed *Walking across Egypt* and *The Night Train*. His writing is known for endearing characters, small-town Southern dialogue, humor, and realistic fire-and-brimstone religious sermons. He has won five Notable Book of the Year awards from the *New York Times*, a Guggenheim Fellowship, a Lyndhurst Award, and the North Carolina Award for Literature. An acclaimed musician and songwriter, he is the Thomas S. Kenan III Distinguished Professor of Creative Writing at UNC-Wilmington.

**Marianne Gingher** has published seven books and writes both fiction and nonfiction. Her novel *Bobby Rex's Greatest Hit* was made into an NBC movie, and she has published widely in magazines and periodicals, including the *Southern Review, Oxford American, North America Review, Oprah Magazine, New York Times Book Review, Washington Post,* and *Our State.* Her latest books are *Adventures in Pen Land,* a comic memoir about the writing life (illustrated by Daniel Wallace), and two editing projects: *Long Story Short,* a flash fiction anthology, and *Amazing Place,* a collection of personal narratives by twenty-two North Carolina writers. A puppeteer, she cofounded Jabberbox Puppet Theater, a venue based in Greensboro, N.C., for salon-style adult puppet comedy. An award-winning teacher and former director of UNC's Creative Writing Program, she is currently professor of English and comparative literature at the University of North Carolina at Chapel Hill, where she also codirects the Thomas Wolfe Scholarship Program.

**Jaki Shelton Green** is a North Carolina poet, creativity coach, and cultural activist. Publications include *Dead on Arrival, Masks, Dead on Arrival and New Poems, Conjure Blues, Singing a Tree into Dance, Breath of the Song,* and *Feeding the Light.* She currently teaches at the Duke University Center for Documentary Studies, in addition to providing writing retreats and travel excursions for women writers through her SistaWRITE business. Awards include 2018 North Carolina Poet Laureate, 2014 North Carolina Literary Hall of Fame inductee, Kathryn Wallace Award for Artists in Community Service, 2009 North Carolina Piedmont Laureate, 2003 North Carolina Award in Literature, and the Sam Ragan Award in Fine Arts.

**Sally Greene** is an attorney and independent scholar in Chapel Hill, N.C. A graduate of George Washington University Law School, she also holds a Ph.D. in English from the University of North Carolina at Chapel Hill. Her work has appeared in the *Journal of Modern Literature, Women's Studies, Southern Cultures,* the online journal *South Writ Large,* and elsewhere. Her edited collection *Virginia Woolf: Reading the Renaissance* appeared in 1999.

**Stephanie Elizondo Griest** is an award-winning author of three travel memoirs, *Around the Bloc: My Life in Moscow, Beijing, and Havana; Mexican Enough: My Life between the Borderlines; and All the Agents and Saints: Dispatches from the U.S. Borderlands,* as well as the best-selling guidebook *100 Places Every Woman Should Go.* She has also written for the *New York Times, Washington Post, The Believer, VQR,* and *Oxford American* and edited *Best Women's Travel Writing 2010.* An assistant professor of creative nonfiction at UNC–Chapel Hill, she has performed across the globe, including in Venezuela as a featured author with the U.S. State Department. Distinctions include a Henry Luce Scholarship to China, a Hodder Fellowship at Princeton, and a Margolis Award for Social Justice Reporting. Visit her website at StephanieElizondoGriest.com.

**Jacquelyn Dowd Hall,** Julia Cherry Spruill Professor Emeritus, UNC–Chapel Hill, is past president of the Organization of American Historians, the Southern Historical Association, and the Labor and Working Class History Association. She is a specialist in southern history with a focus on women, race, and labor and served for many years as founding director of UNC's Southern Oral History Program. Among her many award-winning publications is "The Long Civil Rights Movement and the Political Uses of the Past" (*Journal of American History* 91, March 2005), one of the most widely cited and assigned examinations of the movement.

**E. C. "Redge" Hanes** is the author of two novels, *Billy Bowater,* a story based on Redge's experiences in Raleigh and Washington, D.C., as an advocate for the arts, and *Justice by Another Name,* based on his work on environmental issues in North Carolina. He was born in Winston-Salem, N.C. A graduate of Duke University, he served as an officer in the U.S. Army from 1969 to 1971. After thirty-five years as a business executive, he retired as the chairman of the Russ Companies, an international consumer products company. He was a board member of numerous local and national arts and environmental organizations. Redge lives with his wife in Winston-Salem, N.C.

**Lynden Harris** is an award-winning playwright, columnist, and essayist. A former artistic director of the ArtsCenter in Carrboro, N.C., in 2003 she founded Hidden Voices, whose vision is to challenge, strengthen, and connect diverse communities through the transformative power of the individual voice. Her related play, *Count,* played to packed houses at UNC's Playmakers Theatre in Chapel Hill in 2017. Lynden is a member of the MAP Fund Class of 2016 for the project Serving Life: ReVisioning Justice and in 2014 was named a Founding Cultural Agent for the U.S. Department of Arts and Culture, a people-powered movement mobilizing creativity. She also teaches Stories for Social Change at Duke University. Lynden is a founding team member of the Duke Transformative Prison Project. She lives on a farm in Cedar Grove, N.C., with her family and assorted animals.

**Randall Kenan** is author of the novel *A Visitation of Spirits;* two works of nonfiction, *Walking on Water: Black American Lives at the Turn of the Twenty-First Century* and *The Fire This Time;* and a collection of stories, *Let the Dead Bury Their Dead.* He edited and wrote the introduction for *The Cross of Redemption: The Uncollected Writings of James Baldwin.* Among his awards are a Guggenheim Fellowship, a Mrs. Giles Whiting Award, the North Carolina Award, and the American Academy of Arts and Letters' Rome Prize. He is professor of English and comparative literature at UNC–Chapel Hill.

**Phillip Lopate** is one of the best-known American essayists and literary and film critics. He is the author of three personal essay collections, *Bachelorhood, Against Joie de Vivre,* and *Portrait of My Body;* two novels, *Confessions of Summer* and *The Rug Merchant;* a pair of novellas; three poetry collections; a memoir of his teaching experiences; a collection of his movie criticism, and more. In addition, there is a Phillip Lopate reader, *Getting Personal: Selected Writings.* Recent publications include *Portrait inside My Head* (personal essays), *To Show and to Tell: The Craft of Literary Nonfiction,* and *A Mother's Tale,* a memoir of his mother. He has taught creative writing and literature at Fordham, Cooper Union, University of Houston, Hofstra University, New York University, and Bennington College, where several of the authors in this anthology studied with him. He is the director of the nonfiction graduate program at Columbia University, where he also teaches writing.

**Michael Malone**'s twelve novels include the classics *Handling Sin* and *Time's Witness*. He is also the author of the short-story collection *Red Clay, Blue Cadillac* and of two books of nonfiction. His novels have been translated into many languages. A number were bestsellers. His work has appeared in such periodicals as the *Partisan Review, Playboy, Harper's, New York Times*, and *Nation*. In addition to his plays, he was for many years head writer for network television shows at ABC and NBC. Among his prizes are the O'Henry, the Edgar, the Writers Guild Award, and the Emmy. He taught at Yale, at Penn, and until his recent retirement, at Duke University. He and his wife, Professor Maureen Quilligan, live in Hillsborough, N.C.

**Frances Mayes**'s most recent novel is *Women in Sunlight*. She is the author of three acclaimed Italian memoirs, including *Under the Tuscan Sun*, which inspired the eponymous film; the novel *Swan; Under Magnolia: A Southern Memoir*; and many other books.

**Jill McCorkle** has the distinction of having published her first two novels on the same day in 1984. Of these novels, the *New York Times Book Review* said: "One suspects the author of *The Cheer Leader* is a born novelist. With *July 7th*, she is also a full grown one." Since then she has published four other novels (her latest, *Life after Life*) and four collections of short stories. Five of her nine previously published books have been named *New York Times* notable books. McCorkle has received the New England Booksellers Award, the John Dos Passos Prize for Excellence in Literature, the North Carolina Award for Literature, and the Thomas Wolfe Prize. She has taught at Harvard, Brandeis, and N.C. State and is core faculty in the Bennington Writing Seminar.

**Melody Moezzi** is a writer, speaker, activist, attorney, and award-winning author. Her latest book is the critically acclaimed memoir *Haldol and Hyacinths: A Bipolar Life*. Her first book, *War on Error: Real Stories of American Muslims*, earned her a Georgia Author of the Year Award and a Gustavus Myers Center for the Study of Bigotry and Human Rights Honorable Mention in 2007. She has lived in Raleigh, N.C., and has been visiting professor of creative nonfiction at the UNC-Wilmington.

**Elaine Neil Orr** is professor of English at N.C. State University and teaches in the Spalding University low-residency M.F.A. in Writing Program in Louisville, Ky. In addition to two books of literary criticism, she is author of the memoir *Gods of Noonday: A White Girl's African Life* and of *A Different Sun: A Novel of Africa* and *Swimming between Worlds*. She has published widely in such venues as the *Missouri Review, Image, Blackbird*, and *Shenandoah*. In 2015 she was Kathryn Stripling Byer Writer-in-Residence at Wesleyan College in Georgia, and she is a recipient of a N.C. Arts Council Grant, as well as a frequent fellow at the Virginia Center for the Creative Arts.

**Steven Petrow** is an award-winning journalist and columnist for the *Washington Post* and *USA Today*. He is also a contributor to the *New York Times, Time*, and NPR. Previously, he penned the *New York Times* "Civil Behavior" column and "Digital Dilemmas" for *Parade* magazine and has published in the *Atlantic, Salon*, the Daily Beast, *Los Angeles Times*, and *Advocate*, among other media outlets. Steven is a former president of the National Lesbian and Gay Journalists Association. Among his books are *Steven Petrow's Complete Gay and Lesbian Manners: The Definitive Guide to LGBT Life*; *The New Gay Wedding: A Practical Primer for Brides and Grooms, Their Families, and Guests*; *The Lost Hamptons*; and *Dancing against the Darkness: A Journey across America in the Age of AIDS*.

**Margaret W. Rich**, a native of South Carolina, has lived most of her adult life in North Carolina, where she worked as a professional gardener. A highlight of her gardening career was a summer spent in Monet's gardens in Giverny, deadheading sunflowers and hollyhocks and paddling around in the little green boat you see in his paintings to muck out the waterlilies. She is a graduate of Mills College (1979), where she received a Thomas J. Watson Fellowship for a year of independent study abroad (1979–80). Most recently she earned an M.F.A. in creative writing from Bennington College and is working on a memoir about her life as a single parent during the social upheaval of the 1970s. She lives in Chapel Hill, N.C., with her husband, James.

**Omid Safi**, of Chapel Hill, N.C., is the William and Bettye Martin Musham Director of the Duke Islamic Studies Center at Duke University and a regular columnist for the On Being Project. Born in Jacksonville, Fla., of Iranian descent, Safi received B.A., M.A., and Ph.D. degrees from Duke. Prior to accepting his current position, he was a professor of Islamic studies at UNC–Chapel Hill. He is an award-winning teacher and speaker and has been nominated ten times for professor of the year awards at Duke University, UNC–Chapel Hill, and Colgate University. A specialist in classical Islam and contemporary Islamic thought, Safi is the author of books on American Muslims and debates in contemporary Islam, Sufism, and Persian literature and is in constant demand as a public intellectual commentator in the media.

**James Seay**'s essays and poems have appeared in *Antaeus, Esquire, Harper's, Nation, New Yorker, Oxford American*, and others. He has written five books of poetry as well as a documentary film *In the Blood*, cowritten with director George Butler. He has received the Award in Literature from the American Academy of Arts and Letters. He recently retired from the University of North Carolina at Chapel Hill.

**Samia Serageldin** is a novelist, writer, and editor. Her autobiographical first novel, *The Cairo House*, is set in her native Egypt and was followed by *The Naqib's Daughter* and *Love Is Like Water and Other Stories*. She is also the author of essays and nonfiction in several anthologies and has edited books and written a regular book-review column for ten years. She is an editor and founder of the magazine *South Writ Large: Stories, Arts, and Ideas from the Global South*. Serageldin received her M.S. degree in politics from London University and immigrated to the United States with her family in the early 1980s. She has called Chapel Hill, N.C., home for the past thirty years. For more information visit www.samiaserageldin.com.

**Alan Shapiro** has published many poetry collections, most recently *Reel to Reel*, finalist for the Pulitzer Prize, and *Night of the Republic*, finalist for the National Book Award; and four books of prose, including *The Last Happy Occasion*, finalist for the National Book

Critics Circle Award, and *Broadway Baby,* a novel. Winner of the Kingsley Tufts Award, Los Angeles Times Book Prize, and an award in literature from the American Academy of Arts and Letters, he brought out two books in 2016: *Life Pig,* a book of poems, and *That Self-Forgetful Perfectly Useless Concentration,* essays on convention, suffering, and self-expression. He lives in Chapel Hill, N.C.

**Bland Simpson** is Kenan Distinguished Professor of English and Creative Writing at UNC–Chapel Hill, and he is the longtime pianist for the Tony Award–winning Red Clay Ramblers. His books include *Into the Sound Country, The Inner Islands, Little Rivers and Waterway Tales* (all with photography by Ann Cary Simpson) and *The Coasts of Carolina* (with photography by Scott Taylor). His musical collaborations include the shows *Diamond Studs* (with Jim Wann), *King Mackerel and the Blues Are Running* (with Jim Wann, Don Dixon, and Jerry Leath Mills), *Kudzu* (with Jack Herrick and Doug Marlette), and the three-time Broadway hit *Fool Moon* (with Bill Irwin, David Shiner, and the Red Clay Ramblers). In 2005 Simpson received the North Carolina Award for Fine Arts, the state's highest civilian honor.

**Lee Smith** is the author of seventeen works of fiction, including *Fair and Tender Ladies, Oral History,* and the recent novel *Guests on Earth.* She has received many awards, including the North Carolina Award for Literature and an Academy Award in Fiction from the American Academy of Arts and Letters; her novel *The Last Girls* was a *New York Times* bestseller and winner of the Southern Book Critics Circle Award. *Dimestore, a Writer's Life,* a collection of personal essays, was published in March 2016. For more information, visit www.leesmith.com.

**Sharon K. Swanson** is an award-winning essayist and features writer. Her award-winning documentary film *Landscapes of the Heart: The Elizabeth Spencer Story* was selected for film festivals across the country and has been broadcast on public television in several states. Her memoir, *Free Fall,* about her discovery of stability and love as a groupie in a community of skydivers, is out to agents. Sharon holds an M.F.A. in nonfiction writing from the Writing Seminars at Bennington College and a graduate degree in public administration from East Carolina University.

**Daniel Wallace** is the author of *Big Fish* and, most recently, *Extraordinary Adventures,* his sixth novel. He directs the Creative Writing Program at UNC–Chapel Hill.

# Acknowledgments

This book would not have seen the light of day without the instant, enthusiastic encouragement from two good friends with whom I first broached the idea of an anthology on motherhood: Lee Smith and Margaret Rich. Margaret's mother and mine had passed away recently on the exact same day, half a world apart. Lee Smith, it hardly needs reminding, is a much published and beloved North Carolina writer. Their immediate and unstinting support for the project gave it wings. Lee, as coeditor, reached out to her network of fellow literary luminaries—no one says no to Lee, she is such a loyal friend and mentor. As we each thought of new contributors to invite among our writer acquaintances, and they in turn suggested others, our list grew beyond our expectations.

It has been immensely gratifying that the theme of *Mothers and Strangers* seems to have resonated with everyone we approached, and we would like to thank each and every one of our essayists. It has been a privilege working with you, an education and a pleasure. On my own behalf, I have been called "a horse whisperer for writers" by Michael Malone and "that mean old pope who nagged Michelangelo, but much nicer," by Randall Kenan. I treasure both designations.

Lee and I would also like to acknowledge the team of editors at UNC Press. Director John Sherer green-lighted the project in embryo. Editor Lucas Church worked with us closely, day in, day out over the two years of gestation, guiding the development of the book.

Samia Serageldin